A Man's
Field Guide To Dating

About the Author

Robert A. Wray

Robert Wray is a successful author of computer programming textbooks. A Man's Field Guide to Dating is his first publication in the self-help category. He is the owner and President of netImage, a web design and hosting, e-commerce and publishing firm in Pennsylvania. He has been a public school teacher, college instructor and spent several years as a consultant and trainer before founding netImage in 1996.

Bob is single and spends his leisure time at the beach, swing dancing, playing guitar and working out. He also enjoys skiing, sailing and, of course, dating. He is currently working on a dating guide for women.

Visit the Man's Field Guide to Dating website.
www.dating-guide.com

THE GUIDE

A Man's
Field Guide To Dating

Robert A. Wray

netImage

Mechanicsburg, Pennsylvania

netImage
444 Woodcrest Drive
Mechanicsburg, PA 17055
www.nimage.com

Library of Congress Cataloging-in-Publication Data
Wray, Robert A.
A Man's Field Guide to Dating / Robert A. Wray. - 1st ed.
1. Dating (Social Customs)   2. Man-woman relationships.
I. Title.

ISBN 0-9669723-0-9

This publication is designed to provide accurate and authoritative information in regard to the subject matter covered. It is sold with the understanding that the publisher is not engaged in rendering legal, accounting, or other professional service. If legal advice or other expert assistance is required, the services of a competent professional person should be sought.

— From a declaration of principles jointly adopted by a committee of the American Bar Association and a committee of publishers.

Dedication

*This book is dedicated to my children, Jenna and Eric
in the hope that they will develop healthy, rewarding relationships.*

Contents At A Glance

Table of Contents

Contents

Contents

Acknowledgments

I am very grateful to the many individuals who reviewed my draft manuscript and provided their feedback. I was able to correct many conceptual errors and include some useful enhancements. I want to thank my friends and the women I have dated for enriching my life and providing a sounding board for these ideas. Of course, I thank my family, especially my children, Jenna and Eric — also, my brother Dan, who is my best friend. I love you all.

I have appreciated the many summers spent with the hundreds of crazy singles in Dewey Beach, Delaware. A few weekends there is an education in itself. Of course, sometimes it is just as important to learn what not to do! Thank you, Big Dogs.

Thea Hocker has served with distinction as a copy editor. Bobbi Misiti, my personal trainer, made significant contributions to Chapters 6 and 7. Thanks for your help, Bobbi. You're the best. Many thanks to Bob Rios for his way-cool artwork and Angie Rios for her page layout.

Here are the names of some the wonderful people who have contributed to this effort. I thank them all.

Tammy Wilk, Deb Loving, Mark Hornberger, Liz Knerr, Sarah Koch, Anita Leiden, Kate Panangia, Kate Brossman, Anne-Marie Podgorski, Cynthia Butts, Linda Ricci, Bob and Angie Rios, Kerry Scott, Melissa Rodgers, Mike Bennet, Jenna Wray, and especially Laurie Metzger.

Preface

Why did I write this book? I found myself single again in 1992 after several years of marriage. Like many others I simply stumbled into the world of dating and made lots of mistakes. I also met some wonderful people. The whole process fascinated me. I discovered that most people were as mystified by dating and relationships as I was. I talked about this incessantly with my friends and colleagues. What do women want? Why do we behave the way that we do? Why can't guys commit? You have heard all the questions.

I reviewed the literature in the bookstore. There are many excellent books about relationships — how to fix them, how to improve them. There are some good books about dating. However, most of them were written by women for women. The ones that did address both genders still seemed to emphasize the problems from a woman's point of view. I really couldn't find one that would help me improve my dating life as a man. I thought guys would appreciate a book that approached the subject purely from a male perspective.

I have always enjoyed the company of women and have nurtured platonic friendships with them when I could. Often I would receive desperate calls late at night asking for my advice "as a guy." I thought that it would be a lot simpler if the guy in question were in the loop. Then I could get more sleep. This book includes many of the insights I gleaned from these tearful conversations. Now I can just suggest that her boyfriend read the book before she calls.

I asked dozens of women to read the manuscript before we went to press. Many of their names are in the acknowledgments. They were brutally honest. Because of this, I feel very confident that the ideas presented here are valid. They are telling you what they want. You only have to listen and adjust. I wish I had had this information seven years ago.

Why is the book written in first-person plural? (We) I had so much help from friends and family that I could not represent these ideas and suggestions as purely my own. Much of the information is conventional wisdom. I was not comfortable speaking to you as an individual. Many women contributed their thoughts and feelings to these pages. You get the benefit of their honest perspectives on dating. That is who the "we" is.

I sincerely wish you the best in your search for happiness. Being single and dating can be a wonderful period in your life. It's all up to you and how you look at it. People don't date enough. Guys are afraid of rejection. They don't extend enough invitations. (Women say "no" too often, but that's another story.) It is my hope that this book will have some impact on the problem. Date more. Enjoy yourself. Make as many women smile as possible. I think that will make everyone happier, especially your mom.

Robert Wray
December, 1998

Introduction

We like the term "conventional wisdom." It refers to the type of information you get from your friends at parties. "Hey Ed, I'm looking for a good PC. You're in the business. What do you think?" You will readily accept Ed's opinion — providing that you trust him. It saves you going through the agony of research and sales pitches. That's the spirit of this volume. There is no science here — just a collection of ideas and advice that seem to work for a lot of guys. We did our best to avoid moral judgments, except for the golden rule. You shouldn't do to any woman what you wouldn't do to your sister. (Did that come out right?) Most of it is common sense. Some of it you have heard before — sorry about that. We don't know what *you* don't know. We tried to include everything we could to help you improve your dating life. There is no magic and there are no secrets. Sometimes the problem is simply that you have overlooked some basic detail that prevents a woman from discovering what a terrific guy you really are. The devil *is* in the details. As men, it is not our nature to spend time, money and effort on our appearance and social behavior. Perhaps calling these things to your attention and offering simple solutions will increase your chances with women. What do you have to lose? As it happens, you will discover that working on your weak areas will improve your life in other ways as well. Heck, you might even get a raise or a better job.

This book is intended to assist men who seek to date women. We expect that it would be most helpful to heterosexual men who are approximately 20 to 60 years old. The ideas reflect current social practices between men and women in America, although they could extend to other cultures that are similar. The book does not address issues that may be specific to ethnic or religious populations such as Latinos, Muslims or some Asian cultures. While we respect the traditions and practices of other cultures, we do not pretend to have the experience or knowledge to address the dating behaviors of everyone. However, there are many general ideas and suggestions that may be useful to a broad cross-section of men. Younger men (under 20) or men that are not serious about forming social relationships with women will find very little of interest here. It is our hope that the information contained within will assist the millions of men and women who are struggling to complete this most important aspect of their lives — meeting and enjoying the company of the opposite sex.

What's Your Motive?

We have to pause here to discuss an important point. Why do you want to date? *This book follows the premise that you intend to follow the traditional path of dating — relationship — engagement — marriage.* This may not be the case. That's fine. There are other reasons. We are staying away from value judgments.

You may wish to date to fill up your social calendar and to enjoy life. This is typical among younger guys. You are not ready to get serious with anyone. There is nothing wrong with this as long as you are honest. Make sure that you are on the same wavelength as the women that you are dating. They should know that you are not headed for commitment city any time in the near future. If so, it should be assumed that you are seeing more than one woman at a time. In this case, so are they. This is fair.

As long as these ground rules are in place, you are free to do as you choose without hurting anyone. There are pros and cons. You will have a great time and increase your experience, skills and techniques. The downside is that some women may quickly set their sights on cornering you for themselves. You must be on guard for this. Make your non-committal intentions clear and cut your losses. You will have them. Some people (both men and women) will suspect your motives. You will have a bit of a reputation. People love to talk. All this may make it difficult for you to land dates, especially in a small town.

There is a third possibility. It has to do with testosterone. You are dating to get sex. Now, this factor is always in place. Women understand this. Heck, they expect it. Everyone wants sex on some level. It is a matter of conditions. If your premise is that the purpose of dating is to hit the sack as soon and as often as possible, with as many women as possible, you will have many problems. The fact is that no one likes this kind of behavior. You will be associated with some pretty nasty ladies who may be better at the game than you! Quality women will shun you. Once the word gets around, you may have to start hunting in the next town, fifty miles away. Now, guys will love hearing your stories of conquest but privately, they will keep you away from their sisters and be very nervous about their girlfriends. Quite frankly, buddy, you will have turned into a creep. Clean up your act. You will be happier in the long run. Now that we have had this chat, decide for yourself why you want to date and let's move on.

Is All Fair in Love and War?

Your situation is hardly unique. It just feels that way because you sit and ponder it a great deal. Guys are not in the habit of baring their souls to their buddies, especially if they're having trouble dating. Know that there are thousands of guys in your position. This means that the help in this book can be applied to a vast cross section of single guys.

Is it mean, nasty, manipulative or illegal to use techniques and tactics to win your lady-love? Hardly. First of all, the quest is noble. You would just like to increase the number of dates you are having. You are hoping that something will grow out of one or more of them. What's wrong with that? Remember, the woman wins too!

Second, you are being honest. We don't recommend or even suggest that you use deceit to convince someone to go out with you. However, if you have to stack the deck a bit to impress your lady love, who gets hurt? Minimizing your inadequacies and maximizing your strengths makes perfect sense. Believe us, women are experts at this.

Third, there is nothing new under the sun. The information you will find here has existed for centuries (cyberdating excluded). We have simply sorted, evaluated and presented time-honored ideas that seem to work. Of course, we attempt to coach you and convince you to use them as well. If it was good enough for your grandfather and Clark Gable . . .

You must be convinced of your own success. It's just a matter of time and intelligent effort. While there are no guarantees, what are your options? You can continue as you are and depend on chance or be proactive. You are responsible for your own success. However, we offer you a considerable amount of assistance in this book.

You use techniques and strategies on a regular basis in your daily life to advance your position. Dressing well for a job interview, straightening up your home before guests arrive and smiling at the boss are examples. Why would you not extend this to your dating life?

Of course, people have been playing the romance game in deceitful, and even evil, ways for centuries. Perhaps you have been the unhappy victim of someone accomplished at breaking hearts. Make certain that you do not cross over to the dark side. If your sole intent is to persuade a woman to sleep with you, seek revenge or get in her father's will, you are headed for problems. Using deceit or worse, force, will eventually result in your own unhappiness.

By the way, you may discover that your new skills and philosophy will mute some of the exuberance you have become accustomed to when dating. When you are acting with confidence and determination rather than emotion, your adrenaline levels will naturally be lower. However, this is a more certain path to your goal — successful dating leading to a relationship.

Look down the road and persuade yourself right now that you are going to go through a period of experimentation loaded with mistakes. You will learn from these mistakes and at the end of the road, you will have skills and techniques gleaned from experience. There is nothing more valuable. We can't do this for you. Once you understand this process, each date becomes an opportunity to relax and have a good time while you practice your techniques. Of course, there is always the possibility that you will be surprised with success when you least expect it.

How Are You Doing?

The most likely reason things are not going all that well in your dating life is that you are probably a mismatch with the women you would like to date. *What we mean is that you need to be or become the kind of person you would enjoy dating.* This implies that you should know who you are. You may think that you know but that is not generally something you dwell on. Also, it is difficult to objectively look at oneself. You probably underrate yourself. Make an honest list of your most positive qualities without being openly modest. Are you intelligent? Energetic? Personable? Honest? Affectionate? Athletic? Be as complete as you can. Give yourself enough time to include everything. Be certain to write it down. If you have a close friend or relative that you trust, it would be beneficial if you could ask that person to review your list and make additions.

This exercise alone will begin to increase your confidence. Self-confidence is one of the most powerful attractions for the opposite sex. *Women are not interested in men who appear weak or needy.* If they are, it is because they are looking for someone to rescue. This is not a place that you want to be. You would be starting a relationship on a dysfunctional premise.

This confidence must be grounded in a set of beliefs and a value system. You must be convinced that you are searching for a worthy life partner who embodies the very best. This is an honest and noble quest. You don't want to hurt or deceive anyone. You know that someday you will succeed. It is just a matter of time. As you continue your search you will learn more about yourself, the nature of relationships and the opposite sex. You will eventually bring the value of this knowledge to your life partner. You will continue to work on your weak areas and make yourself even more desirable by *eliminating objections.* The longer this process takes, the more worthy and desirable the type of women you date will be. Time is not your enemy, it is on your side. Your confidence will feed itself as you grow.

You will find a wealth of valuable information in the following chapters. However, the ideas are useless in and of themselves. It is only when you commit yourself to action and success that anything will happen. Read the whole book through once. Then go back and begin to apply the ideas to your life as best you can. Resolve to continue your improvement. You are entitled to enjoy your role as a man. You are entitled to participate in the world of dating and relationships. You deserve to be happy. We are right behind you. Go for it.

Chapter 1
The Long View

*"Happiness is the only good. / The time to be happy is now. / The place to be
happy is here. / The way to be happy is to make others so."*
— Ralph G. Ingersoll, "Creed" c. late 19th century.

A Little Heart to Heart Talk

In your father's and grandfather's day, dating was a younger man's activity.
Typically, you found your one true love, married her and that was that. Today's man needs to recognize a whole new set of realities. People marry later
and experience several serious relationships first. Second and even third mar-
riages are not uncommon. Today's man wants much more than a partner to
raise a family and keep body and soul together. You may not be prepared to
admit it, but here are some of the benefits people hope for in a modern,
healthy relationship:
- Sharing of our innermost thoughts and feelings
- Physical and emotional intimacy
- Unconditional acceptance and love
- Consistent commitment to the relationship, even in hard times
- Nurturing and support for our hopes and dreams
- Opportunity for personal growth

The list could go on, but you can see that things are different today. Unfortunately, many men have been raised in families where nurturing relationships were not the norm. If you were, this means that you may have to
develop or re-teach yourself to be a healthy, desirable partner. When two people enter a relationship with these kinds of skills in place, the chances for success are greatly increased. The dating/relationship model your ancestors
enjoyed is not the norm. Many men find themselves drifting through several
periods of dating and relationships throughout their lives. Nobody prepares
us for this.

Dating is the precursor to a relationship. The way we behave during this phase
will determine the outcome of any relationship that may evolve. Most men

1

don't consider this while dating. They make the same mistakes over and over. Like Sisyphus in ancient Greek literature, who is doomed to push a huge rock up a hill only to have it roll right back down, men stumble through successive dating experiences without satisfaction or success.

Some men bully their way into a relationship and try to control women to discover that the joy and sharing are stifled. The reverse can occur when a man becomes co-dependent and lives to satisfy the whims of his lady. We fall in "love" and have sex after a few dates, only to find that the relationship has evaporated.

Many of us depend on chance and circumstance as well as our hormones to provide opportunities for romance. This is very shortsighted. You will do much better if you are proactive and seek to make an emotional connection that could lead to a relationship. This takes thought, not just chemistry. It also requires time, effort and patience. Of course, it should be enjoyable as well.

It is not as difficult as you think to encounter and date women as long as you have no criteria. You can be infatuated with a wide variety of partners. On the other hand, successfully dating women who offer the potential for a meaningful, fulfilling relationship is one of the greatest challenges you will face. If you are willing to look within yourself and commit to personal growth, you can succeed. It is easy to fault the list of women you have dated in the past as being wrong for you. The truth is that the one consistent factor in all those dates and relationships has been *you! Fortunately that's the one factor over which you have the most control.*

You must also understand the nature of the process as it has evolved in our society and culture. When this is combined with an understanding of ourselves and the nature of women we can take action and determine our own destiny. You are in control if you want to be.

None of us has had a perfect childhood. Often circumstances do not provide fulfillment of our emotional needs as children. We carry this into adulthood and turn to romantic relationships to complete ourselves. These feelings are very deep seated and hidden in our subconscious. As strange as it may sound some men find themselves choosing women who share characteristics with their mothers. They do this because they missed significant portions of their emotional development for one reason or another.

To succeed in establishing a mature, healthy relationship you will have to overcome deficiencies from your childhood and grow as a person. This is intimate, personal stuff. It may require some professional assistance. What is important is that you recognize and accept the goal of developing a nurturing, mutually loving relationship with a woman of quality who respects you and cares for you. If you can visualize yourself achieving this, it will sustain you through the challenge. The way to succeed is to do your best to grow and improve as an individual. Recognize areas that need development and resolve to work on them. There is a great deal of information and encouragement to help you in the following chapters. Accept that this is a lifetime goal. You will continually become stronger and exert more control over your life. You will be more productive. You will discover that you actually enjoy the process.

Stop looking for love. It doesn't work that way. Focus on your self-improvement. Extend yourself to others. Present the best person you can to those you encounter. Love will find you. Women are involved in their own journeys. The quality women that you dream about are behaving the way we have described. That is why you are not likely to find them in bars. They are busy improving themselves and encountering people on a higher level. That is where you need to be. You may discover that they will seek you out once it becomes obvious that you are a man of quality.

Repeated Patterns

Think about your grandfather's day. Reruns of old shows such *as Father Knows Best, Leave It To Beaver* or *Ozzie and Harriet* depict a time when couples married young and grew old together. Times have changed. Today people marry later. They are also likely to have more than one marriage in their lifetime. While it doesn't have to be this way, it would be wise to recognize and understand the patterns. Unfortunately, we lose perspective while we are in the experience.

You start by casually dating. You simultaneously see several women. You are neither serious nor exclusive. You spend a lot of time with friends and by yourself. You have no responsibility to a significant other. This can be a very enjoyable period. Of course, many people complain and are stressed by it.

At some point you discover that you are particularly interested in one woman. We will discuss this at great length later. One of the key problems is that we often stumble into these relationships without any thought or communication. Usually this is because we have become physically involved. You find yourself less interested in other women and prefer to spend most of your time with her. This can get very complicated. An exclusive relationship can evolve into several forms. It can last from a few intense weeks to the rest of your life. You might date exclusively for months or a few years. You could move in together (not a good idea). Of course, many couples eventually get engaged and then marry. If the relationship does not result in a lifelong marriage you will experience the next phase, unfortunately.

If the relationship ends there will be some level of pain on both sides. You will have to go through a process of healing before you can go back to casual dating again. Men often bury their feelings and rush into dating too quickly. Our pride won't let us cry or seek help during this period. If you allow yourself to naturally progress through the stages of grief and heal, you will be emotionally available to date again. There can be many negative emotions to deal with — grief, guilt, remorse, denial, anger or resentment. You must work through all of your feelings in a natural, healthy way. Physical activity, writing, talking with friends and counseling can help.

What is important about all of this is that you recognize and accept the patterns. You may move through them many times. Ideally, you will learn and become stronger as you experience relationships. We offer a lot of help in this book. Reviewing your past experiences and how you handled them is useful. You should know where you are at any time and know where you would like to be. Don't let your hormones lead you. Be proactive. Determine your own destiny.

There are two factors that traditionally drive us into relationships. You are very familiar with the first. Overwhelming chemical changes fog your thinking and evoke primal urges to mate and procreate. The second is our deep-seated need to both compensate for unfulfilled childhood needs and to restore the positive aspects our parents provided. As you can see, there is very little thinking involved. If everything "feels" right, you plunge in headfirst. It won't matter if the woman is not a good match. It won't even matter if she is fatally flawed. As long as your chemistry and subconscious are satisfied you will continue until something stops you. Eventually, something will happen to end it because a relationship with that that sort of beginning never had a chance. Of course, there is the remote possibility that you could get lucky and stumble into a relationship with a quality woman who matches perfectly. You could also win the lottery.

Find a Balance

Think back through your past and try to identify these two factors in your experiences. Do you remember how it felt? Do you remember the lack of control? Do you remember the result? Often this happens over and over again. No wonder men become discouraged! Now that you recognize the feelings and the results, you can make some changes.

Realize that chemistry and emotional fulfillment are absolutely required for a healthy relationship to develop. The problem is that sex must be balanced with other factors. Another problem is that we typically lead with physical attraction. Perhaps you lack a clear vision of what is found in a complete, healthy relationship. Here are some important elements to consider.

Matching Value Systems

These are your core beliefs and lifestyle choices. They come from your upbringing, education, religion and life experience. They are deeply rooted and not likely to change. They are not up for negotiation. If the two of you differ too much in your value systems, the relationship has no hope of succeeding. Values can involve roles, children, work ethic, family, money and sex. This is the really heavy stuff. You can find plenty of examples of failure to match value systems in divorce court proceedings. Do not fool yourself — you can not change a woman's value system to match your own.

Balanced Interest

You must share a common mindset. Both of you must be prepared for a relationship and equally interested. The doors must be open. If either of you has unresolved issues or reasons why an exclusive relationship is not going to work, chances are slim. The interest on her part must be roughly equal to yours. If she is more interested, you will resist making commitments and moving the relationship forward. Perhaps you have had these feelings before. If the reverse is the case, you may find yourself working very hard to draw her closer and become frustrated when she doesn't respond. The two of you need to become a "we" and an "us." When this is the case you can face outside problems together and share intimacies within the privacy of your relationship.

Cognitive Communication

Much of your interaction will be in the form of conversation, discussion and sharing of ideas. Your education levels do not have to be equal. However, your ability to discuss ideas should be balanced. Otherwise, one of you will always feel inferior and intimidated.

If you have chemistry and emotional fulfillment, matching value systems, an equal interest in the relationship and the ability to talk, you have an excellent chance to succeed even with trials and challenges that will surely come. Of course, you'll share a lot of joy as well.

Would you like a simple reality test? Plan and execute some significant activity together and see how it goes. Paint a room. Plan a trip or a party. Fill out a Form 1040! That should help. Was it easy and pleasant? Would you like to do more? Would you be interested in a ten-hour car trip with her? Would she? If the answer is less than enthusiastic, you should re-think your relationship.

When You Are Dating

The trick is to balance your hormones with your gray matter. You should be thinking as much as you are feeling. The feeling part is very easy. It almost takes care of itself. Look. Be honest. It would be possible for you to work up some heat for a very wide variety of women. Every woman has some level of charm and sexuality. The hard part is thinking about the other factors — matching value systems, an equal interest in the relationship and the ability to intellectually relate. It will take time and thought to uncover this information. You are seeking *potential*. However, sometimes you can tell right away. The problem is that it is easy to overlook red flags when your testosterone is controlling the show. It will require discipline and character to accomplish this.

Don't forget that it goes the other way. Dating is a true marketplace. You must exhibit *potential* as a partner in order to start the process. You will both be evaluating each other.

Are You in Love, Lust or Serious Like?

How do you know when you have succeeded? Good question. It is a major problem for many guys. The real question is, how do you know when you have found love? Philosophers have pondered this for ages. While we don't presume to have the answer, here are some observations based on experience.

People that are involved in successful, loving relationships share some characteristics. You would do well to do your own study of happy couples you know. After all, isn't this where you want to be?

First, happy couples are friends. They share their lives with one another — the good, the bad and the ugly. There is an old saying about sharing — "A sorrow shared is halved, a joy shared is doubled." Friends want to spend time together. They miss each other when they are apart. This is the best foundation for a relationship because it will endure. Endeavor to make her your friend first.

Second, successful relationships are built on matching value systems. As we stated earlier, this is complicated. It is often easier to approach it by exception. Because your value system is essential to your identity, you must be certain that there are no serious conflicts between you and your intended. Views on values like religion, parenthood, or lifestyle can make or break a potential relationship. They are best evaluated and identified early, *before* emotional issues cloud your judgment.

A word of caution — do not expect to change her. By the time people reach adulthood, their value systems and mode of behavior are deeply ingrained and difficult to reverse. If any changes do occur, it won't be because of another person's wishes. She will change for her own reasons, not yours. Isn't that true of you?

Finally, you must have emotional chemistry. You know what we are talking about. Unfortunately, too many people lead with this aspect. It is easy to do. Initial infatuation can be very strong and cause you to ignore friendship and values. Big mistake. This doesn't mean that you can't enjoy exciting and even passionate dating. Just don't make the mistake of substituting physical attraction alone for love.

If you believe that your budding relationship is based on friendship, matching values and emotional chemistry, you are well on your way. As long as both parties share generous portions of all three, the relationship has a good chance of success.

The best strategy is to try to cultivate the relationship in the above order. Of course, stages will intermingle. People will often discuss their values on the first date. Infatuation may very well be initially present. That's okay. However, we encourage you to work toward developing a friendship as you learn about her value system. The chemistry will take care of itself. Don't misinterpret an apparent lack of emotional interest as a dead end. Be persistent. In the movie *When Harry Met Sally*, there are some priceless interviews with elderly couples discussing the beginnings of their relationships. Rent it and you will be surprised at some of the stories. Indeed, the script describes ten years of rocky friendship between Billy Crystal and Meg Ryan before they eventually fall in love.

The best you can do is to *choose well*. The classic mistake unhappy lovers make is to choose the wrong person and invest all their emotion and commitment. *One of the benefits of being single is that you still have the opportunity to make an excellent selection.* Don't sit and envy all those who are settled and married. More than half of them will end up paying large sums of money to divorce attorneys because of their poor choices. Do everything you can to avoid this mistake by choosing well; a choice based on friendship and shared values *as well* as chemistry.

Realize that there is another side to the story. A relationship has to work from both sides. While you are choosing, you are being *chosen* (or not)! This means that you must present a worthy potential partner to the woman you are pursuing. A good relationship requires that both parties are happy and satisfied. If you are pleased with your choice and manage to persuade or cajole her into a relationship in which she is *less than* happy and satisfied, disaster is imminent. A relationship is a combination of the desirable qualities and the individual problems of *both* parties. This means you can increase your odds of success by eliminating or minimizing as many of *your* problems and inadequacies as possible. However, we are not suggesting that you should be untruthful — this will only backfire.

Crucial Strategies

You always have to keep the ultimate goal uppermost in your mind. Unless you are dating strictly for fun with no expected outcomes, you are looking for a lifetime partner. If this is the case your best chance for success is to nurture in your lady an emotional desire to be in a permanent relationship with you. It may sound a bit contrived, but you are going to have to be very savvy to accomplish this. You have to think, not just feel. You need to continually analyze what creates good relationships (yours and others') and what destroys them. We will discuss this at length later.

It's a jungle out there. You already know that. Sometimes it seems as though there are no available women. You know that this is not true. Let's take a look at the odds.

Chapter 2
The Odds

"In the middle of difficulty lies opportunity."
— *Albert Einstein*

The Odds

The dating process is statistical. We hate to get cold about this. (You accountant types will love it.) It really is a numbers game. With your standards and self-knowledge in place you face the female population. That's a lot of women. You need to meet as many as possible to increase your odds. If you know anyone in sales, especially people who do cold calls, talk to them. They call on a lot of people and experience a lot of rejection. They depend on the odds to pay the rent. If they make sales on one to five percent, that's more than enough. This is a good lesson for you. If you follow this logic, the more you are rejected, the closer you are to a "sale." Turning this around, you should be very concerned if you are not experiencing rejection. It means that you are hedging your bets and not trying hard enough. Remember, rejection is not personal. Since a woman you have just met knows very little about you, her lack of interest is hardly an accurate value judgment of you as a person. She is not interested for her own reasons that could be completely unrelated to you. Let it roll off you.

If you have Internet access, visit the Web site of the U.S. Census bureau at www.census.gov.

You can learn a great deal about the male/female distribution. It is broken down by state and county. We're not going to quote many statistics here as they are dynamic and don't hold much meaning for you at the national level. (If you live in Wyoming, the odds are much different than in Los Angeles.) However, here are some highlights and insights as of March, 1997.

Female Population Over 18
Total – 101,414,000
Never Married – 20,503,000 – The most likely group depending on your age.
Divorced – 11,107,000 – Your choice, could be a problem — kids, the ex, etc.

Separated – 3,018,00 – Not recommended. Wait until it's final and she has her head together.
Widowed, Married, Other?? – 66,786,000 – Forget it, except for the very small group of younger widows. *Never date a married/engaged woman.* This is big trouble. You can't afford it and you don't have time for it. For that matter, avoid women who are in a relationship. Tell her to give you a call when she is free. Have some standards.

Hence, the probable number of available women over the age of 18 under the Stars and Stripes is 31,610,000. Of course, some of them are 78 years old. So . . .
20-24 Years Old – 8,561,000
25-29 Years Old – 9,468,700
30-34 Years Old –10,708,200
35-39 Years Old – 11,318,400

Now obviously these statistics conflict. There is overlapping. However, it is enough for you to get the idea. Clearly, a large portion of the 20-24 year old group is going to be unmarried. Inversely, most of the 11+ million divorcees are going to be in the more mature brackets. This is not pure. It's just interesting.

If you explore the data, you can fine tune it even further. The number of females in the 20-24 year old group living in the Northeast is about 3,140,000. Want to go further? The number of 29-year-old females living in Pennsylvania as of July 1, 1996 is estimated at 83,777. Of course, we don't know about their availability.

You might want to check out the competition. For example, the number of 29-year-old males living in Pennsylvania as of July 1, 1996 is estimated at 81,872. So what? *In general the distribution of males and females is more or less equal.* However, you may discover that certain areas of the country are slightly out of balance. If you really want to play with the percentages you could consider relocating.

At the national level your competition looks like this:
Male Population Over 18
Total – 92,154,000
Never Married – 25,375,000 – Bad news. There are 4,872,000 excess bachelors running around — probably in the younger age brackets. Many women will consider an older guy. You had better clean up your act. A percentage of these guys are, of course, gay. From the standpoint of the heterosexual, this helps your quest by slightly increasing your odds.
Divorced – 8,208,000 – A little help here. There are 2,899,000 excess female divorcees to consider if that works for you.
Separated – 1,956,000 – Fierce competition. These guys are possessed. We've been there and done that. After several years of marriage they will consider

dating the statue of Venus de Milo. Many women will consider going out with them. The numbers? 1,062,000 excess females. It doesn't help, but since you shouldn't consider dating separated women, (remember they're *still* married) it's probably not significant.

Widowed, Married, Other?? – 59,161,000 – A difference of 7,625,000 Two things here. Obviously, there are a ton of older female widows. Women still outlive us by several years. (Another reason to take excellent care of your health — revenge. Fool them. Outlive her and *you* spend all the money)! The second thing is the shame of our gender. *Married men fool around and single women let them.* It happens all the time. This takes available women out of circulation and increases the competition unfairly. So, if you're married, give this book to a bachelor and don't fool around. Of course, women who are willing to fool around with married guys are probably not good prospects anyway.

Well, the trees were interesting. Now let's step back and look at the forest. *Nationally, there are several million available women who are in your age range.* At the state level, there are thousands. There is a roughly equal gang of competitors pursuing the same group as you. That should put a lot of the whining to rest. While you have reasonable opportunity, you need all the leverage you can muster. Hence, the rest of this book.

Fairy Tales and Love Songs

And what about the fairy tale theme with the knight or prince who shows up as a lady's one true love? Remember the old saying that there is someone out there for everyone if you could only find him/her? Lyrics of popular songs have poisoned the minds and expectations of millions. "I'll know the girl of my dreams when I meet her." Right. No, you won't. *There is no love at first sight.* What happens is that you are initially attracted to someone, probably on a physical level. If it works out, you go back later and claim that it was love at first sight because that's what everyone likes to hear. It makes a great story at your 25th anniversary party. If it doesn't work out it was "just one of those things."

The reality is that there are thousands, perhaps millions of women who would work out just fine as dates or long-term commitments. It is a matter of compromise, readiness, need and circumstance. Don't let this discourage you, but you must realize that you don't end up with the absolute best choice available for a girlfriend or a wife. If you look at it in statistical terms, there must be thousands of women who have more to offer. You just don't have the time and resources to meet them all.

Picture it as a major event like a college football game. You have one afternoon and about 20,000 available women. How many can you get to know well enough to ask out for Saturday night? OK, all analogies leak, but you get the point. So with luck, you could hope to date fewer than 100 girls during your bachelorhood. (We're being generous.) With luck, the average Joe will experience a dozen or so "relationships" lasting more than a few weeks. One or two of these will result in marriages. Maybe. Are you depressed? Don't be — these are just the facts. Check with your older friends and relatives for verification. (By the way, don't forget that the women are also out there meeting, rejecting, accepting, dating and marrying guys constantly — just to add to the confusion!)

So what's a guy to do? If the odds say that you will never meet the many thousand "perfect" girls for you, then *you have to do the best you can with what you've got.* You have to maximize your time by attracting and dating as many worthy women as you can. *If you do nothing — nothing will happen.* An enchanting woman is *not* going to knock on your door next Monday night when you're watching the Philadelphia-Dallas game and say, "Hi Fred, I'm here to change your life. Would you like another beer?"

You are going to meet somewhat fewer than the number of women you try to meet. You are going to date somewhat fewer than the number of women you try to date. You will very rarely be asked out. *You have a problem.* Clearly you need an edge. Actually, you need several. No. *You need every edge you can manage to attract and date the best caliber of woman you are fortunate enough to encounter in this crapshoot.* That's what you will find on the following pages.

The Long Haul

You must be patient. You will have many dating situations that will not pan out. These are not failures — they are mismatches. They are encounters that did not bear fruit for one reason or another. There is no shame in this. On the contrary, these experiences are the best way to grow and improve. There will be times, believe it or not, that you will be the one who is not interested in continuing to date someone. It goes both ways.

Imagine that you are walking down a long road with many other people. The road is very wide. You can wander to the left or right, but the group is headed in the same direction, more or less. On occasion, you bump into someone you would like to walk with for awhile and get to know. After awhile, one or the other of you decides to continue walking alone or in the company of someone else. That is her right. It is her journey, just as you have your own. Sometimes you walk with someone for quite awhile. Hopefully, at some point you will find someone to walk with for the rest of the journey. It happens all the time. This road is our daily lives. The journey is life itself. The short walks in the company of a woman are dates. The longer walks are relationships. The longest walk is, of course, marriage.

When you look at it this way, it helps. The pity is that many people constantly walk alone without attempting to join someone or even speak to her.

You must be persistent. You are not going to give up until you are in a meaningful relationship with a wonderful woman. You deserve it and so does she.

It is up to you to be persistent in your effort. It is said that Mamie Eisenhower turned down Ike's attempts to date her many times before she said yes. Of course, you don't want to be obsessive about this. That's called stalking. On a higher level, you must be persistent in your quest. You must be persistent in your self-improvement and education about the nature of relationships. Read books. Talk to others. If you stop, nothing will happen.

You must be very careful in your selection. Often, the most attractive person you date will end up being the worst choice as a partner in a relationship or marriage. Sometimes very attractive people rely entirely on their looks and neglect the more important parts of themselves. *Remember, when relationships and marriages end it is usually because the partners are not a match, not because one or the other is a bad person — although this is sometimes the case.* Therefore, the trick is to CHOOSE WELL. You must get very good at this. You must have a clear idea of what you want. You must also have a clear idea of what you offer. If you present yourself as someone who is very active and athletic in the hope of landing that type of woman and you are a couch potato, you are headed for disappointment.

Not all the information here will work for you. The characteristics and inclinations of the available male population vary immensely. For this reason we have tried to include everything we could think of from health to dancing. We have probably missed a few points. That's what second editions are for. Use what you are comfortable with and let the rest go. Pass the information on to your friends. We are all in this together. We must propagate the species or go the way of the dinosaur.

People need to date more. The key reason that they don't is the nature of the process. Men are expected to make advances and extend invitations. Women get to say yes or no. However, they must sit and wait to be asked — Mexican standoff. The man fears rejection. It hurts. The woman fears being perceived as aggressive. So, in too many cases nothing happens. As a man you need to shake things up. You must be confident enough to walk up to an interesting woman and start a conversation. Then, if things go well, you must ask for the date. We don't see how else things can improve.

Sometimes sales (that's what initial encounters involve) is about removing objections. If you look or behave like a slob, what chance do you have no matter how charming, deserving or successful you may be? No offense intended. You have to be brutally honest with yourself. Guys are real creatures of habit. We don't change easily. Much more on this later.

The key is to take an honest look at yourself as a package. Any improvements and enhancements you can manage will increase your odds and minimize your competition. Your potential dates will enjoy spending time with you. They may not even realize why. Before they know it they will be asking you to Mom's for Sunday dinner. However, before we get too carried away, there is work to do. It will be painful. You may think, "What's wrong with me the way I am?" After all, if she really loved me, she wouldn't care if I picked my nose every once in awhile. Wrong. She'll just move on to the next guy. She won't even tell you why.

Don't forget that women don't stop looking until they have major jewelry on their left hand. (Some of them continue to look, but that's another book.) So adjust your attitude, dude. You would do it for a great job. We change for our own reasons in our own time. No one can make us change. This is a fatal mistake that women make. They try to find a "fixer-upper" and usually fail. You don't want to be there. Make yourself as desirable as possible up front and she'll have less to bug you about later. (Don't worry, she'll find *something*). The benefit is that you will rise to your true level of marketability. As Ross Perot said, "Put your best foot forward and why not marry over your head?"

How can you expect to find the right woman if you don't know what you are looking for? Have you ever *really* thought about what you want? Spend some time designing your dream girl.

Chapter 3
Your Dream Girl

"I want you just the way you are."

— *Billy Joel*

Is Your Dream Girl Just That — A Dream?

The best time to establish your criteria for the kind of woman you want to date is before you meet her. Once you have met someone attractive and desirable there is a natural tendency to throw all other considerations out of the window. "I don't care if she is still married, she has gorgeous eyes." If you are very clear on your requirements, you can save yourself a lot of heartache. Remember — you can't change a woman. You have to accept her *exactly* the way she is. So you had better be certain that the way she is will be just fine for the long haul.

You should be in a good frame of mind when you do this exercise. Go someplace where you will not be disturbed. Make sure you have a few hours without any responsibilities on your mind. A park bench, library, bookstore or coffee shop should do just fine. You can use the chart below or develop your own.

Start with the qualities you require in a friend. Why are the friends you have now so important to you? (It's OK to include guys.) Dependability, honesty, sense of humor, intelligence are possible qualities that come to mind. Put these characteristics in your own words. Example: "I like it when someone knows enough to leave me alone."

Next, consider value systems. What about religion? Attitudes about family, children, politics, alcohol, sex and other serious issues are critical to a potential relationship. You can use your own inventory as a starting point. Potential dates do not have to match your value system perfectly, but if there is too great a difference between hers and yours, a red flag should go up. These are the areas that can make or break a relationship.

15

You will probably not have to work too hard on emotional attraction. You will feel it or you won't. However, it may be helpful to make a prioritized list as a reality check. Is it really so important that your lady be a blonde? Behavioral aspects are probably more valuable here. Do you like a person who is very affectionate or do you find mushy stuff annoying? Remember that emotional attraction can develop over time. If friendship and similar values are in place there is always opportunity to grow chemistry between two people. The reverse is not true.

Try to paint a picture of the type of woman you would like to meet. *Write it down.* You should have two columns. One is a list of the absolutely essential characteristics she must have. Be careful here. These are the deal-killers. Examples are religion, views on children, height, age, health, values, type of personality, education, or level of physical activity. These are areas where you will absolutely *not* compromise. They should have a lot more to do with *who* a person is than her physical characteristics. The reason these criteria are there is because they must match your own. You should have a solid reason for each one.

Some examples:

She *must* be a Roman Catholic — You are of this faith and would insist on raising your children as Catholics.

She *must* be a college graduate — You have a master's degree and really enjoy intellectual discussions on a wide range of topics.

She *must* not have any children — You have made a decision that you do not want to be involved in raising another man's kids and want to have a few of your own.

She *must* be 5'9" or less in height — You are 5'7" and a two-inch difference is about all you can handle.

Notice also that these criteria are not adjustable or not easily so. She either has kids or she doesn't. Clearly a person can get a college degree later, but are you willing to wait for that? Once you have this list you should use it to narrow your choice of dating partners. There is no sense wasting each other's time if there is no possibility of a match.

Religion can be a critical issue in a relationship. Many people are non-committal about it. Others have very strict rules about marriage and children. The clergy and the family will expect the intended spouse to raise the children within the faith and to perhaps convert. This will be obvious early on. Don't ignore it. Others may be satisfied if both parties attend worship services together on a regular basis. What you need to understand is that religious differences will intensify as the relationship grows. You need to address it early and move on if you can't reach agreement.

Family lifestyle is also very important. Do you expect your wife to stay home and raise the kids. How will you balance her career, yours and the family? Will you entertain a lot? How much time do you need away from the home playing golf or seeing your buddies? What about her? A great deal of marriage counseling time is dedicated to these issues. Know what would make you comfortable. Know how you expect her to feel. Use this knowledge when you are considering a relationship with a woman.

How do you feel about personal development? Are you quite happy with yourself just the way you are? Do you strive to grow and continually remake yourself? Another big topic in marriage counseling is change. "He's not the same guy I married" or "she doesn't want to try new things. I'm bored." Look back over your past and hers. Is there a pattern of growth? Better to understand this now, than to suffer later.

Other possible requirements might include being a nonsmoker or social drinker; interest in and support for your career; an ability to resolve differences (good temperament), a resident of the area; being financially responsible; or having a life vision or commitment to personal growth.

The second column includes those things that would be nice to have. Again they should not be trivial. Men who will only date redheads with long legs really need to sit down and think about this. On the other hand, if you are a professional athlete, your future sweetie had darned well be a real fan of your sport. You must be willing to compromise on some of these criteria, but not most of them. It is reasonable to include some physical preferences as long as you are prepared to be flexible when you find someone who exceeds expectations in most other ways. If you are attracted to a great smile or someone who is petite — that's reasonable. If you are demanding a great body, you had better have one, too! We think you get the idea, but here are some examples:

She *should* be a tennis player — You just love the game and play a lot.

She *should* have a good sense of humor — You are the guy always telling jokes at the party.

She *should* be petite — You are not that big yourself and enjoy dancing with and hugging a smaller gal.

She *should* like country music and line dances — You were born and raised in El Paso and don't understand people from New York.

Absolute Requirements	It Sure Would Be Nice If . . .

Be sure to spend some time envisioning your relationship with your dream girl as well.

What do you see the two of you doing?

What kinds of feelings will you experience?

Location, Location, Location

Long-distance relationships have an extremely low chance of succeeding. You should avoid the heartache for both of you by sticking to the female population within a two-hour drive of your place. This only makes sense. If things do start to heat up, how can you be part of her daily or even weekly life if you live four hundred miles away? Phone, fax and e-mail are not sufficient. You have to be there on a regular basis. Choose local women or relocate.

Age

How old should a date be? This is a very interesting topic. Beyond the obvious legal limitations, the only concerns should be compatible stage of life, and the perceptions of society. Americans are much more restrictive than other cultures in this regard. It seems to be universally accepted that men are often older than their mates. This is not absolute, of course. It's just the way things are. In some cultures, this age difference is encouraged. The reasoning is that a more mature man has the experience and resources to properly care for a wife and family.

An important consideration is the maturity of each party. There are men who mature at an early age, although this seems to be atypical. It is generally accepted that girls and women mature more quickly than their male peers. Some men seem to physically age more quickly than others. On the other hand, today it is not uncommon to find men in their forties and even fifties who have the same appearance, interests and vitality as much younger guys. These are some of the factors affecting age differences. Obviously, it comes down to the individuals involved. There are characteristics associated with every stage of life. If you share the same life stage, the odds of success are higher.

There is also energy level, for lack of a better term. When people are young, they typically have more energy than later in life. Some people lose this energy early. Indeed, some never seem to have it at all. Others keep a high-energy level for most of their lives. This is an area where a high-energy man might be more comfortable with a younger woman.

Now we are not making a case either way. What is essential is that you must honestly evaluate your own "age" and decide upon an appropriate age or stage of life for your potential partners. You must also look out twenty years or so.

Chronological Age

First, consider mortality. Nobody likes to think about it, but women live several years longer than men on average. If you add an age difference, your beloved will spend perhaps ten years or more as a widow. While this is commonly accepted, it's something to consider before you get too serious. Reviewing your family history may be helpful when determining your prospects.

You should consider parenthood as well. A younger woman will want to start a family and can afford to wait a while, perhaps into her thirties. If you are older, you should project your age through the childhood of your potential offspring to see how this will pan out. For example, a forty-year old man gets married to a twenty-eight year old woman. They decide to wait a couple of years to start a family. The man is forty-two when his wife becomes pregnant. He is forty-three when the first child is born. (There may be other children.) He is forty-nine when the child enters school. He is sixty when the child graduates from high school and enters college. He is sixty-four when the first child graduates from college. One problem is that college expenses are conflicting with saving for retirement. By the way, his wife will be twelve years younger at each milestone. Also, remember that women statistically outlive men by five years or more.

When you look at things this way, it probably makes more sense for a man to marry an older woman! This does happen, but not often. Society seems to be most comfortable with a difference of five to ten years. Beyond the common sense factors discussed above there is some age prejudice alive and well in America. There is the "dirty old man" or "cradle robber" image associated with an older guy and a younger woman. Of course, this depends on the appearance and energy level of the man. Also, women harbor feelings that older guys should be reserved for the troops of their eligible older sisters. We say chart your own course. Determine the age group where you are most comfortable. How old are most of your friends and associates?

Biological Age

Some people are blessed with good genes. They stay youthful and energetic for decades. When combined with good habits (no smoking, minimal drinking), exercise and proper diet, some can appear many years younger than their actual years — effective grooming and youthful clothing also help. Do you attend your high school reunions? You should for a number of reasons. Here you will find ample evidence of this phenomenon. Some classmates will still look like the day they graduated, while others look like their grandfathers. The bottom line is that you can control all the factors mentioned except your genetic programming which is the most powerful.

It is difficult to be empirical about this. There is no finite way to determine your biological age. It is totally subjective. The best you can do is play "Guess how old I am?" from time to time and average the responses.

Social Age

Make a list of as many of your friends and associates as possible. These would be the people you gravitate to and spend the most time with. A group of at least ten would be best. Add their ages and divide by the number of people. You could consider this your *social age*. How does it differ from your chronological age? How does it compare with your biological age? If your social age matches with your younger woman it will increase your odds for success. Age differences will fade over time. Consider the difference between 25 and 35 when compared to 45 and 55. If you are older than your partner you may have to face other potential problems. You may be in better shape financially. Money still means power, no matter what anyone tells you. You may assume a fatherly role in the relationship which she may resent. You may discover yourself behaving in ways that are not the real you in order to keep up with her younger lifestyle. Of course there may be overriding positives such as strong compatibility and matching value systems that will minimize these negatives. It really is up to the two of you.

Children

This is a huge issue. *You must have an opinion about it.* You don't need to express that opinion on the first date, but it's just good to have one for a number of reasons. The older you are, the more critical the issue becomes. Some women are already mothers. How do you feel about this? If you are absolutely certain that it is unacceptable, fine. Just have an opinion. You cannot expect to seriously date a woman with children without your lives becoming intertwined. It is something you must accept. They are a package deal. Of course, they probably have a natural father. That's a whole other program. Some guys love the idea of a built-in family. There is a lot of complexity here. We are just asking you to give it serious thought. There is no sense starting down the road with a woman with children if you are not going to be able to deal with them.

If you have children, you have a challenge as well. Your dates are going to have to have this information fairly soon. It could go either way for you. We do not recommend that you introduce a date to your kids until well into a relationship. It is not fair to the kids or to her. Children bond easily. You are probably divorced, so they are already going through a lot. They don't need to get attached to your girlfriend, only to have you move on in a few weeks. Keep your dating and your fathering separate. *Also, make sure that your fathering comes first.* We know this is tough, but that's what good Dads (and real men) do.

As childless women approach their late thirties many of them begin to panic. You have heard of the ticking "biological clock," no doubt. While medical science is doing incredible things with reproduction, there are serious problems for a woman at this stage of life. The longer she waits, the less likely it is that she will conceive. There are procedures to help, but they are expensive and marginally successful. Additionally, later pregnancies carry more risk for the baby and the mother. What does all this mean? It has an impact on dating. Time is now an issue for these women. They must find the right guy who will be a good husband and father and want to have children right away. That's a lot of pressure. You need to be aware and sensitive to this when you are involved with her. The dating cycle is compressed. She will not be willing to give you several years to make up your mind. Also, you need to be fair and not trifle with her affections if you are not prepared to move at a faster pace. As always, honesty and communication go a long way. You will have to have frank discussions fairly early on. Another consideration is that some women in this position might behave more desperately than they would have ten years ago. You must take this into consideration.

If you are certain that you do not want children, that is your right. You will severely limit the pool of women who will be willing to seriously date you. It is something you will have to accept. If you really mean what you say, get a vasectomy. It is a very simple procedure — it just sounds bad. There is a reversal procedure that has a high percentage of success, but it is expensive. You should postpone such a serious decision until your thirties. Of course, you will have to communicate this to any woman you get serious about. There are women who are very serious about their careers or who don't want to be moms for other reasons. There are just not that many of them. She may have elected to have a tubal ligation, which will prevent her from conceiving.

If you are younger and are not a father now, your options are wide open. You have time. You can date whom you please. Know this — most women want to be mothers. It's a natural fact. You don't have to face this right away, but once things get serious it will come up. Here is where you should have an opinion. Do you want them at all? Do you want them sooner or later? How many? It is best to have a general idea of what you eventually want. It shows responsibility on your part. That is always attractive to women.

Ex-Husbands and In-Laws

If there is a man in her past who had a significant relationship with her, you may have to contend with some fallout. He could be an ex-husband, a former fiancée or even a long-term boyfriend. If there are *no children involved*, she should have resolved all their issues before getting involved with someone else. This is a good measure of her emotional health and maturity. If the ties are still in place — watch out. You want a clear field. You deserve it. Sometimes he will still be in contact with her parents and family. She may still be in contact with his. Decide how much of this you are willing to tolerate. After all, are you hauling all this baggage to her doorstep? Courtesy and civility are one thing. Spending Christmas with this guy and his family is another.

Children are an entirely different matter. Understand something very clearly. *Kids always come first.* If she is a mom, then she is a mom first and your girlfriend second. It has to be that way. Those kids have a dad and he has to be big part of their lives. That makes him a big part of *your* life if you get serious with her. This is a package deal. It is not an easy road. That doesn't make it impossible. It will take a lot of maturity, commitment and patience on your part to make things work. Maybe she is worth it. Also, you need to accept his family as part of the kids' lives. They may be in-laws from Hell. You will have to be accommodating and pleasant in order for the kids to maintain their involvement with his folks.

If you are a dad, then you can reverse engineer the last paragraph. She has to be willing to embrace the whole program. Kids require constant care and attention until the age of eighteen. They will always be a part of your lives as adults. Think very carefully about all of this. That cute little five-year old will be arguing with his mom for the car in eleven short years. By the way, how will things work if the two of you have one or two kids of your own? Will all things be equal for all the kids — yours, mine and ours? *The Brady Bunch* was just a TV show. Be very careful.

The List

How do you use the list? Simple. Memorize your "I gotta have" list and don't get involved with a woman if she fails on one or more of the points. You may have to ask some questions first. Now you see why it is so important to make sure that the absolutes are absolute. With an extensive list, you are going to eliminate a lot of great women. That's the way it goes. Better now than later. As you begin to date keep an eye on the "it sure would be nice if" list. Try *not* to be too distracted by the physical chemistry at this point. We are not saying you shouldn't enjoy it — just don't give up your list for it.

The last point about your list is that it should be flexible enough to change and grow as you do. Your dating career may span several years. You will be growing and improving all the time. What seemed important at the beginning may seem trivial in a few years. Evaluate your list every few months and include some insights from your dating experiences. Maybe it is not so important that she is a good dancer or likes football after all.

Another tip as you are preparing this list is to think carefully about all your past dating and relationships. What qualities really pleased you about each woman? What were the deal killers? Make a list of every woman you have ever dated. What was desirable about each one? What was it that ended the relationship? Include the characteristics of some women you *wished* you had dated as well. You will find some good clues here.

Name	Qualities	Problems

We have been having fun with the idea of a "dream girl." The reality is, of course, that there is no perfect match for you. She doesn't exist. You really shouldn't be searching for her. Instead, focus all your attention on this golden period of your life. It should be exciting, satisfying and beneficial. You can grow more during your single years than at any other time in your life. You have total control over your time and behavior. Use this power to learn about yourself and relationships. You have the luxury of preparing yourself for a great relationship. It's as if you know that your friends are going to throw you a surprise party at your house sometime in the next six months. You don't know when it will happen, but you have plenty of time to prepare.

Your Choice

A few points are in order here. You can be *exclusive* or *inclusive* in your selection process. This means that you can decide not to date anyone unless they meet all of your critical qualifications. Stated another way, you will eliminate anyone who would not qualify as a wife. If you have a great deal to offer as a potential mate this may be okay. On the other hand, there are some advantages to dating a wider circle of women:

1. The more you date, the more you increase your skills and confidence. There is nothing wrong with going out with someone without any expectations. Actually, it can be very enjoyable — because there is no pressure.

2. You can never have too many friends, especially women. You will find that women form strong circles of friendship. If she becomes your friend and thinks you are a worthy candidate, she will refer you.

3. It's the right thing to do. Spread the joy. Be a nice guy. It's good for you. You would be surprised how seldom women who are not super-models are asked out.

4. Your criteria will change as you date more. You will move closer to a more accurate definition of what will make you happy.

5. *You just never know.* In spite of all your analysis and pre-conceived notions, you may discover yourself dating, then falling in love with the most unlikely woman. In that case, pass this book onto a friend and accept our apologies and congratulations. Where you end up is a lot more important than how you got there.

Once your criteria are in place you will encounter a wide range of women who meet your qualifications. Some will barely make the cut. Some will excel in every category and knock your socks off. A large number will fall somewhere in between. So how high should you set your expectations? This is really tough. There is some internal psychology at play here.

You need to recognize that the small circle of intelligent, charming, drop-dead gorgeous women at the top of the food chain will not be particularly interested in you because you don't meet *their* criteria. However, somewhere south of that it will be possible for you to have success. You will, of course, be challenged to the maximum extent of your capabilities when encountering these women. At the same time, your adrenaline levels will be off the scale. This is good. You need to have a bit of a challenge or it's just no fun.

The inverse situation goes something like this. You may meet a woman who barely qualifies as a potential partner but is very attracted to you. She pays a lot of attention to you and is very complimentary. She makes it very clear that she would love to date you. How does this make you feel? Well, nice, of course. Everyone loves this type of attention. However, there is very little challenge, no intimidation and no thrill. It probably won't work. Weird, isn't it?

Once you have given some serious consideration to the type of woman you would like to date, it is time to turn your attention to yourself. The next few chapters will focus on your self-improvement. Let's start with some self-assessment.

Chapter 4

You

"Man is the artificer of his own happiness."
— Henry David Thoreau, Journal, January 21, 1838

Don't Be a Weenie

In a good match both partners are interested in pleasing each other. You can get a sense for this very early in the dating process. *Watch for signs of inconsiderate behavior or unkindness. Don't tolerate it. It will not change.* If she is rude to her friends, family or co-workers — you're next. On the other hand, she should not be meek and easily manipulated. Sometimes men gravitate to women like this because they are easy conquests and can be controlled. This is a character flaw on the part of the guy. You will not have any respect for a woman who is too meek and has low self-esteem. Again, she will not change and you will regret it when she is clinging to your leg as you try to escape.

The best combination is a woman who is receptive to your initiatives, but who is still challenging. She may only accept you as a friend at first. That's okay. Actually, that's the best place to start. Give it some time — perhaps a couple of months. The strongest trees grow very slowly. Weeds grow very quickly.

A successful relationship consists of two people who match on several levels. Adults are fully developed and only change on their own terms. Therefore, everything required by both parties must be in place beforehand. This is what makes it so difficult. Men are walking around with a key and women are walking around with a lock. While it is true that many keys will fit inside many locks, most of the combinations will not work. What is amazing is that so many couples will attempt to match and stay together even if the lock doesn't open. Don't let this happen to you.

Read the verse about marriage in *The Prophet* by Kahlil Gibran. He compares a married couple to two trees that stand next to each other. While their roots and branches intermingle, they are independent entities.

25

If you accept the principles contained in this book and are concerning your-self with friendship and matching values, it becomes easier to locate candidates. They are busy improving themselves and involved in activities that develop and nurture the body, mind and spirit. It doesn't have to be serious. What is clear is that bars are probably not the best bet. Volunteer organizations, community events, galleries, museums, charities, church groups and college courses are a few examples of high value hunting.

Looking at the Guy in the Mirror

We're not talking about your appearance here, although we will. If you want to become a desirable dating partner you will have to make necessary improvements from the inside-out. The good news is that you are probably a pretty nice guy to begin with. You have many fine qualities such as honesty, sincerity and a capacity for love. Maybe you are shy or needy. These are the types of improvements you will want to concentrate on. You can work on the outside as well, although some characteristics cannot be changed. The important thing to remember is that your internal qualities will always win out over your appearance. A worthy woman of quality will place more value on character than looks in the long run. You may have to go deep inside yourself to discover your goodness, but the process itself will increase your self-confidence and therefore, your attractiveness.

Have you ever seen a very attractive woman with a man of average or less-than-average looks? Have you ever noticed that this situation seems to be more common than the reverse? There is a reason for this. Women are probably more advanced from an evolutionary standpoint than men. After all, we start all the wars and fill the jails. They are raising most of the kids, many times by themselves. Women look for things that go deeper than looks. If you have a solid value system, some personality and humor, and have worked hard to secure a life for yourself — you have the right stuff. *Love is blind.* Women will look past a big nose or bad complexion if you have the rest of the package. While this is not a universal truth, there are enough women who feel this way to make your efforts worthwhile. Of course, it will never work unless you have faith and believe it.

Look at it this way. Beauty is in the eye of the beholder. Another way to say this is that women will create their own image of you and your looks in their imagination. If she decides that you are very worthy and desirable based on character, personality, and the way you treat her, she will make you handsome in her own mind. This is exactly where you want to be. Love lives in her internal emotions, not on your face or biceps. Turning the situation around, if you *were* great looking, but lacked the more important elements, you could not possibly sustain a relationship with any woman of quality. In this sense, you can be way ahead of most Hollywood stars. (Check out *their* track records!)

By the way, if you are seeking true happiness with a woman, you may want to take a hard look at your own search criteria. Take a tip from the ladies and switch your priorities. A great looking pair of legs is a truly beautiful thing, but a sincere, caring woman who really loves you will sustain you through good times and bad.

Take Stock

You need an inventory of yourself to make any progress. This will be tough, but well worth it. You must also periodically revisit your inventory to assess your improvement and make adjustments.

POSITIVE QUALITY	COMMENT
Values	Honesty, caring, generosity, etc.
Intelligence	
Personality	
Career	
Social Abilities	
Achievements	
Capacity for love	
Physical Appearance	
Emotional Capacity	

Begin to think of yourself as a work in progress. You are completely comfortable with your value as a human being. You have your priorities in order, you treat other people with respect and consideration and you are happy to be walking down the road of life. You have nothing to apologize for. What others think of you or how they treat you does not alter your view of yourself.

You are striving to improve and know that you will succeed. It's simply a matter of time and effort. The guy you will be in one year will be much more desirable than the guy you are today, no matter what. The women who meet you then will be very fortunate.

The secret of power is inside you, not in the outside world. Comparing yourself to others is futile. They are no better or no worse than you. They are on their own journey. It doesn't matter. Your strength is that you are completely worthy of love exactly the way you are. Knowing this will put a smile on your face and a spring in your step that is very attractive to the opposite sex. This confidence comes from your self-knowledge — not from the way that others treat you. The beauty of all this is that when you encounter women that are also well-adjusted and self-confident, you will be attracted to each other on that level. This is much more valuable and enduring than physical attraction.

The power of this knowledge will sustain you as you endeavor to make other improvements in your self-inventory. Your deficiencies will seem less important and will not impede you as much. You will have the strength and confidence to apply the required effort to eliminate weaknesses as an obstacle.

Convince yourself that you will be in a constant mode of change and improvement for the *rest of your life.* The idea that you can work hard for a few months, achieve some success and then coast should be abandoned right now. This will give you the patience that you need. If the job is never going to be done, you will not appear impatient. Women are attracted to men who seem to be on the move and changing all the time. It keeps them off balance and creates an air of mystery. You are constantly evaluating your experiences, good and bad. You learn from them. You adjust. If one thing doesn't work, you try another. You're not afraid to start over. You NEVER give up. You are determined to succeed. You will not be denied. This is the most powerful force in the cosmos.

As Calvin Coolidge once said, "Nothing in the world takes the place of persistence. Talent will not; nothing is more common than unsuccessful men with talent. Genius will not; the world is full of educated derelicts. Persistence and determination alone are omnipotent. The slogan 'press on' has solved and always will solve the problems of the human race."

Good Looks or Looking Good?

Let's face it. Some guys are blessed with natural good looks. You see them in the movies and on TV all the time. Now, we are not placing undue value on this factor, but you have to be realistic. The first thing any woman will notice about you is your looks. Isn't it the same for you? If the woman is intelligent and insightful, she will try to learn more about you given the opportunity. If a woman immediately rejects you based on your looks (or lack thereof), you have lost nothing. Let her move on.

Having said all of that, you would be foolish to ignore your looks. They are your calling card. You need to work very hard to make the best of what you have. Now, looks are composed of factors that you can control (and improve) and those that are out of your control. It would be wise to acknowledge the factors out of your control and accept them. Here are a few examples:

- Height — Unless you are seventeen, that's it, guy.
- Bone structure — If you are very slight or put together like a WWF star, you'll have to accept it. Of course muscle mass and body fat percentage are another matter.
- Facial shape and appearance — Unless you have major plastic surgery, your chin, nose, ears, forehead, etc. are permanent.
- Hair — If you are bald or nearly so, that's the card you were dealt. Thanks, Granddad.

You get the idea. The good news is that the aspects of looks that *really* matter are controllable. You will find details and specific advice later in the book, but wardrobe, fitness and grooming can all be greatly improved to make you look your best. Part of the trick is to be consistent and pay attention to these factors constantly. You never know where you will bump into Miss Right. Have you ever had that experience? You roll out of bed, throw on your worst T-shirt and shorts and stumble down to the store for some coffee and WHAM! There she is in line in front of you. She looks at you like you are slime. Never let this happen to you. Always be in a position to seize opportunities, by checking your appearance on the way out of the house.

You have to know who you are and do your best to improve yourself. You have to know what kind of person you are looking for. You have to have the resourcefulness, persistence and discipline to search until you find a match. This is really what it's all about. Of course, there are hundreds of details in the process. However, as long as you are focused on the goal stated above you will succeed. *The most important thing is to try to make the right choice!* Fortunately, because you are single you have the opportunity to do just that.

Take your time, take stock of yourself and make all the improvements you can. Thoroughly enjoy the dating process. Properly set your expectations for the women you encounter. Be clear about your wants and needs. Be realistic. You will have to settle for something less than perfect. After all, how close are you to perfection?

Your attitude and mental health will be much better when you focus on your own development and well-being. The ancient Greeks used to pursue a balance of mind, body and spirit. Strive for this, rather than moping about the number of dates you haven't had. Concentrate on developing all three. Get very busy with this. Everything else will fall in place. Think about the journey and the process, not landing the woman you want. Stay the course. Have you ever been sailing? If not, the challenge and pleasure of it is the time spent on the water, not the destination. You must constantly adjust the sails, check your course heading and improve the performance of the boat. You are never able to go straight from point A to point B. Currents, wind shifts and physics will require you to zigzag your way across the water. You enjoy the sights, sounds and feel of the journey. It is a beautiful thing. Does it matter where you end up? Well, maybe, but the whole point is the quality of the time spent on the journey. Think of dating in this way.

Talk privately to guys who have had a successful single life and are now in a healthy relationship. They may reveal that although they are quite happy, they sometimes miss the single life! They will actually envy your position. This doesn't mean that they are unhappy or would trade places with you. It means that it is very possible to have a happy, exciting life as a single man. Embrace this. Work to make this one of the happiest times of your life. Stay the course.

We think it is a good idea to keep track of your progress and ensure that you are doing your best to improve and meet your goals. We will be discussing many of these factors in the following chapters. Look at the checklists in the Appendix. These checklists may prove useful to you. Keep the first three on your desk or in your appointment book. Put the last three on your bathroom mirror. Add rows and modify as you see fit. Eventually these points will become habits.

Before we consider cosmetics and appearance, let's work from the inside-out. You need to address your essential health first.

Chapter 5
To Your Health

"We should pray for a sound mind in a sound body."
— Juvenal, Satires (10:356), c. 115 AD.

Suck It Up, Buddy

You need to be the kind of person you would like to date. Depending on your current status, there is probably work to do — perhaps a great deal of work. You would probably appreciate a date that is healthy and fit. Men are very interested in the condition and appearance of a woman's body. How is yours? You enjoy the company of women who are well groomed and attractive. What do you see when you look in the mirror? Are you more interested in a very needy person who is not in control of her life and constantly in crisis mode? What do you have to offer? The dating scene is a pure marketplace. The buyers and the sellers are both buying and selling. You must leverage every advantage you can to increase your chances. We have attempted to consider every possible objection a woman might have to dating a man. Perhaps you are in fine shape. If not, suck it up and get to work. The rewards are well worth the effort.

Health

This is the most important section of the book. Without your health, you have little hope of a happy life, let alone a successful dating career. You need the confidence, energy and enhanced appearance of a well-maintained healthy body to attract the same. You have heard much of this before, but here it comes again. If you gain nothing else from this book, we hope you take some steps to improve your health. If you are a triathlon champion, please skip to the next chapter with our apologies. Otherwise, please continue.

Serious Business

The 10 Leading Causes of Death, 1995

1. Heart Disease	32%
2. Cancer	23.3%
3. Stroke	6.8%
4. Chronic Obstructive Lung Disease	4.5%
5. Accidents	3.9%
6. Pneumonia and Influenza	3.6%
7. Diabetes	2.6%
8. HIV	1.8%
9. Suicide	1.3%
10. Chronic Liver Disease and Cirrhosis	1.1%

Source: National Center for Health Statistics, U.S. Dept. of Health and Human Services

We know this is unsettling, but you can't date if you are dead. You will discover that the suggestions to follow will not only improve your chances of a long and healthy life, but also increase your appeal as a dating partner.

Let's analyze these chilling statistics a bit. Some of these causes of death are under your control. The two worst, heart disease and cancer, account for over 55 percent of the death rate.

#1 *The risk of heart disease, the cause of one out of every three deaths, can be greatly minimized by exercising, eating well and controlling cholesterol.* Of course, hearts can fail for a variety of other reasons.

#2 Cancer is very complicated. For men, the top three cancer sites in order are lung, prostate and colon/rectum. Most of the lung cancers are smoking related. *Don't smoke.*

You must have a regular prostate exam by your doctor. It is unpleasant, but only takes about 30 seconds. There is a new blood test that can help detect the disease as well.

Colon cancer can be detected early with a simple scope procedure that is recommended every five years for middle-aged men. A diet high in fiber and low in red meats reduces the risk of colon/rectal cancer. *You must talk to your physician about all of these issues.* We are only pointing out the statistics and how you can improve your chances.

Lung disease, #4, is very much smoking related. *Don't smoke.*

#5 Most accidental deaths are a result of car collisions. Men are three times more likely to be killed. Don't drink and drive. Wear your seat belt. Keep your car in good repair. Be careful.

#8 You are probably familiar with the warnings concerning HIV, but here they are again. *Always wear a condom.* Don't be an IV drug user. Don't frequent prostitutes.

#9 Men are five times more likely to commit suicide than women. Keep yourself in good mental health. Seek help when you feel that you cannot cope with your life circumstances.

#10 Many liver deaths are associated with heavy drinking. Drink in moderation, if at all.

What you can easily see is that you can significantly reduce the most common causes of death by leading a healthy lifestyle, exercising some caution and regularly visiting your doctor.

You need a good physician to watch over your health. Visit him at least once a year. Do you know what your cholesterol level is? Heart disease is the number one killer in this country. You are the only one who can lower your risk. Your doctor will work with you to adjust your diet, increase your level of exercise and prescribe medication if required. High cholesterol levels are an extremely reliable indicator of future heart problems. You must get it under control. He will monitor the health of your prostate and colon. These are the two highest risk cancer sites for men. It's nice to have a male doctor close to your age. He can more easily sympathize with your problems as he is likely to be experiencing some of them himself.

Life Expectancy

These figures include the entire population and are calculated from the year of birth. The older you are, the longer you can expect to live. A man who is 70 years old has a better chance of seeing 80 than a man who is 25. These figures are for all men and are generic. Factors such as genetics, location, smoking, race, occupation, and lifestyle will have a significant impact on your life expectancy.

Age	Life Expectancy
20	74.2
25	74.6
30	74.9
35	75.4
40	75.9
45	76.5
50	77.1
55	78
60	79.2
80	87.3

It is commonly recognized that women enjoy a longer life expectancy than men. Here are some statistics to demonstrate it.

Year of Birth	Men	Women
1950	65.6	71.1
1960	66.6	73.1
1970	67.1	74.7
1980	70	77.5
1990	71.8	78.8

Some numbers you should know up front:

Your cholesterol count. It should be below 200. Check with your doctor.

Your blood pressure. There are two numbers. In general, the lower the numbers, the better. Check with your doctor.

Your resting heart rate. Check it as soon as you open your eyes in the morning. Find your pulse, count the heart rate for one full minute. Again, the lower the better. This is a good indicator of cardiovascular fitness. As you improve, your resting heart rate will decrease. Some professional athletes have resting heart rates as low as 40 or 50. This means that their hearts are so strong and their distribution systems are so clear that pumping blood to a body at rest is a breeze.

Smoking

Don't smoke. What will it take to convince you? If you don't think you are killing yourself early, check with your life insurance agent. These guys don't fool around with life expectancy. They are the masters. He will bet you hundreds of thousands of dollars that smoking will introduce you to the Grim Reaper before your time and he has the numbers to prove it. Visit some emphysema and lung cancer patients or talk to their widows, if you have the guts. See your doctor about a nicotine withdrawal program. While patches and gum are available, there is a promising product called Zyban that has a good success record. It is actually an anti-depressant that has the side effect of reducing the urge for a cigarette. After you succeed, you will feel great, smell great and immensely increase your dating potential. You can easily prove this for yourself. Look in the personals section of the Sunday paper at "Women Seeking Men." Count the number of times non-smoking is mentioned. Divide by the total number of ads. Any questions? *Most women do not want to date a smoker.* The number increases every day. Why reduce your odds? The number of smokers continues to decline in this country. The tobacco companies are on the run. Get with the program, sparky.

Tobacco:

- Stains your teeth
- Stains your fingers
- Causes halitosis
- Causes wrinkles
- Imbeds odors in your clothes, hair, car and house
- Causes dust and dirt
- Burns holes in things like women's clothing and couches

By the way, tobacco is tobacco. Women do not make distinctions. Pipe smokers look real boring. Snuff? You must be kidding. Who wants to French kiss a spittoon? Cigars are very trendy right now. Even women are in on the act. Resist, pal, resist. Unless you have a chance with Madonna, you will be banned to the deck to smoke your stogie and come out smelling like a wet Golden Retriever.

You can save major bucks if you quit. Cigarette prices continue to rise and the trend is likely to continue with the major tobacco company lawsuits in process. One pack a day at $2 for a year? $730 will buy a great Armani suit on sale or finance a $60 date each month. Do all of us a favor and quit. We don't want to pay your medical bills as you lay wheezing in a cancer ward.

Drinking

"He that drinks fast, pays slow."

— Benjamin Franklin, Poor Richard's Almanac, 1733.

Drinking is a complex issue. No one likes a drunk, including you. So what is a drunk? When is too much, too much? This can be tough. First, some serious stuff. A call to Alcoholics Anonymous can give you some signs of the disease. Do you drink alone? Do you drink in the morning? Do you black out? You need help now. Forget about dating. Get your act together so you will be alive to meet your grandchildren. Here is an agency you can contact:

The National Council on Alcoholism and Drug Abuse, Inc.
12 West 21st Street
New York, NY 10010
(212) 206-6770

The vast majority of women will be quite comfortable with a non-drinker or a social drinker. A social drinker will have one or two drinks on social occasions, but will not get drunk. It's that simple. This enables you to carry on a witty conversation and drive home. She feels safe and isn't worried about you winding up with a DUI. You will not embarrass yourself in front of her friends and family. You have discipline, character, strength and class. Good stuff.

If your lady slugs down four shots of tequila followed by a martini or two — look out, brother. Is this what you really want? While you may be headed for a quick conquest, what are you going to do with her the next day? If she's really into alcohol, she won't be happy unless you are too. Wish her the best and turn her loose.

If you decide to imbibe, here is a suggestion. Drink wine. Order a bottle with your meal (about two glasses each) or by the glass. If you love beer, fine. It has more calories, hence the term "beer-gut." Mixed drinks are a possibility. Wine has more class. You will notice that many women order it. White is more popular than red. Try a Chardonnay, white zinfandel (sweeter) or cabernet sauvignon. Merlot is a popular red wine. When you order, ask for a recommendation. Once you find one or two brands that you enjoy, you can order with some confidence. The truth is that it really doesn't matter that much. She will appreciate the fact that you are decisive and know what you want.

Special occasions are more special with sparkling wine. It doesn't necessarily have to be champagne, which can be tricky to purchase. The cheap stuff tastes like it. The expensive stuff may be out of reach. Try Asti Spumanti. A bit sweeter, but the same effect. Be sure to chill it before serving at home.

There is some recent evidence that very modest drinking (a glass of wine a day) can have a positive effect on health. The jury is still out. One thing is for certain. Alcohol is a depressant. We know it doesn't feel that way when you have a buzz, but it's true. Guess what effect a depressant has on sexual performance? That's right. So, while it lowers inhibitions, it also lowers your ability to deliver. Food for thought.

Sleep

"Early to bed and early to rise makes a man healthy, wealthy and wise."

— Benjamin Franklin, *Poor Richard's Almanac,* 1738.

Your body requires a reasonable amount of sleep each night to repair and rebuild tissues, including muscle. This can vary between six to eight hours a night or more. You can test this on a Friday or Saturday night. Make sure you won't be disturbed and note the time you go to bed. Sleep until you wake up naturally (This is a good opportunity to check your resting pulse rate.) How many hours did you sleep? How do you feel? Of course, you can sleep too much. The most important thing is to get at least your minimum each night on a consistent basis. As you work out more you will find that your body needs more sack time. You will also notice that regular sleep makes you look much better. You can tell when someone is not sleeping well by telltale bags under their eyes and a lethargic attitude — not very attractive.

Now that we have considered the serious aspects of your health, let's see what can be done to improve your vitality and appearance. You probably guessed what's next. That's right — *exercise.*

Chapter 6
Exercise!

"Every man has two doctors — his right leg and his left leg."
— Anonymous

The "E" Word

Is your waist larger than your chest? Do you find yourself out of breath walking up a flight of stairs? Has it been a while since you could look down and see your manhood when you're in the head?

YOU HAVE TO EXERCISE. It is the single best thing you can do for yourself. There are no shortcuts. You must do it. It doesn't matter what you do as long as you are working your body. The best exercise develops your cardiovascular system. Walk, jog, ride a bike, take an aerobics class or swim. These exercises, when done properly, raise your heart rate at a safely consistent level. Your heart rate is very closely related to the amount of oxygen your system can deliver to keep your muscles working. There are charts available that will tell you what is an optimum and a safe pulse rate for your age. You want to keep your pulse at 65 to 80 percent of capacity for thirty to forty-five minutes. This should be done at least three times per week.

If you make a commitment to do this for the rest of your life, you will be making the best possible investment in your health. Get some help from your doctor and do some reading. *Invest in a simple heart rate monitor — about fifty dollars.* Although you can learn to check your pulse the way nurses do, it's much more convenient. It consists of a transmitter that is strapped around your chest and a watch-type display. You simply glance at your wrist to see your current heart rate. In this way you can ensure that you are not exceeding your target rate while still challenging your system. *The benefits of effective cardiovascular exercise are immense:*

- You will reduce the risk of heart disease — the number-one cause of death in America
- You will have more energy

- You will be capable of participating in other activities such as dancing or volleyball
- You will lose fat, hence, you will be more attractive
- You will increase muscle, hence, you will be more attractive
- Your clothes will fit better, hence, you will be more attractive
- You will be a better lover

Here's an idea. Compare the number of hours you spend watching TV with the number of hours you exercise. What is the percentage? What benefit did you ever get from a rerun of *Mork and Mindy?*

Exercise releases testosterone! Isn't that great? Not only will you look more like a stud, you will have the chemicals to prove it.

Remember: *YOU REST — YOU RUST.*

Schedule your workouts as appointments and don't break them. You are making an appointment with the new, improved you. The guy who is going to look much better and be more attractive to women who haven't had the pleasure of meeting you.

Join a health club or gym. *You should visit the club at least three times a week.* One way to ensure this is to line up a reliable workout partner. This assumes that you won't be jogging or riding a bike at home as an alternative. Make it a goal to get up to 30 minutes of exercise most days of the week. *The point is that you need three sessions of aerobic activity lasting 30-45 minutes every week for the rest of your life.* That's right — for the rest of your life. Why kid yourself? You can't work very hard for a few months, meet a short-term goal and then slide backwards. The keys are consistency and stick-to-it-iveness. If you can do more down the road — that's fine. This is the most important point of the book. Nothing else will do more for you than regular exercise. Nothing.

Why is aerobic exercise so important? A strong cardiovascular system offers many benefits. The most critical is the reduction of the likelihood of heart disease, the number one cause of death among adult males. Therefore, it is your best bet to extend your life. You will have the energy to pursue your heart's desire and participate in physical activities. You will lose weight. Aerobic exercise is an extremely effective means for weight control, even more so when combined with resistance training. You will build muscle mass and lower your percentage of body fat.

It is interesting how this works. A common misconception is that the exercise stands alone as a one-for-one means of burning calories. For example, eat a piece of cheesecake — run five miles and you are even. Not quite. What happens is that you raise your heart rate considerably during the exercise. There is a powerful post-training effect. Your metabolism remains elevated for hours afterwards. Therefore during your normal daily activities, including sleep, you will burn more calories than a sedentary person.

Do you remember those toy cars that would "rev up" as you rapidly rubbed the wheels on the floor faster and faster? You would then let go and the car would zip across the floor, powered by the spinning flywheel inside the car. This is a good analogy for the post-training effect. You "rev up" your body for 30-45 minutes and it continues to pump during the rest of the day. As time goes on you will notice that your resting heart rate, which you should check as soon as you wake up, will gradually reduce. This is because your heart is getting stronger and doesn't have to work as hard to do the same job — a good sign.

Don't forget to stretch your leg muscles as well as your low back, shoulders and chest following your run, bike ride or step exercise. Stretch your calves, hamstrings, quadriceps, hip flexors and gluteus muscles. Hold each stretch for 30 seconds. Have someone at the health club show you some good stretching exercises. This protects your muscles from injury. It also feels great.

Weight training is also very beneficial and we will talk about that soon. However, nothing replaces the aerobic workout schedule. Before you start any of this, you should consult your doctor. We don't want you to hurt yourself. You may have medical conditions that would be aggravated by an exercise program. If you have been very sedentary for many years, you may have to begin by simply taking a brief walk three times a week. That's OK. You have to start somewhere. Any exercise is better than none. It all starts with one step. Again, please be sure that you are not at risk by consulting your doctor and following his recommendations before you start.

Contact a personal trainer if you can afford it. Even a single consultation including an evaluation and a suggested workout program would be beneficial. It will reduce the risk of injury and increase your results. Schedule checkups once a month to stay on track. The Hollywood stars have a trainer visit them at home several times a week. This, of course, can get very pricey. Perhaps you could afford one appointment a week, at least at the beginning.

Decide whether you prefer working out in the morning or the evening. The only way to really figure this out is to try both a few times. There are pros and cons either way. It has a lot more to do with your schedule and general disposition than anything else. The most important thing is that you continue to work out regularly. Figure out what works and make it convenient for yourself. If you can find an experienced workout partner it really helps. It will motivate you and make the workout more fun. Strike up some conversations at the gym when you see some guys, or better yet women, who seem to be there the same time as you.

Join a health club this week. Visit several that are close to your home. If it is too far away, you won't go. Find one that has aerobic classes, a cardio-fitness center (tread mills, bikes, etc.) and some weight training equipment. Don't pay for a pool or racquetball courts unless you intend to use them. Most clubs will give you a free pass or two. Do this at several clubs. Observe the clientele. How do they look? Is it mostly Arnold Schwarzenegger types? Do the people seem serious or is it a country club scene? Compare until you find a club with the right mix. Ask your friends for recommendations. The problem is that you will be signing up for a year and it is not cheap. Costs range from $300-$500 per year. There are often monthly plans that include automatic billing to your checking account. Shop carefully, but do it. Also, this is an excellent place to meet women. Make a good choice. *By the way, this is a great source of conversation.* It is very cool to be able to discuss the gym you chose, your favorite exercises, etc.

Buy a few decent exercise outfits on sale and invest in a good pair of cross training athletic shoes. You want to look good and feel good when you are there. Your work out must be a positive experience. You should look forward to it. It should be a high point in your day.

Health Club Etiquette

- Strip all weights from the bar or machine when you are done and put them away.
- Wipe down equipment when you are done, especially if you tend to sweat. Some gyms provide paper towels and a spray bottle. If not, carry a small towel for this purpose.
- Be courteous and share the equipment. Don't spend more than 10 or 15 minutes on a weight training station or 20 to 30 minutes on a cardio device if others are waiting.
- It is appropriate to ask another member if you can "work in" on a machine in use. Of course, they may say no. Be willing to allow this yourself. You need friends at the gym.
- Don't slam or drop weights. Don't let machines slam down during reps. Take care of the equipment and report problems to the management for everyone's safety.
- Make sure you know the general rules of the club and follow them. Things like use of the lockers, towels, and membership cards are important. You want to make friends here. *It is a very important part of your life now.*

Getting Ripped

Weight training is an important aspect of your physical fitness program. (There is also flexibility which can be maintained and enhanced with stretching exercises.) The benefits of weight training should be obvious. The general principle is that if you effectively challenge your muscles in a consistent, focused way, they will respond by gradually getting firmer and increasing in size.

General Guidelines

Get someone to show you proper form for each exercise. This is critical. If you do an exercise improperly it is not only unsafe, it will offer no benefit. Often, the personnel at your health club will do this if you ask. Strive for slow, perfect form on every repetition every time. Pushing out reps using poor form will not yield results. It is better to do five perfect reps slowly and correctly, than ten sloppy ones quickly.

Do each exercise very slowly and do not let the muscle rest between the reps. When contracting the muscle, the positive motion, count to two. On the way back, the negative motion, count to four. It is actually the negative motion that offers the most benefit. An example would be the bench press. In this exercise you lie on a bench and hold a barbell with weights above your chest. Pushing the weight up by straightening your arms is the positive movement. Lowering it to your chest is the negative movement. You will not be able to start with very much weight nor do many reps this way. However, the results will come more quickly.

Recover between sets for a minute or so and drink water frequently. Get some help from the club staff or a book. Keep a written record of your workout. Include the number of reps and the amount of weight. Then you will know where to start the next time and you can monitor your progress. Watch yourself in a mirror to observe your form and for motivation.

Legs and Gluteus

These are the largest and most powerful muscles you have. After all, they carry you around all day. Working on the legs will improve your ability to run and do other cardio exercise. For this reason, they are probably the most fit of all your muscles regardless of your condition. Men generally do not have to worry about fat accumulation here.

The best exercises for this group are the squat and the lunge. These are combination exercises that hit your quads, hamstrings and glutes. It takes a great deal of energy and cardiovascular fitness to perform them. You should get someone qualified to help you with your form. Calves can be exercised with calf raises. There is typically a machine available for this. There is also a hamstring machine for the back of your thighs.

Pay special attention to your glutes. Women enjoy seeing a firm butt on a guy, although they may not admit it except among themselves. You would be surprised.

Abdominals

Nothing defines a man's body better than a firm set of abs. You can achieve a true 'V' shape. Once you succeed, you will have significantly reduced your body fat since the waist is a good barometer of your fitness. Just look around you. A protruding gut sends a very bad message and is a limiting factor in your appeal. You look bad, feel bad and lack confidence. Do some ab work every workout. Don't do sit-ups. Do crunches and exercises that train your abs to stabilize and support your spine. Most aerobic classes will include some ab work.

Purchase a tailor's tape measure and check your waist measurement every month or two. This is the most important measurement for improving your appearance. The reason is that fat accumulates here *first* for most men. If your waist is under control it is unlikely that you will have significant problems anywhere else.

Lats

These are the large muscles at the top of your back beneath your shoulders. Lats will fill out quickly and increase your upper body appearance. Since they contribute heavily to the 'V' shape, they produce the interesting effect of reducing the relative size of your waist. Cool. The best exercise is a pull-down using a machine for the purpose.

Middle Back

These are the muscles between your shoulder blades and are tricky to work. They can give you some nice definition. Also if you tend to sit over a keyboard all day, as many of us do, it can help with your posture.

Pecs

These are your chest muscles. Next to your abs, they can add the most dramatic effect to your look at the beach. The bench press is the definitive exercise for your pectorals. It also helps in other ways. By the way, it can be very dangerous. ALWAYS have a spotter who knows what he is doing when you do exercises using free weights. Most people will be happy to help you out if you ask. (Why not ask a woman to give you a hand?) If you are not at the gym, the good old pushup works just fine.

Shoulders

There is a saying that "shoulders make the man." Shoulders give you bulk high on your frame and help you fill out a suit. Since they are close to your face, they can have a big effect on your appearance. They are tough to work. The overhead press is the grandfather exercise for the shoulders. Lateral raises with dumbbells are effective in a different way. Lateral raises help to define the muscle and give you a nice shredded look at the area where your arm and shoulder meet.

Triceps

Typically novices will ignore the triceps, which are the back of your upper arm, in favor of the biceps — mistake. The triceps will really round out and increase the upper arm. They take on a nice definition to boot. You can work them with dips. Take it easy at first. They are usually underdeveloped and will poop out fast.

Biceps

This is what everyone thinks about when they talk about muscles. Remember when you were a kid and you would make a muscle to show your older brother or dad? OK, they are part of the whole look and need to be worked, but many overdo it. Use dumbbells or a straight bar to do curls slowly and with good form.

There are many other smaller muscles such as the inner and outer thighs and the forearms that the pros will work on. As an amateur, you will find that the exercises listed above combined with aerobic activities will round you out nicely.

Fighting Fat

Do some reading, get some help and stick with it. The results are very gratifying. You will have an incredible competitive edge. There are too many of your brothers who have just given up. Americans as a group are in terrible shape. Lower your body fat with consistent aerobic exercise. Do weight training a couple times a week and set a goal of six months to a year. You will be amazed. By the way, limit measuring your progress. Check your waistline every couple of months. You should notice a difference in your jeans and slacks after a few months. Yes, *months;* you must be very patient. Keep an ideal future image of yourself in mind and hang in there. You are building a body for you and the women you will be dating a year from now. If your waist is coming down, everything else will fall nicely into place. Testosterone is good stuff.

Your body fat percentage. Ask around the health club and find someone qualified to do this. It requires some training and a special set of calipers. When done properly, your skin is "pinched" in four or more locations and measured several times to strike an average. These four numbers are put through a standard formula to determine your percentage of body fat. The best long-term goal to improve your appearance is to lower this percentage.

Ignore the scales. Your weight can vary greatly depending on water content, time of day and muscle development. (Muscle weighs more than fat. By the way, people who have a high body fat content can float more easily than those who don't. If you have trouble floating in a pool, good.) It will take months to lower your fat percentage even a few points. It takes patience and persistence. Set a realistic goal for six months. Top college wrestlers, marathon runners, professional body builders and male models can have percentages in the range of 3-9 percent. This is extreme and unrealistic. *You need to consult with your doctor or a fitness professional to set realistic, healthy goals for your age and body type.* However, it is important to accept that this is the best measurement for presenting a more attractive image. If you want an ideal to strive for, look at professional tennis players and decathlon athletes. For the most part, they have the look.

The way to lower your body fat percentage is consistent, aerobic exercise for 30-45 minutes, 3-4 times per week. Your metabolism will gradually increase and you will become a fat-burning engine, even when you sleep. Obviously, you need to adjust your diet as well. However, the exercise is critical. It is the only path to success. Diet without exercise is a recipe for failure. Diet aids are dangerous and just don't work. Your body will return to its original condition as soon as you stop.

If it were easy, everyone would do it. If it came in a bottle, everyone would have a great looking body. Just walk down the mall and count the number of guys you would be willing to trade bodies with. This is a sad commentary on our society, but it is the truth. Unless you are blessed with great genes, or you're still eighteen with human growth hormones flooding your blood stream, you will have to work for it — every week for the rest of your life. The benefits are incredible. You will live longer. You will look your best. You will have more energy. You will enjoy life. *Do it.* NOW.

Yoga

Yoga is not just about meditation and stretching. That is a misconception that many people have. Yoga:
• builds strength
• improves posture
• increases internal awareness
• reduces stress
• can be both challenging and relaxing
• reduces the risk of injury
• helps "rehab" common ailments such as low back pain, knee pain, shoulder injuries, and neck pain

Yoga offers a way to bring balance to your whole being: physically, mentally, emotionally and spiritually. There are many different types of yoga. Some focus on the physical, meditation, the spiritual, or relaxation. We suggest that you try Ashtanga yoga, commonly known as "power yoga." It has a challenging physical aspect and increases internal awareness as well. Celebrities such as Sting are big fans. There are many books available. If you decide to try it be certain to find a qualified yoga instructor. One of the benefits of yoga is that it can be done anytime, anywhere and without equipment. If you travel, you can do it in your hotel room. The investment is minimal other than finding a class and a good instructor or purchasing a book and a yoga mat.

How does yoga fit into an exercise plan? If you are already exercising three times a week, you could start by ending your workouts with about 15 to 20 minutes of yoga. Then you could progress to adding one yoga workout or about one hour to your plan each week. You could then add more yoga, depending on your time and goals. Talk with a personal trainer to help you decide what is going to best meet your needs.

How do you fit all this exercise into your life? If you are not exercising at all, here is a good starting plan.

- Try to start with 30 minutes of exercise three times each week. It is best to start walking two of those days, and do some strength training one day. Target all the major muscle groups with one set each. Always include some stretching at the end of every workout. *What is most important first is establishing the habit of exercise!*
- After you have accomplished this for three months, lengthen one of your walking sessions to include both walking and weights. This will give you one day of walking, one day of weights and one day of both. Follow this for up to six weeks.
- Your next goal should be to increase your walking time on your walking-only day. Increase it in five minute increments to forty-five minutes or one hour, depending on your time availability. Follow this schedule another six weeks.
- Next, on your lifting only day, increase the intensity (weight) of your exercises. Work to momentary muscle fatigue within 8-12 reps.
- Follow this for two to six weeks, then increase the volume on this day by adding a second set to your exercises. At this time you may feel that you can add another day of exercise or a yoga class.

This plan will give you a well-rounded exercise program to keep you improving. You should try different cardio workouts. Walking is a great starting point, but give biking a try. Try a group fitness class or a stair climber. After you have gotten to this level of exercise, you will want to change your lifting routine approximately every three months. You do not have to change all the exercises each time, just some of them. This will keep you growing. Your body will adapt to certain movements if they are done all the time. To keep progressing, you must surprise your body with different things. This will also help keep your motivation levels peaked.

Now that you have vowed to make exercise a permanent part of your life you will need to provide fuel for your body. Hang on. You will need as much discipline to improve your diet as you did to start exercising. They are both lifelong goals. Put down that brownie and read on.

Chapter 7

Fuel

*"Look to your health; and if you have it, praise God,
and value it next to a good conscience;
for health is the second blessing that we mortals are capable of;
a blessing that money cannot buy."*

— Izaak Walton, The Compleat Angler, 1653.

Fuel for the New You

*D*iet is important. We are more careful about the fuel we put in our cars than the junk we stuff in our faces. Your exercise program can erase many sins but why not help the cause as much as possible? When we say diet we don't mean you should go on a "diet." That just doesn't work. The implication is that you can go on a diet and when you reach your goal, you go off the diet. This is ridiculous. The result is a yo-yo syndrome. *You need to change the way you eat for the rest of your life.* You need to have standards. You need to view food as precious fuel.

The Enemy

Fat in all its ugly forms. Let's see. You are trying to lower your percentage of body fat, but you're still gorging yourself on pepperoni pizza? Right. Nature has programmed us from caveman times to ingest fat and store it against hard times. Of course, your ancient ancestors had to run all day just to get a scrap of sirloin. The genetic message we are left with is that the stuff tastes great. Those days are long gone but the memory lingers. Learn to identify it. If you rub some food on a napkin or paper towel and it turns clear, it's fat.

Fortunately, the government is helping you here. Current labeling standards are great. There is a simple test for this. You want to eat foods that are less than 30 percent fat. Every label has to include the total calories and calories from fat per serving. Divide the fat calories by the total calories. (OK, try to round off as best you can.) Never throw anything in your grocery cart that is 30 percent or above. Remember that the ingredients are listed in quantity order. If the first or second ingredient is partially hydrogenated soybean oil, give it to someone you don't like. Hydrogenation is a process that turns "good" fat into "bad" fat. It is essentially the same as saturated fat, just more processed.

If it isn't in the house, you are not likely to munch on it. Keep foods such as potato chips, cookies, most crackers, ice cream and pastries out of the kitchen. Whole milk has lots of fat. Even 2 percent milk is a problem. Learn to drink skim milk. You'll get used to it. Look for safer snacks like popcorn, low-fat yogurt and fresh fruit. When a woman eventually inspects your kitchen, you will score points. There are a few important exceptions, such as olive oil. Some fats are acceptable and are needed by the body to store fat-soluble vitamins. At the end of the day, the total amount of food that you have consumed should be less than 30 percent fat (ideally 20 – 25 percent). So, if you must have a smear of butter on your toast, it certainly is acceptable; just make sure that everything else you eat is within the acceptable fat limits. Please make sure not to make the same mistake the majority of the public makes when attempting to eat a low fat diet — low-fat cookies, low-fat cake, low-fat ice cream, low-fat potato chips. Most of these low-fat foods are loaded with sugar and empty calories. You will not lose weight or inches eating a low-fat diet that consists of these types of foods. Time and time again science has proven that a diet *naturally* low in fat, rich in whole grains, fruits and vegetables, moderate in low-fat sources of protein with only small amounts of un-saturated fats, is what promotes longevity (and a trim waistline).

Red meat. There is plenty of saturated fat here (that's the really bad stuff) — also, lots of cholesterol. Eat skinless white chicken, turkey and fish instead. You need protein to build muscle but you don't want to make it a high per-centage of your diet. Extra lean cuts of red meat in 3-ounce portions can cer-tainly be part of a healthy eating program one or two times per week.

Sugar. The problem with sugar is that your body gets fooled by all the emp-ty calories and it knocks your system out of whack. It stalls your progress. The sugar you do consume needs to be inside a food such as fruit so that your body must work to digest more slowly than the straight stuff. Resist eating candy. Chocolate is a double whammy of fat and sugar. Have a banana. If you're a real chocoholic, try using it as a reward once a month for sticking to a healthy eating program.

Salt. Sodium can be a problem. Ask your doctor. Get out of the habit of put-ting salt on food. Throw away your salt shaker. Most of your sodium intake comes from the processed foods you consume. Sodium content must also be listed on labels. Keep an eye out for this. Better yet, avoid processed foods when possible.

Processed Foods and Chemicals. Food suppliers are out to sell product. Quite frankly, they could care less about your appeal as a date. They will load products with whatever will move them off the shelf. This includes preserva-tives, color, texture enhancers and even wax. Eat whole foods whenever possible. A simple baked potato is a beautiful thing — lots of vitamins and minerals, low calories and loaded with complex carbohydrates. Take a hard look at the ingredients on a package of potato-based snacks. Things like maltodextrin, monosodium glutamate, disodium phosphate, artificial color yellow 5, lactic acid, disodium inosinate and disodium guanylate are not required for good health.

Bad Combinations. In general we are talking about treats and sweets. Unfortunately, the better it tastes, the worse it is. While this is not always true (fresh corn on the cob), combinations of fat and sugar are to be avoided. Eventually you will begin to acquire a taste for healthy foods. After drinking skim milk for several months, you will find that a glass of whole milk will choke you. Ice cream, candy, baked goods, and processed meats are killers. Why take one step forward and two steps back? This is how you got dumpy and lumpy in the first place. Do your best to gradually reduce and then eliminate them. Keep them out of the house. Don't buy them at the store. (By the way, never go food shopping when you are hungry.) Don't frequent places that sell the stuff. Learn to automatically say no when they are offered. A good response is, "I'd love to, but I just can't afford it." Then pat your gut. Aunt Jenny will understand.

The Good Stuff

Drink water. It really helps in lots of ways. Super models and guys who have had kidney stones will testify to this. It keeps your system flushed and keeps the body's H2O percentage in sync. Your body will keep your fluid levels correct if it has a consistent supply of water. Is your urine strong smelling and dark yellow? Bad sign, guy. As Nixon said, "Make one thing perfectly clear." A common recommendation is eight glasses a day of aqua pura. Diet soda doesn't count. That's about 64 ounces a day, or a two-liter bottle. It's not as much as it seems. If you're awake for 16 hours, that's about 4 ounces per hour which is about a teacup. Never pass a water fountain without taking a big drink. Keep a glass close by while you work. Make it a habit for the rest of your life. Carrying a water bottle is very hip these days.

Take a multi-vitamin every day. While the debate rages among the experts, vitamins are cheap insurance. Your body will dump what it can't use. Also, many doctors recommend taking an aspirin each day to reduce the effects of high cholesterol. It thins the blood and improves the flow of oxygen to your tissues. Talk to your doctor about this first, as aspirin can be tough on your stomach lining.

Carbohydrates

Carbohydrates include simple sugars such as honey as well as complex wheat and grain products such as cereal, bread and pasta. Whole-grain carbohydrates should comprise approximately 60 to 65 percent of your diet. Note that whole-grain carbohydrates do not include white bread made with bleached flour and fiberless pasta.

There are lots of low carb/high protein diets out there today. However, these diets do not promote a healthy way of eating. They severely reduce calories and push lots of protein. Too much protein is associated with an increased risk of heart disease, osteoporosis, some cancers and kidney damage. It will also leave you feeling a little tired since without adequate carbs the muscles and brain are left with few reserves. This has a negative impact on energy levels, strength gains, and endurance. The body prefers carbs for fuel and it needs carbs present to burn fat. Fat burns in a carbohydrate flame. If you are too low in carbs, your body must convert protein to carbohydrate. There goes some of that muscle tissue you have worked so hard to build.

Balance is the key! Too much protein is not good, too many carbs are also not good. A good balance is:

60 – 65 percent carbs
15 – 20 percent protein
20 – 25 percent fat

Fiber

There are two types of fiber — soluble and insoluble. Soluble fiber is found in beans, fruits and vegetables. Soluble fibers help remove fat and cholesterol from the blood stream. Insoluble fibers are found in whole grains such as oats, whole wheat and barley. These fibers are good for the colon. They reduce the risks of cancer by keeping things moving down there. Remember that colon/rectal cancer rates for men are very high.

Fiber also is very filling. Eating fiber with your meals will make you feel fuller on less food and you will stay fuller longer. Do this test. Take a piece of white bread and crumble it up; then take a piece of whole wheat bread and do the same thing. The white bread will be an ugly little ball. It makes great fishing bait for bottom feeders. The whole wheat bread will maintain its mass. Which do you want in your stomach?

Fresh Fruits and Vegetables

Fresh fruits and vegetables provide fiber, important nutrients and vitamins. They are also very low in calories and fat (except for avocados and coconut). Fruits and vegetables also provide fiber and "phyto-chemicals." These are compounds that occur naturally in all fruits and vegetables and help reduce the risks of cancer.

The average person does not consume nearly enough fresh fruits and vegetables. Try to eat at least two, preferably four, different fresh fruits every day. Remember that variety is good. Try not to always eat the same fruits. The banana is the most consumed fruit, and although it is a powerhouse food, it should not be your only choice. Buy what is in season and try some of the exotic ones. Some fruits with high nutrient value are guava, kiwi, oranges, strawberries, cantaloupe, watermelon and mangoes. Fruit juices (100 percent only) can be one of your servings but juice does not provide fiber. Orange and grapefruit are the most nutritional juices.

Try to eat at least three, preferably five, different vegetables every day. Try to make one of them raw. When you cook vegetables they lose some nutrients. However, cooked vegetables are better than no vegetables. When you make a salad always use mixed greens (romaine, fresh spinach, or spring mix salads). They provide more nutrients than iceberg lettuce. A recent national survey revealed that the two most frequently consumed "vegetables" are French fries and ketchup. Are you looking for a way to edge out your competition?

Protein

Most Americans eat plenty of protein! You may think that you need more because you are exercising. The average American eats 50 percent more protein than needed. So you probably do not need more because of your exercise. Excess protein does not create muscle. It is either burned for energy or turned to fat. Studies have shown that endurance athletes and body builders do need more protein, but they have a higher food intake so they usually get enough. To calculate how many grams of protein you need each day, multiply your weight in pounds by .4. For example a 150-pound man needs about 60 grams of protein daily. If you are overweight, you may actually need less. If you are taking in more than 120 grams of protein a day, reduce your intake! Remember, too much protein will increase your risk of heart disease, osteoporosis, some cancers and kidney damage. If you are an active exerciser and work out at higher intensities, multiply your weight by .5 to .6 to calculate your protein needs. The best protein sources are lean meat, chicken, and fish. One ounce supplies six to eight grams or protein. Other sources include:

Dairy products (1 cup = 8-12 grams)

Eggs (6 grams per egg)

Beans (1/2 cup = 7 grams)

Nuts (1 ounce = 6 grams – watch the fat!)

Until it becomes second nature, remember that good nutrition is not a sacrifice but a choice and a matter of common sense. It must become part of your lifestyle. A wonderful side benefit is that women appreciate a guy who is careful and informed about nutrition. It makes a great topic for conversation.

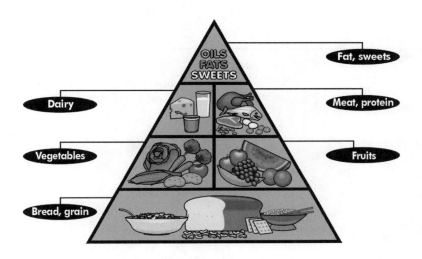

The Food Pyramid

The USDA developed the eating-right pyramid to overcome the shortcomings of the "basic four groups" because of the overemphasis on meat and milk products. The pyramid keeps the concept of the basic four but refocuses emphasis on grains, fruits and vegetables. Each of the five groups in the pyramid — breads, vegetables, fruits, dairy, and protein — provide the basic nutrients you need for good health. Following these daily recommendations will provide all the essential nutrients needed to fuel your body.

The base of the pyramid includes six to eleven servings of breads, cereal, rice and pasta per day.

Next is two to four servings of fruit on one side and three to five servings of vegetables on the other.

Then two to three servings of milk, yogurt and cheeses and two to three servings of meat, poultry, fish, beans, eggs, and nuts.

At the top of the pyramid are fats, oils, and sweets. These are to be used sparingly. Some foods high in fat and sugar are acceptable when eaten as part of a healthy diet. Remember, moderation is the key!

We are constantly reminded of the many benefits of proper diet and exercise. Your goal is to improve your dating life. Eating well will not only improve your health and appearance; it shows discipline and responsibility. You exhibit intelligence and are well-informed. All of this contributes to your appeal in the eyes of the women you will meet.

You are well on your way to a more attractive body. Let's consider some of the details involved in taking good care of it.

Chapter 8
Neat and Clean

"Health is not valued till sickness comes."
— *Thomas Fuller, Gnomologia, 1732.*

You Only Get One Set of 32

You *need a good dentist.* You must see him twice a year. Bad teeth are an instant turnoff. A great looking smile is a major advantage. Halitosis and ugly incisors can be prevented. You must brush several times a day and floss at least daily. Have your dentist or hygienist show you how if you don't know. This is the best way to prevent halitosis. Avoid raw onions and garlic before a date. Always carry breath mints. Never chew gum unless you're playing baseball.

Do you have "happy teeth?" Even if Mom and Dad could not afford an orthodontist, it's not too late. If you can afford it, many adults are straightening out their smile. It's no big deal these days. Several months of minor inconvenience and expense could make a huge, permanent difference in your appeal. The cost is generally around $1,000 over a year or so. (By the way, maybe it's just us, but many female dental professionals seem to be attractive — added bonus.) If your teeth are really in bad shape your dentist may suggest caps. These are very expensive but may be the only answer in severe cases. There are plenty of movie stars flashing caps at cameras.

Are your teeth the same color as your kitchen floor? Did you ever notice that movie stars seem to have snow-white smiles? How do they do it? Simple — they have money. The secret is a whitening process most dentists can provide. It consists of using an 11-16 percent peroxide solution in a custom set of dental molds. (Forget the drug store brands. The solution is too weak and the "molds" don't fit.) The price is typically about $350. It's worth saving for. In the meantime, use a good whitening toothpaste, limit your coffee intake and please tell us that you're not smoking!

Cleanliness

Come on. Do we have to say anything here? Your mom taught you this. You need a shower every day. Wash your hands frequently to reduce disease, especially after using the restroom. OK, OK, enough. Do you use a good deodorant and anti-perspirant every day? BO is a killer. Check the armpits of your shirts at the end of the day. Are they stained or damp? Do they smell like corned beef and cabbage? You must address this. Switch brands until you find something that works. By the way, get an unscented type. You don't want to cover your odor with a cheap fragrance and you don't want to compete with your good cologne.

Always flush toilets and urinals. Always wash your hands when leaving a restroom. It's the right thing to do. It helps protect your health. Also, that guy standing next to you in the restaurant men's room might be your date's cousin!

Snoring

Do you snore? You may not be aware of it if you do. It doesn't have too much meaning until you find yourself sleeping with a special woman. Of course, if you get married it will be a major issue. Many women feel very strongly about this and well they should. You could find yourself within earshot of others on a trip or vacation. There are a few things you can do. Besides earplugs for her, look into the plastic nose strips that you see professional athletes wear. They gently pull your nasal passages open and increase the airflow. A more severe solution is a surgical procedure that your doctor can tell you about. It has been noted that changing your sleeping position or the type of pillow you use can offer some relief. Beyond that, be prepared for some serious negative response to this annoying condition.

Gas

We hate to bring this up, but . . . you have to be very careful here. Let's be blunt. Our digestive systems will release gas in both directions. This happens to everyone on the planet — no exceptions. Super models pass gas. They just won't admit it. Women are very sensitive about this. Men find it amusing. They have since sixth grade. Gentlemen do anything they can to conceal this in the presence of ladies. You should too. The obvious solution is to excuse yourself and let it rip in the men's room or outside. Don't try to sneak one by. The risk is too high. Belching should be controlled. Mask it with a napkin and excuse yourself if necessary.

Sneezing and Coughing

Always cover your mouth and turn your head when this happens. Nobody appreciates you spewing saliva all over the place. Say "excuse me." By the way, don't go on a date if you're sick. She'll understand and appreciate your consideration. It would be nice if you had a tissue when this happens. If you don't, excuse yourself and go wash your hands. If she sneezes, be sure to say "bless you."

Hiccups

People are not usually offended by hiccups. It can be amusing, unless you are the victim, of course. Hiccups are an uncontrollable spasm in the diaphragm, the muscle used to draw air into your lungs. This may be because of some irritation in the stomach or esophagus. There are abundant home cures for hiccups including eating sugar and scaring them away. This can be the source of some entertaining conversation. One cure that seems to have some merit is to hold your breath and pinch your nose while taking small sips of water as long as you can. This seems to deprive the diaphragm of oxygen and cause it to relax. In any case, they will go away in a few minutes. You can smile and ignore them.

Yawning

Yawning is a reaction to a shortage of oxygen to the brain. Typically this is because of a lack of sleep. Of course, a particularly boring speaker may convince your body to shut down, causing you to yawn. Yawning is not as intrusive as sneezing or a coughing (you're inhaling, not exhaling), but it can be offensive. She may think that she is the cause "Am I boring you?" Yawns can be stifled to a certain degree. If it happens, cover your big mouth and immediately offer an apology. Blame it on a late night, early morning or tough day. Reassure her that it is not her company. The problem is that you don't get one yawn. They come in a series like waves. Worse yet, for some reason they are contagious. Too much of this will lead to an early end to the evening. Next time try to get a decent night's sleep before the date.

Nasal Hygiene

Keep your pipes clean. Always carry a pack of facial tissues with you and keep them in your car. Try not to blow your nose in her presence. Excuse yourself and go to the men's room or outside to take care of business. Look in the mirror and make sure everything is clear. Hankies are really gross. Don't use them. Think about it. You blow your nose, then stick it in your pocket? Yuck. Sniffing, snorting and spitting?

You must be kidding. These are all related to handling internal mucus situations. It sounds gross and women hate it. Go to the men's room and do whatcha gotta do out of earshot.

Watch the pick! This is embarrassing, but. . . *don't pick your nose, or anything else*. Scratching and picking will reduce you to Cro-Magnon status in her eyes. There is a famous Jerry Seinfeld episode about this. As he is rubbing his cheek, his date sees it from the opposite side and dumps him. Take care of your nasal hygiene in private.

Auto Etiquette

It doesn't have to be fancy or expensive — although a nice car does give you a bit of leverage. What is important is that it is in good repair and is clean. If your muffler is bad or the engine is running rough, she'll wonder what your problem is. Aren't guys supposed to be good with cars? If you can't take care of your car, what about other things down the road?

You should recognize that you will be spending time in your car during your first few dates. It will be a big part of her first impression of you. Women are usually fastidious about keeping their cars sparkling clean. You should be too. If she has a nice outfit on, she doesn't want to sit in a seat sticky with last summer's milkshake spill — or worse. Clean it up as if you were going to sell it. If you have the money, get your car detailed. It will retain its value and it will be a pleasure to drive. There is a reason they call it "detailing." It is because the pros attend to every detail of the vehicle. You can do it yourself if you have the time and inclination. It only requires a few inexpensive products and a nice afternoon. Put a game on the radio, don't answer the phone, pour a cold drink and get to work. Don't try to do this three hours before your date. It's better to do it a day or two before.

1. Wash the outside of the car with a commercial product, a clean sponge and lots of water. Do the wheels with a stiff nylon brush after washing the body.
2. Wax the body if you can. Spray the tires with a dressing to shine them up. Pay attention to the wheel covers. Polish any chrome surfaces.
3. Remove all trash and accumulated items such as sneakers and magazines. If the items should stay in the car, put them away neatly. Clean out the glove compartment and the trunk. She may wish to put her purse or sunglasses away.
4. Remove the floor mats and vacuum. You may need to scrub them with a carpet cleaner, then let dry.
5. Thoroughly vacuum the inside — first the seats, then the floor.
6. Wipe down all interior surfaces with a cleaning product. Pay close attention to places that she is likely to touch such as door handles and buttons.
7. Spray vinyl areas with a silicone-based product to shine them up. Very carefully clean all glass surfaces. You may have to do this several times if they are in bad shape. Pay close attention to her side of the car. If there is a vanity mirror on her side, it should be spotless. She'll use it. If there isn't, get one for the visor.
8. Always keep tissues, breath mints and an empty litterbag in the car.
9. Get some music. The radio is OK but a tape player is better. You can improve the background with a continuous set of good tunes. A CD player is preferred because the sound is better and selection is random. The ultimate is a multi-disk changer in the trunk but this item is expensive.

10. Consider a very light quality fragrance in the car. Put some potpourri in the ashtray since neither of you will be using it, right?
11. Once you have the car in good shape, try to maintain it with regular attention. Be very careful with food and drinks. Obviously, you will have a rule about anyone smoking in your car.

What Turns Women Off – The Seven Grooming Sins

Ask them. While the answers may be obvious when you think about it, it is easy to let things slide. Old habits die hard. Constant attention to detail is required. Some things women just hate include:

Halitosis – Usually regular brushing and flossing should keep this under control. However, raw onions, garlic or other strong foods can cause bad breath. Sometimes you are not aware that you have it as it can be difficult to detect in yourself. Always keep strong breath mints handy and use them frequently.

Unclean teeth – No excuse here as you can easily check the mirror in the men's room.

Body odor – Regular showers and an effective deodorant/antiperspirant should do the job.

Greasy, dirty hair – It should be washed every day. This is something we sometimes skip and it shows.

Dirty fingernails – Get those clippers out once a week. Scrub with a brush if required.

Needing a shave – Wait until the last minute before you shave. Experiment with different brands and methods until your face feels like a baby's behind.

Messy, unkempt appearance – Your clothing must be perfectly pressed. Check every detail very carefully in a full-length mirror before you walk out the door. It is critical.

Dirty clothing – Come on. Trying to sneak by wearing a shirt with a stain will get you nowhere fast.

It may seem as though we are overstating this. Trust us. These turn-offs mean a lot more to women than they do to us. Be meticulous in your attention to detail. You will be rewarded. (By the way, can we introduce you to a nice girl with stringy hair, bad breath, BO, hairy legs, spinach in her teeth, wearing a wrinkled skirt with a stain? She has a great personality and a sense of humor. Any takers?)

Once you have the hygiene basics covered, it's time to put the icing on the cake. You will need to pay close attention to your grooming and clothing to complete the package. This is a very important aspect of your market appeal.

Chapter 9
Body Work

"Eat to please thyself, but dress to please others."
— Benjamin Franklin, Poor Richard's Almanac, 1738.

Hair

Keep it clean. Dirty hair looks bad and smells bad. You won't fool anyone, especially a woman. They are hair experts. If you have dandruff, get rid of it and keep it under control. There are several effective products on the market for this. Find a good hair stylist and tip her well. (Yes, *her* — you're better off.) Although a barber is great for sports stories and talc, they're typically out of touch with what women find attractive. Besides, it's a great idea to go to a salon where there are lots of women. Did someone say networking? Get to know your stylist and insist on appointments with only her every time. Schedule every three to four weeks depending on how fast your hair grows. Confide in her and let her know you are available. Who knows? This lady has attractive women parading past her all day long. She'll enjoy the challenge and you become a walking advertisement for her. Be sure to tip her at least 15 percent, preferably 20 percent. (By the way, be a good tipper in general. It shows style, it's the right thing to do and it comes back to you in excellent service.) You will do better with a shorter hairstyle. Although some women like long hair, the percentages favor a well groomed, shorter mop.

If you can afford it, buy recommended products from your stylist. You may find that there is a difference. If not, ask her to suggest a good drugstore brand of shampoo and conditioner and use them consistently. Develop a dialogue about the condition and appearance of your hair. Be open to some experimentation. Ask her to teach you how to use a hair dryer and styling products to keep you looking good until your next appointment. You may need to purchase a hair dryer and a styling brush. Consider using a mousse. It will help to hold your hair and add life to the texture. Pomade is a heavy preparation that can be used to keep hair in place and add some shine. Consult your stylist about these products. Do you have a hand mirror to check out the back of your head? Shave the back of your neck every week or so. Carefully trim from the hairline down. It will keep you looking fresh between haircuts.

By the way, if this is a full-service salon, consider a professional massage as a treat from time to time. Massages are expensive, but very enjoyable. They give you a feeling of well-being.

There is a certain percentage of women who will not consider a man who is bald or has thinning hair. That is their right. You have your hard criteria as well, don't you? It is not an overwhelming percentage. However, it is a fact. *Accept it.* That's the way it goes. Minoxidil may help. It takes three to four months and about 60 dollars to find out. It will not work for everyone. Minoxidil is available over the counter. It comes in two strengths and is only effective on the top area of your head (the "monk" look). Some men report success with Nioxin or Kevis products. There is some promise in the drug, Proscar, but is has the potential side effect of lowering your sex drive. Nature is cruel. It is probable that science will provide more relief as time goes on because the revenue potential is enormous. Stay tuned.

Forget toupees or hair weaves. Ask Marv Albert. *Never comb hair over anything but other hair.* A "comb-over" looks really bad. Instead, keep your existing hair neatly trimmed. Overcome this disadvantage by being fastidious about every other aspect of your appearance. This is the best you can do. Women will be more attracted to a great guy in excellent shape who is a bit thin on the top than a Suomo wrestler with a prolific mane.

You could consider surgical micro-plugs. In this process, tiny pieces of scalp containing three or four strands of hair are "farmed" from hair-rich areas such as the back of your head. They are then tediously inserted in the bald areas where they take root and grow. It is expensive, time-consuming and involves an embarrassing developmental period where you look a bit strange. The results can be satisfactory. Consult your physician for a recommendation and a referral to a qualified practitioner.

Women are extremely conscious of their own hair. It is a critical part of their self-image. They will be impressed if your hair is well groomed and always in place. Make an effort. It will yield results.

Gray Hair This is, of course, a natural process to be expected. Sometimes it happens prematurely. Steve Martin is an example. Steve made the decision to just go with it. Of course, he is an extremely talented, attractive and rich movie star. If you begin to get a little snow on your roof, you will have to decide what to do about it. Without question, it will make you look older. If you consider this to be a problem, the obvious solution is to dye your hair. Once you decide to do it, you have a maintenance project on your hands.

Ronald Reagan pulled it off into his eighties. You will have to freshen up the color at least once every two weeks. A professional will charge fifty dollars or more to do it for you. You can learn to do it yourself for less than ten dollars. It will take some practice and perhaps some help at first. A good solution is have a professional do it once or twice and then take over yourself. You will have to continue once you start — probably every one or two weeks. Women have been doing it for decades. It's really not a problem, just a decision.

Mustaches and Beards Facial hair is a touchy area. First of all, mustaches and beards are high maintenance items. You have to keep them neatly trimmed or you will look like a zoo resident. Also, they have to be kept clean. The darn things collect stuff like breadcrumbs and soup. While many women insist on a clean-shaven man, some like a moustache or a beard. Sean Connery aside, facial hair works better on younger men. If you're an older guy, a hairless face will make you look younger. Also, if your complexion is bad or if you have some unfortunate scarring, a beard may help. Of course, you may have to consider dying your facial hair if you dye your hair — another hassle. If you want to play the percentages, shave. If you begin dating a woman with hairy preferences, you can always grow something for her. It could be fun.

Unless you have a full beard, (and you should re-think that) you should be freshly shaven anytime you go out in public. You just never know. It's part of your public image. You could be at the mall with a five o'clock shadow and run into a honey you have been pursuing. Wham — you're down 16 points in the first quarter. Tough to recover. It's happened to us. Women understand this concept very well. They would not consider going anywhere without their armor. You need to get in the habit of being prepared each time you leave home. Purchase an inexpensive full-length mirror and put it in a convenient place near your closet or front door. Take a quick inventory on the way out — hair, face, clothes? Are you in good enough shape to meet the girl of your dreams? It could happen.

"Other" Hair As we age, we lose the hair on top of our head and it migrates to our ears, between our eyebrows, and in our nostrils. Women notice everything. All of these must be removed. This is a real pain but it must be done. Buy a small pair of cosmetic scissors and a good pair of tweezers. You will also need a magnifying cosmetic mirror. Use the scissors to trim the nasal hair as close as possible. Please be careful — a wound here is dangerous, painful and slow to heal. You will need to do this weekly. Having hair hanging out of your nose is a real turn-off.

Use the tweezers and the magnifying mirror to remove hairs from your ears. Carefully inspect them including the back. (Sooner or later, she will notice — yuck.) Again, this is a weekly task. You can do it while you're watching a game alone. (You may as well remove any excess earwax with a cotton swab while you're at it.)

Do you have eyebrow hair hanging down in your eyes? Either ask your stylist to trim them up for you or use your scissors and a comb to remove the really long ones. You'll look younger and more svelte. A "mono-brow" is a very scary thing. It makes you look mean and prehistoric. If you're an NFL linebacker, this is good. Otherwise — remove it. Regular use of the tweezers and mirror will do the job. Also check any other areas of your face not covered by regular shaving such as the tip of your nose. We know this is gross but what can we say? By the way, can you imagine what women would look like if they did absolutely no maintenance along these lines? Whoa.

Why Do They Call It A Manicure When Women Usually Get Them?

Nails must be neatly trimmed at all times. This is something else that women notice and speaks volumes about you. Buy a good pair of nail trimmers and use them every two weeks. If your job exposes your hands to grease and grime, you may have to give them extra attention with a brush and some heavy duty soap, such as Lava. If you have the money and the inclination, a professional manicure can be nice. (Hey, it's just an idea.) Please tell us you don't bite your fingernails. You will need a larger pair of clippers to handle your toenails. Your feet are ugly enough; at least keep the nails from turning into dangerous weapons.

To Tan Or Not To Tan?

Sun is the greatest enemy of your skin. A tan looks great, but it's just not possible to go the George Hamilton/Zonker route anymore. First, there's cancer. Skin cancer is on the rise and is preventable. Don't use tanning beds. When in the great outdoors, use a good sunscreen with at least a 15 SPF. There is plenty of information out on this subject. Pay attention. We realize that guys are not used to smearing goo on their skin. Get used to it. It really helps. By the way, there are some fairly effective "sunless" tanning products available. They basically dye your skin on a temporary basis. Most Hollywood stars go this route — your choice. Don't spend a lot of money on them. If you check the label you will find that they all use the same chemical.

Second, there's cosmetic damage. By the time you hit your late 40s or early 50s your face could look like a saddlebag. You will look older than your years. (Smoking plays a major part here as well. You did *quit* didn't you?) You don't need this. If you're an older guy (you remember disco) consider using a high quality facial cream at night. It will do a lot to smooth some of the effects. You may want to consult a dermatologist if you can afford it. There is a preparation called Retin-A that works wonders on a wrinkled mug. Laser resurfacing is a recent but expensive solution for improving a ravaged face. The high-tech light is carefully focused on damaged areas exposing fresh skin underneath. The results can be dramatic. Healing time is two weeks to a month and the cost can be three thousand dollars or more. In all likelihood, health insurance will *not* cover this. If you have the problem and the money, consult a reputable cosmetic surgeon.

Do Women Make Passes at Guys Who Wear Glasses?

This is not necessarily a problem unless your frames are cheap, out of date or just plain ugly. Glasses do not bother most women. However, how would you feel about contacts? They're a bit of a hassle and an expense but could improve your appearance. Also, there are some new surgical procedures that can permanently reverse some vision problems — see your doctor. If you decide to continue wearing your specs, consider new frames and spend some bucks on them. It will probably set you back one hundred and fifty dollars or more for an attractive, high quality pair, in addition to the lenses. Since they are an integral part of your face, it's worth it. Observe the frames the stars or GQ models are wearing for some clues. Avoid those metal aviator types with the shaded lenses that change with the light. They look geeky. Get a female relative or close friend to go with you to pick your new frames. Never buy or wear the drugstore brands. They look like they cost twelve dollars.

Tattoos

Most women will prefer a man without tattoos. They are quite popular today and some women have them. If you have one, it is permanent, of course. Be prepared for rejection by a certain percentage of ladies. No value judgments here — however, it is a limiting factor. If you are trying to decide whether to get one, please take this into consideration. Don't do it while drinking or with a bunch of your buddies to avoid peer pressure. Think about it carefully and do it because you really want it and you believe it will look great. Never get a tattoo with a name other than Mom or the Marines. Things change.

Jewelry

Less is more. If you are going to wear it, be sure it is high quality. Cheap gold looks like cheap gold. Women can tell. They are experts. In general, if you are not wearing it now — don't bother. Save your money for some good clothes instead. Most women prefer that *they* wear the gold. Women are fond of saying "never date a man with better jewelry than you." The exception is your watch. Buy a decent one with a good leather or metal band. Don't wear plastic athletic watches on a date.

Earrings

There are some women who will find this attractive. They are very young and/or involved in a trendy lifestyle/culture. If you are playing the percentages, earrings will classify as a negative factor. One benefit is that earrings can be temporarily removed and the hole will probably not be noticed. If you have one now, consider not wearing it until you have tested your marketability with naked earlobes. You can always put it back in if you feel that it is an integral part of your persona.

Body Piercing

(See earrings) Clearly this is a more severe ornamentation than jewelry or earrings. You will be appealing to an even smaller pool of available women. You need to decide if it is in your best interests. You will increase your odds by removing the silver ball in your tongue, even if only temporarily.

Clothing

"Every girl's crazy 'bout a sharp dressed man."

— ZZ Top

Clothes make the man. Well, maybe. They sure can help. Since they cover 90 percent of your body you need to pay attention. This is another area men don't enjoy addressing. We tend to dress for comfort. The more ragged the jeans, the better. You probably have stuff in your closet from high school. Let's hope you don't wear it. What you should do is go through your closet and drawers and sort out anything you haven't worn in over a year. Make sure it's clean and donate it to a charity. (You can get a tax deduction for this.)

Now take stock of what you need. Clothing is a major investment. It can be spread out over time. You can gradually build your wardrobe. Women pay very close attention to what a guy is wearing and draw conclusions. We know it doesn't seem fair, but it's true. Ask your sister. A few guidelines here. *Buy quality items.* It pays in the long run. They look much better when they are new and will last much longer than inexpensive stuff. Cheap clothes look bad when they are new and worse later. They lack style and detail and are made of poor materials. Good clothes are made from wool, cotton and silk. They also feel great to wear. You will notice details like strong seams, extra pockets and belt loops, or lining. You can find better labels in discount stores. When you are shopping for an item, start at the top. Look at the most expensive brands and work your way down. There is a difference. Unless it's an emergency or a piece of clothing that really doesn't matter, wait until you can afford something that will add value to your closet.

Make sure you buy the right size. What is your collar size? Do you wear a small, medium, large or extra-large shirt or sweater? What about jackets and suits? Are you a 38 short, a 40 regular or a 42 long? Are you sure? Get measured. Jeans are sold by waist and inseam length. What are yours? Sizes can vary considerably from brand to brand. You really need to try them on and get them altered. This adds to the cost but is necessary. (Uh, don't forget to remove the labels, including those four little pieces of white thread near the belt loops.)

You need a least one good suit. It may take a while to find the right one and pay for it, but make it a goal. It should be made of 100 percent wool and be very dark. You can use it for a variety of situations including weddings and New Year's Eve. Buy it on sale but spend as much as you can for a top label. It will last for years. Your new suit should fit perfectly. This is key. Buy it where there is a good tailor. Ask around. Be sure to tip him. It will eventually pay off. Buy a good quality white shirt. Be sure to buy the right neck size. Check with a tape measure. Invest in an expensive (about forty dollars) silk tie. Learn to tie a double Windsor knot. You will look great. You will also need a pair of dark dress socks and a pair of good dress shoes, preferably black. These should always be freshly shined and ready to wear.

Slacks should fit well. Be sure to buy the correct waist size. Why kid yourself? Use a tape measure and check at about your navel or a bit below. Don't suck it in. If you buy a pair that is too small, your gut will hang out over your belt and you will look worse. If there's a problem here (the statistics say it's likely), then start working out and lay off the doughnuts. For the time being, you will have to wear the right size and wait for better days. You'll look better. Tight slacks look terrible, unless you're a rock star. Make sure that the length is right. Longer is better. If the inseam is too short, you end up with the high water look. Ugh. The cuffs should just hit the top of your shoe in the front. A good tailor is a big help here. You can get slacks altered at many dry cleaners. By the way, if you can afford it, having your slacks cleaned and pressed at the cleaners is a great idea. You will have a nice crease and a very sharp look.

Khakis work very well. Select other neutral shades such as gray and dark blue. Stay away from loud colors. Cuffs are an option — your choice. A good pair of jeans is also a requirement. They can fit tighter, but be careful here as well unless your waist is ten inches smaller than your chest. (A good goal, by the way. Some insurance policy medical exams include this criteria.) *Buy a few good belts* (leather, not scotch). Some extra money spent here will add a nice touch. Men don't get to do much in the area of accessories. You need to maximize your opportunities.

Sport shirts and sweaters are your opportunity to play peacock. You can be bold with color selection as long as you are buying quality brands. Sticking with the better labels will keep you from looking bizarre. Long-sleeve sport shirts are preferable because they can be used all year round. They also look a bit dressier than short sleeves. Polo and rugby shirts are great if you have the waistline to wear them. Consider darker solid colors. Walk through the most expensive men's stores in your area and pay close attention to the mannequins and displays. Each year there are a few colors that are in. Take note and try to include these colors in your ties, shirts and sweaters. Check yourself sideways in a mirror for the honest truth. Sweaters are expensive, so select carefully and look for sales. Make sure they are not too small. Have your shirts cleaned and pressed at the cleaners for a polished appearance — hangers, no starch, please.

Women love shoes. We don't know why, but it's true. Remember Imelda Marcos? Naturally, they will be looking at yours. Again, you will be judged here. We have actually heard of women passing over guys because of bad shoes. Wow! Men often ignore the condition of their shoes. Are they in repair or are the heels run down? This is easily remedied. Many dry cleaners will repair shoes. Keep your shoes shined and use sole dressing on the edges and sides of the heels for a nice effect. Selection? You have a lot of latitude here. Avoid clogs, sandals and mountain boots, except for their intended purpose. For dating you want to send a message of casual style and quality. As always, this will cost a bit. Try to observe stars, magazine models and guys around town who are well dressed. You will notice some styles that are appealing to you and that will enhance your image. Gradually build a small collection of nice-looking casual shoes. She will notice if you wear the same pair every night.

Go a bit crazy with your socks. You don't get that many chances to flash some color. Show some personality above your shoes. Women love it and it may become a conversation point. Just make sure that they are high quality. Since they are a low-cost item, you can afford the best.

Hats can be OK. They can also make you look very strange. Baseball-type caps are acceptable on the right occasions. Wear them to the beach or a game, not on a date. If you're young enough, it can be cool to wear the hat backwards. British racing caps will make you look more mature, if that's what you want. Other hats can be very risky. An "Ike Eisenhower" fedora will make you look *real* old. Remember, Indiana Jones was set in the 1940s. If you get into Swing dancing a "Frank Sinatra" Stetson could be fun. Anything else such as a knit cap or hunting hat, will make you look like a clown.

Buy some good cologne. You will have to spend a bit of money. (Ask Mom or Sis to get you some for your birthday or Christmas.) In general you get what you pay for. Women are very sensitive to this. They invest a lot in smelling just right. Sending a good first impression to a woman's olfactory nerves is a very powerful message. When using cologne, less is more. Just a spray or two is fine. She should barely notice your classy fragrance. (This will make her lean closer to enjoy the scent.) You don't want to smell like a drugstore counter or a locker room. Magazines like GQ and Esquire often have "scratch and sniff" ads for better fragrances. Shop at an upscale department store. They have lots of testers. You can stop in there before going out and try one. Keep trying until something strikes your fancy. Better yet, you may find that a lady or two may comment on your selection. Just be sure you know what you're wearing and can pronounce it. Ask the salesperson. (By the way, these places are notorious for hiring attractive sales help.)

Pheromones are scents emitted by animals as an attraction for mating. There is some research claiming this occurs in humans through the genitals, armpits and other apocrine glands. Some manufacturers are selling pheromone scents. The jury is out on this.

Buy a good pair of sunglasses. You should be very style conscious about this selection. Save some money. Buy the best pair you can afford. Seventy five dollars will put an attractive pair on your face. UV protection is important. Sunglasses protect your eyes and relieve squinting that can lead to crow's feet. Never wear them inside. Keep them in a case when you aren't wearing them.

Outerwear is important in inclement weather. A coat or jacket covers lots of territory. If it's cheap or shabby, it doesn't matter what you have underneath. You look like Columbo and you lose. This stuff can get very pricey. Shop carefully and watch for sales on high-quality brands. The upside is that a good outer garment will last for years. (Keep an umbrella in your car. It's nice to huddle under it while you dash to her door in the rain.)

Problems

If you feel especially helpless about clothes shopping, try to persuade a female friend or relative to accompany you. Be sure she dresses well herself and has some taste. Offer to treat her to lunch. Keep a small notepad in your pocket to jot down ideas for later purchases. Rather than shopping a few times a year, always keep an eye out for ideas to increase your wardrobe. Two good times to shop are right after Christmas and in late summer. Watch for sales.

Some colors to avoid include sky blue, orange, yellow and most shades of green. Avoid looking like a box of crayons. Navy, maroon, wine, beige, khaki and black are very safe.

If you are a big guy, you have a special set of problems. People, especially women, will be wary of you. Your imposing size naturally intimidates. The solution is to dress as softly and warmly as possible. Try to attain a "big ol' teddy bear" look. Avoid high profile clothing and sharp contrasts between tops and slacks. Instead, blend the two with similar lighter colors. By the way, don't forget to adjust your demeanor as well. Speak softly and gently. Be as warm and sincere as possible. Also, try to sit rather than stand to level the difference and increase eye contact.

Small guys will have to compensate in another way. They must wear high-profile clothing with sharp contrast to draw attention to themselves. Be neat to a fault and favor bold, darker colors. Vertical stripes can help. Smaller men need to develop strong self-confidence and a deep commanding voice. They should concentrate on their posture to minimize height differences. The Richlee Shoe Company in Frederick, Maryland offers a line of height increasing shoes.

If you are very thin, consider clothing with a lot of texture and heavy sweaters. Horizontal stripes may help. Layer clothing when possible. If you are young enough, the open flannel shirt look is useful. If you have a weight problem, be certain that your clothing is loose enough to mask it. Black is your best color, especially in slacks. Be very careful with sports shirts as they can reveal too much waistline.

Now you are looking good. Continue to pay close attention to your grooming and appearance consistently. The next area to consider is your general behavior and style. You need to act as good as you look.

Chapter 10
Style

"Success is getting what you want. Happiness is liking what you get."
— *H. Jackson Brown*

Cleaning up your act and improving your appearance is not an especially difficult task. Making improvements in your lifestyle and behavior will take a lot of effort and time. However, the rewards will be considerable.

Posture

Posture is critical. It offers great benefits. The Marines know it. Take a good look at these guys. Although they may be extreme, they have the idea. Try standing against a wall in your bare feet. Put your heels, buttocks, shoulder blades and the back of your head flush against the wall. Level your head so you are looking straight ahead. How does that feel? Try sitting that way. Drive that way. It can be very tiring, but what it will do is train you to have a properly erect posture. The best examples are ballet dancers. Look at Barishnikov. The shoulders are pressed down as well as back. Floating the rib cage above the pelvis helps many people understand not to let their rib cage drop to their pelvis and their shoulders to round forward. Keep your spine long, think tall; think a little air in each vertebra of the spine. Rent *American Gigolo* with Richard Gere. There is a scene where Richard's character has an amusing discussion about posture with a frumpy police detective.

Walk the Walk

Walk briskly with energy. Always look as if you are going somewhere even if you are not. Keep your head erect and your shoulders back. Walk as if you are going to a podium to receive an Olympic gold medal. Never shuffle or hang your head down. Look straight ahead. Be aware of your surroundings. Don't rock from side to side or shuffle. Let your arms swing naturally. Look people in the eye as you pass. Smile and say hello, especially to women.

Personal Appeal

Some people seem to just have it. Their pleasant easy-going nature is irresistible to others. They light up a room when they arrive. Things seem a bit boring when they leave. Everyone wants to talk to them. You know people like this. Study them. Observe their behavior and mannerisms. It has nothing to do with physical beauty. Consider Danny DeVito or the late John Candy. While these men are not considered sex symbols, their charm and personal appeal is considerable. Find examples closer to home.

You don't have to have a personality transplant. As with your personal appearance, you can make minor improvements to increase your appeal and still remain true to yourself. More on this later.

Your Smile

People just don't smile enough. We don't mean to make you a grinning idiot or a used car salesman. The secret is timing. You need to turn it on and off at the right time. Careful here — this sounds fake, but allow us to explain. You have pleasant feelings and thoughts all the time. You wake up and see a great day outside. You pet the dog. You read Doonesbury or Dilbert. You find ten dollars in a pair of pants under your bed. You go the gym and see an empty treadmill next to that cute redhead you've been interested in. (Now we're getting somewhere.) In all these instances, especially if you are alone, you would just enjoy the moment and maintain your typical poker face. It's easier. What's the point of working out those facial muscles if no one can see it? Plenty. It's conditioning. Allow yourself to express warm and fuzzy feelings by smiling when it feels right. Always. People will actually begin to catch you at it. They will wonder what you're up to. After a while it will become second nature. *You will begin to smile more.* Of course, when the moment is over, you need to relax. People will think you're doing a Jack Nicholson impression if you don't.

Work on your smile. Nothing expresses warmth more than a sincere smile. Do it often. Share it with everyone. It should be engaging and captivating, not contrived — heartwarming, not forced. Your smile will be a natural reflection of your frame of mind. Learn to control your thought patterns and set your mood before you go out. Maintain your inner feelings of calm happiness and it will be reflected all over your face, but most of all in your smile.

Now that you're smiling more frequently, how does it look? Check the mirror. We know it seems weird, but you need to pay attention to how you look to others. It only makes sense. Actors are trained to do this in order to be convincing. You will have more confidence if you are certain of your appearance. Are you showing some dental enamel? Come on. Let it rip. A smile without some teeth is more of a smirk. Try opening your jaws slightly so your teeth are not clenched. Your smile will more be relaxed and natural. Try a few head positions while you're at it. Do you have a good side? Most people do. If you really want to go the distance, here's a great idea. Find out who is the best professional portrait photographer in town and schedule a session. Tell him you want him to pose you so you will look great for your girlfriend in Paris. He will take a whole series and you can select a few for purchase. This costs less than you might think. A great looking photo of you in a classy frame could be a nice gift for a woman at the right time.

Now that you have this valuable skill, you need to use it every time you see the object of your affection. From the moment she sees you see her, your mood and appearance should perk right up. After all, aren't you happy to see her? Sure you are, so show it. Get that smile happening and keep it working. Speak with energy and enthusiasm. Immediately tell her how great she looks. No woman can resist an opening compliment. Surely, you can say something sincere about her appearance. Once is enough — don't overdo it. Compliments should be used like spice in cooking. Keep your eyes focused on her face while you speak. She is the only person in the room. Immediately start asking about her interests and life. A few open-ended questions should do the job. ("What's it like working in a large corporation? I've never done it.") Everyone likes to talk about themselves. The secret is to encourage them. Take a tip from Jay Leno and Dave Letterman.

Don't look too serious, Are you frowning? Look at the spot between your eyes. Do you see wrinkles?

Learn to smile, not like a grinning idiot or at the inappropriate time, but frequently. Have a good word for all.

Tics

We are not talking about nasty little bugs. Tics are involuntary mannerisms that can be annoying. Usually they show up when you're nervous, such as when you're on a date. Perhaps you shake your foot or leg incessantly. You might constantly clear your throat, or say "uh." In general, it is a good idea to keep your hands away from your face. Often you will not even realize that you have a tic. However, it can be very annoying to someone who doesn't know you well. Ask a good friend or relative or videotape yourself. Once you recognize the problem, it should be easy to correct. It is surprising how a simple thing like a tic can turn a woman off, but it's true.

Attitude — Prevail as a Male

You must work on this. Attitude is an air that comes from within. It cannot be contrived. When your life is on track, it shows.
- You are healthy.
- You are self-confident and know where you are going.
- Your career is going fine and you are in control of your finances.
- You enjoy life and sincerely like people.

- You have friends.
- You are interested in everything around you.
- You pursue your own happiness with no apology.
- People are fortunate to know you and be in your company.
- You hurt no one.
- You are honest and approachable.

You can talk yourself into this frame of mind. It is a form of self-hypnosis. Many athletes such as high jumpers do this before they compete. They use visualization. You can watch them repeatedly walk through each step of their approach with intense concentration. They are literally seeing themselves clear the bar. When they actually jump, the action is automatic. Their mind is free and they are doing what they have programmed themselves to do.

Have opinions. Express them. Think them out ahead of time. Don't rage or act eccentric, just thoughtful and interesting. Sometimes she will agree with you. When she doesn't, it should be clear that you are not concerned about her assessment of you. What we mean is that you insist on maintaining your independence in spite of anyone's opinion. Women cannot generate a lot of passion for a man they don't respect.

Humor

You should have a good sense of humor. What does this mean? Well, you enjoy jokes and see the humor in things. Be careful about telling jokes. Don't try to be the Jerry Seinfeld of the evening. Avoid long, drawn out stories that you find amusing. If you know a quick, funny topical joke, that's fine. One or two a night is OK. The essence of a good sense of humor is to make an occasional amusing comment on the fly. This is not easy. You know others who can do it. Listen to them. It has to be spontaneous. One way to start is to turn the focus on yourself and your human frailties. If the topic is the stock market you could say, "I know a surefire way to make a stock's price go down. I just buy a few shares." It may not be a belly laugh, but it is mildly amusing. That's what you want. The real masters of comedy such as Steven Wright, have a dry sense of humor. Work on it with friends and associates before you spring it on the ladies.

Be a Good Sport

Guys are supposed to be sports enthusiasts. This is not to say that women are not. It's just that the Y chromosome seems to give us a predisposition to competition. Unfortunately for many of us, we become spectators after the last high school game. The couch and the remote do nothing for your fitness level and isolate you from the other gender. Parlay your love of sports and your desire to date by becoming more of a participant. Besides, you need to use that body you have been working so hard on at the gym.

Volleyball This game is a sure-fire way to increase your odds. It's fun. It's co-ed. It is often played on the beach in *swimsuits*. Any questions? It is excellent exercise. Although it is not truly aerobic (too much stop and go), there is plenty of stretching. Risk of injury is low compared to some other sports such as skiing. Watch some pro games on TV. Look at the physiques of the play-ers. The basics of the game are simple. Join a novice league at your local recreation board. Learn to play well enough to move on to better competi-tion so you don't embarrass yourself. Coed games are often six to a team and an effort is made to keep the ratio even. It is very common for teams and groups to retire to a local pub to celebrate or whine. Learn to play volleyball.

Skiing This is a very expensive sport. Depending on where you live, you may have to travel to the good slopes. Of course, you are already familiar with op-portunities in your area. You will need decent equipment, although you can rent at first. You will need some attractive clothes; and these can set you back a few dollars. There are serious safety considerations here. If you don't learn golf well enough, you simply *look* bad. If you don't learn to ski well enough, you could *feel* very bad. Take lessons. They are offered in groups at a very rea-sonable cost. There will be women in your class who are as inexperienced as you. You can practice your basic snowplow together, then retire to the lodge for apres ski. This is a wonderful tradition where skiers get together to party and discuss the day's successes and trials. In upscale resorts it is often done in a hot tub. Wow. A ski vacation to a resort in Colorado or Vermont can be an excellent opportunity to meet healthy, personable and generally available women. The best way to accomplish this is through a local ski club, if you are in the northern climes. (Ski lines are really cool. Most lifts demand two-per-son occupancy. If you play it right you could spend fifteen minutes or so in beautiful surroundings alone with a dozen single women a day. What more could you ask? You can meet them for drinks later on in the hot tub.)

Biking Ditto to most of what we said about skiing and volleyball. In addition, this is a truly aerobic activity. The bike can be expensive and you will need a helmet and other padding. This can be a solo sport for pure exercise, but why not take advantage of the social aspects of an organized club? The sport is somewhat seasonal, since you can't bike safely in snow and ice. It presents a balance for skiing. If you are in good enough condition, you get to wear some sexy looking clothing.

Running Clubs This is a more social approach to a typically solo sport. Be-sides group runs, there are meetings and social gatherings. You can expect the fitness level of this crowd to be above the norm. Membership is inexpensive and so is the sport. You will need excellent shoes and some nice outfits. You get to wear cool colors and styles. This is an excellent aerobic activity. Check with your doctor before you get too intense. Build up gradually and stretch afterwards.

Golf The sport is quite popular and offers excellent social opportunities; however, it can be expensive and the proper dress is very important. Lots of women participate. As you may know, people usually play in foursomes. This could work nicely. You will need some instruction to avoid looking foolish. It is possible to get to the point where you can play a respectable round in short order. The business opportunities of golf are well known.

Tennis You get a good aerobic workout, nice outfits and lots of one-on-one interaction. It doesn't have to be expensive. You will need good shoes, an acceptable racket and a place to play. Tennis has a lot of style and many women participate. You don't have to have great skill, just be able to return a volley most of the time. Women look great on a tennis court.

Racquetball Think of it as indoor tennis. It is much more intense, and requires skill and fitness. Court time can be expensive. Of course, you can play year-round.

Billiards There are lots of upscale billiard parlors in operation these days. They are clean and a perfectly acceptable place to take a date. In addition, you may find candidates enjoying a game of eight ball who are willing to share a table. Of course, you will need some basic skill at the game in order to hold your own. This is easily accomplished by asking a buddy to give you some tips. You can catch tournaments on TV and watch an instructional video.

Table Tennis When played socially, this game is a good mixer. It takes some skill to at least keep a volley going. Try to get into a mixed doubles game.

We have not discussed other sports such as softball, soccer or martial arts. Evaluate the benefits of each and try a few until something clicks. If you can find one or two that include the opportunity to meet women, so much the better. At the very least, you will increase your fitness level and have some good topics of conversation.

Music Is a Great Motivator

Develop a collection of your favorite CDs and tapes. Play them often. Keep your music going in the house, especially if you live alone. Listen while driving. Sing along. Get a walkman. Listen while you walk or jog. It will improve your frame of mind. The right music can pump you up before working out, going on a date or meeting friends. Music is good for your soul.

Become a Culture Vulture

Art is not typically our strong point. There can be significant advantages to understanding a bit about the humanities. It gives you a bit more polish than the next guy. You are more worldly and have more class. You can attend concerts, plays and exhibitions with some level of appreciation. You will discover that there is a high percentage of women at these events. Also, the women who are there are generally a cut above the ladies at the local bar. Force yourself at first. It may be less painful than you think. See if we are correct about the advantages. By the way, many of these opportunities are free or very inexpensive.

Here is some help. Art takes a variety of forms including painting, sculpture, music, dance, theater, literature. There is a lot of interrelationship among them historically. A number of style periods are generally recognized and used to group artists and their works. These periods are not precise and often overlap. Each period has a set of characteristics that can be observed in the works of the time. Here is a very brief review of some of them.

Baroque – Early 18th Century
Classical – Late 18th and Early 19th Century
Romantic – Mid to Late 19th Century
Impressionistic – Early 20th Century
Modern or 20th Century – Mid 20th Century to Present

One way to become familiar with the periods is to spend an afternoon strolling through a world class museum such as the National Gallery of Art in Washington D.C. or the Art Institute of Chicago. The works will be arranged and identified by these periods. Initially your goal should be to become generally familiar with a dozen of the most important artists and some of their works. Over time you can gradually increase your knowledge by attending events every once in awhile. Eventually you will know the difference between Bach and Beethoven and immediately recognize a Van Gogh. You will also be much better at Trivial Pursuit.

Nervousness

This is tough. We could tell you to relax, but what does that mean? How do you do it? The trick is to recognize and accept your trepidation. When you act in spite of your concerns, you show courage. This is actually a very attractive quality. People love to cheer for an underdog. *If you condition yourself to respond to your nervousness with immediate decisive action, it will eventually disappear.* Remember the first time you tried the high dive or roller skates? Now, *that's* nervous. It probably took a dozen tries before you were completely at ease. After awhile you were not only calm and relaxed about diving or skating, you became confident and maybe even a bit cocky, in spite of belly-flops and skinned knees.

Consider each encounter with a woman to be a training exercise. You don't expect to really succeed in landing a date. Your expectations are low. *You just want to practice.* If she rejects you — so what? You were just being friendly. That's the worst that can happen to you. This repeated experience will eventually enable you to be calm and cool. The sweating palms will go away.

Hollywood Secrets

If your successful experiences with women have been very limited, you may have to create an alternate personality until your actual experience catches up. One way to do this is to become an actor and play the part. There is nothing dishonest about doing this. It will still be you relating to the woman. You are just going to play some mind games with yourself to improve your social skills and make yourself a more worthy partner. After reading this, you may wish to take an acting class or become involved with a community theater group. This is not a bad networking experience, by the way.

Perhaps you have heard of method acting based on the work of Stanislavski and Lee Strasberg. Many famous actors use the principles outlined here to convince us that they have become the characters in the script. Shelley Winters, the famous actor, said that you have to able to "act with your scars." You must find similar experiences in your own life, and be first willing, and then able to relive those experiences while playing your part. Your assignment is to approach a woman and play the part of a warm, sincere guy with lots of potential as a romantic partner. You must try to find an event or parallel situation from your life experience, and recreate it using an emotional memory.

Have you ever had a warm feeling upon hearing a certain song that was popular while you were in high school? This happens to many people. You hear every word, note and nuance of the song because they are embedded in your sensory memory. Perhaps that song is linked to some wonderful times. You might recall your senior prom, the first time you made love or the time you won a big game. The point is that warm emotional responses are involuntarily triggered from your subconscious simply by hearing the music. The same thing could happen when you are looking at a picture, smelling fall leaves burning, tasting fresh baked apple pie or feeling the warm sand beneath your feet.

The first tool you will need is a set of actual memories from your past that are parallel to the role that you are playing. Times when you were on top of your game, when you were warmly received or made a deep emotional connection with someone would work well. You were confident, warm and sincere. Everything was going your way. You made a connection with someone that was meaningful for both of you. Really search through your past to find a few outstanding examples of times when you felt this way.

Memory	Sight	Sound	Smell
Senior Prom	Dress, decorations	Song	Perfume

Touch	Taste	Emotion	
Hair	Punch, lipstick	Warmth, confidence	

Try this exercise at home. Sit alone in a comfortable chair with no distractions. Try to recreate the remembered event. The more specifically you recreate the objects of the memory, the more fully the emotional memory will work. You are attempting to bring back the emotional frame of mind that existed when you experienced those great feelings. Concentrate your full attention on the sensory aspects of the of the memory. Describe the location in as much sensory detail as possible. What were you wearing? Recreate the clothing in your mind. What color was it? Feel the material. Describe the texture. What time of year was it? What was the weather like? What was the time of day? What objects were around you? Use all your senses to touch them, see them, hear them, smell them or taste them. If you dedicate your sensory memory fully to exploring these aspects of the event, without regard to the resulting emotion, you may find yourself reliving the event emotionally.

Pour yourself a drink in your favorite glass or cup and use all your senses to study it each day for ten minutes. Think of as many questions about the glass as possible and use your senses to answer — very much like the game Twenty Questions in reverse. Eventually, it should be possible for you to recreate the sensory image of the glass anytime, anyplace. Practice doing this until you can recreate it at will. Can you imagine what it would be like to be a prisoner of war in a small cell, alone for years? Do you think you would be able to recreate the walls, floors and ceiling of your cell years later? Unfortunately, you would link these very detailed memories to some horrible events. Now imagine if you could summon a mental state that would make you confident, sincere and charming when approaching a woman?

Sense memory is the remembering by the five senses of the impressions you experience in everyday life. These impressions are stored in your subconscious. You can learn to recall sensory impressions from the subconscious by concentrating on the stimuli associated with them. It is similar to Pavlov and his dogs. Have you ever been very hungry, thought about your favorite food and discovered that your mouth actually watered. This is an example of your senses remembering the taste of the food and responding accordingly by activating your salivary glands. Ever reach into a dark closet and pick out the clothing you want to wear just by touching it? Your senses remember the touch of the material of that particular article of clothing.

If you believe that what you are doing is real, the woman will also believe it. The sense memory exercise is a key to unlocking the door of imagined reality. Faithfully executing a sense memory exercise each day will aid you not only in believing the truth of your "performance" but also in developing stronger powers of concentration.

By creating a particular place in a sensorial way, you can have an honest emotional response and you can use that exercise to produce the same emotional response in front of a beautiful stranger. After practicing this exercise many times, it only takes a few seconds for it to work.

However, you must never go for the emotional state, only for the associated stimuli that have in the past helped produce the emotion. By concentrating on all the sensory memories present when you had a socially successful experience, the emotional state will bubble up from your subconscious. You cannot will emotions. In life, emotions are produced of their own accord as a result of certain stimuli.

Another actor's trick it to do a substitution or personalization. Sometimes actors must play someone who is in love and their partner is a stranger or an actress they don't care for. If you have worked on recalling pleasant memories of past loves or high points in your life, it will be possible for you to substitute that image for the woman you are approaching. Think of the power you will have. You can turn this beautiful stranger into your high school sweetheart and present confidence, warmth and sincerity.

An Excellent Suggestion

Hand out free compliments. If you are not quite ready for prime time, select the woman you would most like to approach and give her a freebie. Screw up your courage, walk up and deliver the warmest, most sincere compliment you can and walk away. No risk. She will be delighted. It may be the only compliment she gets all night — or all month for that matter. Once you walk away you will immediately have her attention and interest. Obviously, you cannot walk down the line doing this or it will lose its meaning and effectiveness. You may also get thrown out. However, if you're discreet, you could compliment two or three women a night. At the end of a month you may have approached a dozen women or more with great success. How can you fail? By then you will be an old hand at it. You may discover that one or two women may actually strike up a conversation and invite you to join them! *If you get a positive response, do everything you can to capture the moment in your sensory memory in order to recreate it at will the next time you want to approach a woman!*

Another important aspect of self-confidence is your financial condition. If you are constantly worried about paying bills, it is difficult to relax and enjoy yourself. The knowledge that your finances are under control will increase your peace of mind.

Chapter 11
Your Bottom Line

"If you don't know where you are, a map is of little value."
— *Anonymous*

Women prefer a man who is financially responsible. *This does not mean that you have to be rich.* You just have to have your act together. You should not be in a fiscal crisis most of the time. You should be able to pay your bills and set a bit aside for the future. Is that too much to ask? You will be happier, more confident and much more attractive if you are not living from paycheck to paycheck.

Where Do You Get Your Mail?

Don't live with your parents unless you are desperate. When your desperation is resolved, move out. You don't stand a chance if Mom is still making your bed. This should be obvious. Women take a very dim view of guys in this situation. You could be a "mama's boy." If you don't have enough earning power to at least pay for a room somewhere, how are you going to support a relationship with her? Also, it will be extremely difficult, if not impossible, to entertain a date or have a party at your parents' place. *Move out.*

Obviously, the best situation is your own apartment or home. It offers great advantages. You can decorate your place to reflect your excellent taste. Don't have any taste? Get your lady friends and relatives to help. By the way, do not overdecorate. Less is more. Empty space has value. Women will view this as a blank canvas they may paint one day. Once you have your own place your appeal increases. You have substance. You are a man of property. Cool. You have privacy. Enough said.

The next best alternative is to share an apartment or house with some roommates. Often guys will advertise when someone moves out. This keeps your expense down and you have some guys to hang with — more economical, but privacy is limited. On the other hand, you have a built-in social framework. (Don't share living quarters with women. Your dates will wonder what's up.) Parties are more likely. These guys will have friends, sisters, cousins and co-workers. It's OK to date *their* co-workers but not your own. One other thing — never date the ex-girlfriend of a friend you want to keep. We don't care what the guy says, it will irk him and change your friendship for the worse. You need all the friends you can keep. It's just not worth it.

Entertaining at home. Make dinner for her. She will love it and tell all her friends. It will set you apart from your competition. Do as much of the preparation ahead of time as possible. A crock-pot is a big help. Ask your Mom, sister or a friend for an easy, tasty recipe. Be sure to make a salad. Hot rolls are great. Some chocolate-covered strawberries for dessert and you are a hero.

Your place must be perfectly clean. Take care of this several days ahead of time. Pay special attention to the bathroom and the kitchen. Get a female friend or relative to inspect your work. Details count. Do you have pictures of old girlfriends around? Get rid of them. However, pictures of family, friends and vacations can be good sources of conversation. Put clean hand towels in the bathroom. Flowers and candles are nice. Music is critical. It sets the mood, provides a topic of conversation and fills in those awkward gaps. Get a CD player. If you can afford it, a multi-disk changer is great. You can load it up with six hours of music and forget it. Choose a variety. You can always skip a disk.

Get a Job

It is very difficult to attract women if you are between jobs or in a similarly unsettled employment situation. There is a basic problem here. Women seek a man of strength and resource. *It doesn't mean you have to be rich, just responsible.* If you are not being responsible for your own career, how are you going to take care of a family later on? *Women like ambition.* It is also very healthy for you. You don't have to be in the job you were meant for, but you should be striving for it. *Have some passion about your future.* Know where you're going. Be all that you can be. (Sorry, we got carried away there.)

Seriously, if you have plans and are doing something about them, that's OK. You are a work in progress. If you always wanted your own restaurant, you are studying the competition, looking for the right location and talking to investors. It doesn't matter if you're not finished with culinary school. Sure, you are still a student, but you are a student with a dream and a future — very appealing. She wants to be able to talk about this aspect to her family and friends. Give her something positive to say. If you have been working part time at a convenience store for quite awhile and don't have any particular plans to improve your lot in life, you will eliminate a large percentage of potential dates. It's just the way it is. Get some job counseling. Start doing some long-term planning. Ambitious, successful people can tell you about their future. *You need a vision.*

Thoreau wrote, "most men lead lives of quiet desperation." Does your future consist of Wednesday following Tuesday? Have a dream. Have several, but have something. You don't have to aspire to buying out Bill Gates or making the NBA. Perhaps you would like your own business or some further education. It really doesn't matter and it certainly can change. Try this. How do you see your life one year from now? What about five years? Close your eyes and paint a picture. Don't put limits on yourself. Now *there* is some fascinating conversation. When you are done telling her about yours, ask her about hers.

It is even more effective if you communicate a vision that you will *achieve with or without her.* You don't have to be snotty about it. What you want to convey is a sense of independence. She will have a natural inclination to reel you back in.

Finances

As we mentioned several times, *women are attracted to men who are responsible, stable and have resources. This does not mean you have to be rich — just responsible.* Obviously, it is in your best interest to have control of your finances. Most people do not. Unfortunately, personal financial management is not included in a typical American education. Pity. We usually pick up concepts from family, friends and experience. While this is a complicated topic and is best left to professionals in the field, we offer some basic advice.

The biggest problem most people have is that they really don't have a clear picture of their financial position. They just stumble from paycheck to paycheck hoping that things will work out. They borrow or use credit cards like addicts. They put off saving until better times. Time is their enemy. Their ambiguous financial position worsens and they eventually find themselves in real trouble. If this sounds too familiar, you need to take action. By the way, do everything you can to avoid declaring bankruptcy. This is a very severe blow to your future. You will be branded for years. It should be the absolute last resort.

You will not be able to achieve your dating potential in this condition. You will lack confidence and the disposable income to show your sweetie a nice time. Remember, you are expected to fund the courtship. The cost of a typical date can range from twenty to one hundred dollars or more. If you find a gal you're sweet on, you'll probably want to see her at least once a week. You'll need an extra one hundred dollars a month, minimum. It would be very foolish of you to spend this money if you can't afford it. You will constantly be uncomfortable worrying about the cost of this and that. You will be in an inferior psychological position.

There is hope. Just like losing weight, it will take time — probably a lot of time. However, you don't have to completely straighten out the mess you're in. You just need to get to the point where you are comfortable tipping waiters and buying flowers. Of course, you need to know when you reach that point, which means you need to know your true financial condition. A brief arithmetic exercise once a month will help.

Where Does Your Cash Flow Go?

Study several months of your checkbook registers. Draw a vertical line on a sheet of paper. On the left list the average monthly deposits to your account. On the right list each expense you pay on a regular basis. These include rent, insurance, car payments, loan payments and minimum credit card payments. Be careful to include any quarterly payments (divide them by three). Since your taxes are typically deducted from your paycheck, you will not have to consider them here. However, if you make a yearly tax payment, divide by twelve and include it on the list. Leave out food, clothing, gas, etc. for now. Add up the income on the left and the fixed obligations on the right. We sincerely hope that the figure on the left is larger! If not, you are in major trouble, guy. You will have to take on another job, move, sell some stuff or some combination of the above. *You will have to put your social life on hold for a while.*

Your income is probably larger than your fixed expenses. Subtract the expenses from your income to calculate your disposable income. Of course, required items such as food and gas are going to have to come out of here. Make a list of your typical necessary expenditures at the bottom of the page. Be realistic. It may be tough to figure food and clothing. Do your best to come up with an honest monthly average for each of these and then total them. Subtract this from your disposable income. This figure is the amount that is truly disposable. More on this later. Don't spend it yet.

Prepare a Detailed Debt List

Put these headings at the top of a new sheet:

Name   Balance   Interest Rate   Minimum Payment   Payments Left

List each debt that you have. Include credit cards, car loans, student loans, store accounts and personal debts. You will have to examine statements to find the data. Try to put them in order by interest rate. Only mortgages and home equity loans are tax deductible. List them last.

Figure Your Debt/Equity Position

Draw a vertical line on another sheet of paper. On the left list everything you own — your car, furniture, stereo, the fair value of your house, etc. Include the amount in your checking, savings and investment accounts. These are your assets. Now list all your debts from your list on the right. This includes credit card balances, mortgage, student loans, car loans, back taxes, etc. Total each side. Subtract the debt total from the assets. If the number is positive, congratulations. You now know what you are worth. For many people, the number will be negative. This is not fatal. It will take years to make the number positive and that's OK.

Ten Most Wanted

Study your debt list ranked by interest rate. Make the minimum payment on the accounts on the bottom of the list. Consider this a hated *Ten Most Wanted List*. Divert as much disposable income as possible to payments against the top account on the list until it is paid off. Then, move on to the second "worst" account in terms of interest. Of course, you must stop buying on credit. Freeze all your balances. Never use the cards unless it is an absolute necessity. If you have to buy a new transmission for your car, you are better off taking out a small loan with your bank. Join a good credit union if possible. Their rates are much more favorable than commercial banks. When windfall amounts such as tax refunds come in, use them for debt reduction instead of a new sound system for your car. It may take several years to wipe out the list but it is well worth it. When that happy day comes, continue to apply your debt reduction allowance to your savings.

Of course, the whole point of this strategy is to increase your personal confidence and enhance your dating potential. It is surprising how confident you will feel when your financial situation is clear to you and you are making progress toward a realistic goal. Obviously, you will be comfortable spending a reasonable sum on your dating budget as well. You will hold your head up a bit higher and it will show.

Pay Yourself First

This is a tough one. It depends on your age, responsibilities and life position. Most people save little to nothing. A minimum goal for anyone should be five percent of their monthly income. Ideally, it should be more like 15 or even 20 percent. However, few people are fortunate enough to be able to put away that much and still eat. The point is you must get in the habit of saving *something* every paycheck, even if it's ten dollars. *Pay yourself first, put it away and don't touch it.* An IRA is a great way to start. This will permit you to sock away up to two thousand per year, tax protected. Check the new Roth IRA as well. If you are unfamiliar with the stock market, consider a strong mutual fund. It would be wise to get some professional advice from someone you trust. You may be able to have an amount automatically deducted from your paycheck. This is painless because you never see it and it requires no action on your part. Millionaires will tell you that this is one of the most important keys to accumulating wealth. Having a nest egg that is growing every year will give you a lot of satisfaction and really increase your self-confidence.

Savings and Debt Reduction

Establish an action plan, monitor it and stick to it. *Debt reduction and savings are the keys.*

OK, now for the hard part — you need to analyze your situation. This can really be tough.

You have to pay your taxes. You have to pay your fixed expenses such as rent and car loans. Your variable expenses such as food and clothing can be studied for possible reductions. Eat home more often. An interesting fact is that fresh fruit and vegetables and complex carbohydrates are much less expensive than meats and processed foods. *It is actually cheaper to eat a healthy diet.*

The area you must study most closely is your disposable income. You must include two categories here that may not be currently addressed — *savings and debt reduction.* Take a small percentage of your available income and diligently put it into savings without fail. This is critical. It is as much habit development as financial sense. The second category, debt reduction, will do a great deal to improve your financial condition. *Making the minimum payment on credit card accounts makes no sense at all.* This figure is established by the creditor for their advantage — typically five percent or less of the balance. They prefer that you pay outrageous amounts of interest, as high as 21 percent, for the longest possible time period because it means more profit for them. Always exceed the minimum payment by as much as possible. A good rule of thumb is at least ten percent of the balance if possible. This has the multiple effect of reducing the principle faster, lowering the amount of interest you are paying, freeing your credit line for more worthy purposes and making more funds available for savings. Of course, this takes discipline, patience and time.

What is Your Credit Rating?

You can find out easily. It is extremely important. Like insurance, a good credit rating is something you want to have, yet not use unless absolutely necessary. When you miss a payment or default on a loan you get a black mark on your record for years. Many people can get your credit record. Visit the local agency and insist on a copy. There will be a small fee. If you find discrepancies, insist that they be corrected. This is extremely important.

Insurance

You obviously need car insurance. Don't make claims unless you have to. It will keep your rates down. Life insurance is for your survivors. Who would be financially hurt if you died? If the answer is nobody, then don't spend the money on life insurance. If you need it to protect a child or a dependent relative such as a parent, buy term insurance. It's a better buy than whole life.

Investments

You should have an IRA, either the traditional type or the new Roth plan. Additionally, you should put your savings to work in something more beneficial than a bank savings account or CD. Financial geniuses know that the stock market has performed consistently well over the years.

Credit Cards

We love them and we hate them. They are required to reserve hotel rooms and rental cars. They are handy for purchasing through 800 numbers and on the Web. Their responsible use is great for building your credit rating. You know the dangers. People run up a high balance, then make minimum payments and suffer for years. *Always pay off the entire balance every month.* When you make a purchase, set aside the money from your checking account to pay for it. Imagine every credit card purchase as cash out of your pocket. Credit card abuse is the most common financial problem today. Don't get trapped.

Learn to Pay Cash

Control yourself. Don't buy on impulse. It's good training for dating. If you want a new stereo, shop carefully and wait until you have the cash. You will make a better purchase and save hundreds of dollars. If you face an emergency car repair and you don't have the cash to pay for it, use your credit card, but vow to pay it off as soon as possible. Avoid any luxury spending until you do.

Consistent application of these principles will gradually improve your financial position. You will develop the kind of discipline required to be a good provider. Your dates will sense this. You will become more attractive. However, all this self-improvement will be of little use if you have fatal personality flaws. Let's look at the dark side of male behavior.

Chapter 12

Are You a Jerk?

"It is a man's own mind, not his enemy or foe, that lures him to evil ways."

— *Buddha*

Don't Be a Jerk

How do you know if you are a jerk? Well, most jerks know that they are because people have been telling them for years. They just don't care. Of course, these are the hard-core jerks. You may just have some jerk-like tendencies. This, of course, is more subtle. The best thing to do is to ask. Hopefully, you have a confidant or two in your life — a relative or close friend you can confide in. Simply ask, "Hey Joe, do you think I act like a jerk sometimes?" This gives Joe some room to help you out without losing your friendship (and the twenty bucks you owe him). Ask him to describe your errant behavior. Accept what he says without challenge and encourage him to go on. (Of course, there is always the possibility that Joe is a jerk. You'll have to ask someone else in this case.) This will be painful but you will probably be listening to some hard, cold truth. You can then institute some changes by reversing your jerk-like behavior to improve your chances.

If you are a jerk or have jerk-tendencies, you are doomed until you change. It's just that simple.

Women are used to dealing with jerks. They have "jerk-radar" and special jerk avoidance strategies. They discuss this among themselves all the time. If you want to have some fun, ask them about it. They will tell you some amazing stories. You know, the worst-date kind of thing. If you still need help, here are some jerk behaviors and jerk adjectives.

Jerks

- are full of themselves.
- expect sex on the first date. That is the point of a date, after all.
- expect sex on every date after the first date. That is the point of a date, after all.
- know that women are inferior to men.
- believe that they are the answer to every woman's prayers.
- depend on muscles, money, macho, mouth and meanness to conquer women.
- think that manners, politeness and chivalry are for weenies.
- define all of life experience in terms of themselves.
- know it all.
- aren't about to change for anyone.
- swear a lot to show how cool they are.
- use a lot of sexual comments in their conversation.
- call women mama, bitch, chick, sweetheart or baby.
- think they are God's gift to women.
- are stuck on themselves.
- talk about themselves a lot.
- don't listen.
- compliment themselves.
- like to show off.
- dominate the conversation.
- put down others.
- can't keep their hands to themselves.
- talk about other women and their conquests.
- lack manners.
- use cliches as pick-up lines.

Jerk Adjectives

Addicted	Compulsive	Macho	Revolting
Aggressive	Conceited	Materialistic	Rude
Antagonistic	Condescending	Mean	Self-absorbed
Argumentative	Contradictory	Miserable	Self-centered
Bitter	Crude	Nasty	Selfish
Boastful	Drunk	Negative	Slick
Boorish	Dull	Obnoxious	Smoking
Boring	Egotistical	Obscene	Too talkative
Bragging	Hostile	Obsessive	Unhappy
Brazen	Immature	Offensive	Unpleasant
Chauvinistic	Indifferent	Opinionated	Violent
Cheap	Insincere	Possessive	Weak
Childish	Loud	Pushy	Whining
Cold-hearted	Lying	Raw	

Eliminate the possibility that any of these adjectives could be applied to you. This will do wonders for your appeal. It is quite surprising how likeable we can be if we just don't act like jerks.

Are We Pigs?

You have heard the unpleasant saying, "All men are pigs." Don't put too much stock in it. Either the women are having some fun at our expense or they have been recently wounded by one of our more thoughtless brothers. Understanding the basis is important, though. Historically, men have been obsessed with the appearance of women. Artists and poets have immortalized it. Many scientists believe this has more to do with biology than chauvinism. Our ancient genetic programming compels us to mate and propagate. Males strive to find fertile partners and to mate with frequency — hence, the natural inclination toward the female that exhibits healthy physical manifestations. Females, on the other hand, search for potential fathers with resources. Now all this is just anthropological theory. However, if you accept the premise, here are some ideas concerning male perceptions of beauty. You will find that women typically disagree with most of this. We hope to help you understand what is going on in your libido. In this way, you can control it and move up the evolutionary scale.

Thin is Not In

As much as women rant and rave about the popularity of the super model's waif-like appearance, it's not our fault. This *Vogue* look is cherished by the fashion community who pander to the tastes of wealthy women. We prefer the fleshier look of the Victoria's Secret model. Most guys are *not* interested in wrapping their arms around a skeleton. It's preferable to see some movement when she walks down the street. Women who are determined to become a size 4 when they are a size 8 are not doing it for us. They are doing it for themselves for a very unhealthy reason.

Symmetry Counts

The left side should look the same as the right side. As strange as this seems, a lack of sameness on each side will be psychologically perceived as inferior. This is manifested in the face and the body. Typically this is not a problem. This symmetry projects a healthy prospect. The lack of it suggests physical inferiority.

It's All About Balance

Guys love numbers. However, what floats our boat is not the figure on the bathroom scale. Women are constantly talking about losing five or ten pounds. It doesn't really matter. What does matter, according to history, is the ratio of her hips to her waist. Stay with us. The magic number, .7, works like

this. The hip measurement is unlikely to change a great deal. You can work
with a waist. (So can we!)

Hips	Waist
30	21
31	21.7
32	22.4
33	23.1
34	23.8
35	24.5
36	25.2
37	25.9
38	26.6
39	27.3
40	28

Now the decimal fractions are a bit absurd but the notion is not. This pro-
portion produces a very attractive appearance that projects health and a high
probability of child bearing. This .7 ratio is present in most beauty contest
winners but not on the runways of Paris. By the way, we can turn this around.
Your chest should be proportionately larger than your waist. Strive for a difference of ten inches. You can increase your chest by working out but reducing your waist measurement will yield much more worthwhile benefits.

True Beauty is Under the Skin

You really can't judge a book by its cover. You must have proved this to yourself over and over again. Before we all get in too much trouble here to a large
extent, it's not what you have — it's what you do with it. We are also attracted to energy, vigor and charm. The way a woman behaves and moves
kicks in big time after your first look. We are, after all, highly evolved intelligent creatures capable of thoughtful involvement with others. After the hormones subside you have to relate on another, more meaningful level.
Underneath all that feminine charm is a real, live person. Enjoy the excite-
ment but move on to getting to know her and making her your friend as soon
as possible. We just want you to understand what is going on in your subconscious. If you end up stuck in first gear, the party will end sooner than you
would like.

Now that we've had this little talk, it's time to get out there and start meeting women. Where do you start? Well, one thing is for sure — it's not in your
living room.

Chapter 13
Out and About

"Life only demands from you the strength you possess.
Only one feat is possible: not to have run away."

— Dag Hammarskjold

You Really Do Have to Get Out More

Force yourself. Get off that couch, turn off the television, get cleaned up and get out. Use any flimsy excuse. Be constantly busy and on the run. Get to know your town very well. When a new place opens up, be one of their first customers.

Your opportunities for potential relationships are directly proportional to your social exposure. When you break out of your self-defeating cycle of depression and isolation you create positive energy. You will meet new people you will enjoy, lower your anxiety and increase your optimism. From this vantage point, the world seems like a better place and you can convince yourself that there are many worthy, potential partners out there. This confidence will also permit you to pass up relationships that may not be right for you.

Actively seek occasions and activities that will enrich and not simply entertain you. You will grow as a person and cultivate a positive outlook. While you are engaged in these activities you must *practice* your interpersonal skills. *Practice* approaching interesting women. *Practice* relating to them. Learn about their character and personality and reveal some of yours. *Practice* determining if there is any dating potential. How can you fail if you are only *practicing?* Of course, if something should happen to develop, so much the better. Enjoy the process and have a good time. You deserve it. You are a positive, worthy guy. If you have been wise enough to participate in worthwhile activities you will be absorbed, relaxed and confident. You will be amazed at how much more attractive you will seem.

Most communities have a local recreation board. The school district or the municipality may sponsor it. Sports leagues, classes and workshops are offered most evenings and are very inexpensive. Drop by and take a look. Pick up a schedule. You could sign up for a coed volleyball on Wednesday nights for twenty five dollars. Check bulletin boards, newspapers and radio stations. Clubs are often crying for volunteers to help keep the ball rolling. Get involved. If you don't care for the situation, move on.

Re-examine your childhood and adolescent interests. Remember all those clubs they used to have in school? There must be something you were always interested in. What do your friends, associates and co-workers do in their spare time? Ask. Work very hard on this. It is extremely important. *This personal development is probably your best path to new potential relationships.* You can easily fill up your schedule with extra work hours and chores. Perhaps you are avoiding the issue. If you don't have time to take a photography class or golf lessons, you probably don't have time for a relationship — food for thought.

You have become very comfortable with your current existence. It is familiar. You come home from work, grab something to eat, look at the mail, and fall asleep in front of the tube. There will be a normal psychological resistance to changing this pattern. Initially you will be uncomfortable. Take it slowly. Schedule one activity for one night a week. If you don't really enjoy it, try something else. After a month or so, add another activity. Busy people are happy people. Eventually you will view a night at home alone as a treat!

Get Around Town

Get involved with one or two community groups or events. Ponder your interests and opinions and select one that you can support. You are then more likely to meet people with similar interests. Charities are great. It's the right thing to do, enhances your image and puts you in contact with many people. It could be as simple as participating in a "Walk for (fill in the blank)." This is very simple. You sign up, contribute or solicit contributions, show up and enjoy the event. You will meet all kinds of people. Quality folks frequent things like this. Get your own little group together from work or among your friends. Nurture a reputation as a social catalyst. After the event, you can suggest gathering at a local pub or restaurant.

Watch the paper for art exhibitions, music performances or plays. It's OK to attend events such as these alone. You will be more informed and the networking opportunities are great. Learn who the better local bands are. Call up some buddies and go to see them.

Bookstore/coffee shops are excellent places to frequent. There are often events like music, book signings and lectures. They are a great place to be seen and increase your cultural frame of reference.

Take any opportunity you can to attend parties. Always bring a little something for the host/hostess. A bottle of wine, some flowers or a dish will do. Be as courteous a guest as possible. Parties are great places to network. Eventually, you can get to the point where you can throw your own.

Do you like horses? Many women love them. We've noticed that riding stables are a magnet for women equestrians. If the sport appeals to you, a few lessons could yield some nice benefits. Of course, it can be a bit pricey depending on your area.

There are some worthy organizations that have chapters just about everywhere. Attend a meeting at most or several of them and decide if you would enjoy participating. Take a quick survey of the availability of single women. Keep trying until you find one or two that you like. Membership is usually not expensive. You can adjust your participation to suit. They will be pleased to accept any time that you are willing to contribute.

Some organizations that you may want to consider include:

The Society for the Prevention of Cruelty to Animals
Young Democrats
Young Republicans
United Way
Greenpeace
Sierra Club

Has a waitress caught your eye? If not, visit a wide variety of restaurants and coffee shops until one does. Become a regular. Tip well. Make small talk. Try to visit when traffic is at a minimum — either early or late. She will be more likely to talk. The nice thing about this situation is that you can really take your time since you know her schedule. Only proceed if your attention is welcome. Don't become a pain or worse. She's very busy and trying to earn a living. On the other hand you could become a real bright spot in her day. Over time you may be able to suggest that you take her someplace nice where they will wait on her!

Personal Ads

They can work. The odds are slim and you have to know what you are doing but it is possible to meet quality women using the personals. It takes a lot of homework and plenty of dead-end phone calls and meetings. It also takes thick skin. What we like is that, unlike dating services, it is a true marketplace that you can control.

There is a certain stigma associated with doing this. Many people take a dim view of the personals. They believe that it is for losers or freaks. This is partially true. You may wish to keep your activities to yourself for now. Ultimately what matters is that you find some worthwhile women to date. It doesn't really matter how you meet them. Eventually you may have to explain when people ask where you met her. Worry about that later.

Get copies of some major magazines that feature personals such as The Washingtonian, Los Angeles, Boston or the New York Review of Books. Carefully read the men's ads. You need to get a feel for the competition and look for clever ideas to borrow. Concentrate on the lead lines. This is the most important part of the ad because it must attract attention or she will keep going down the column. By the way, you may want to start with a word that is early in the alphabet as the ads are often listed alphabetically. Many women never get to V or W. You need to be clever and reveal something about yourself here. Make her smile and wonder what kind of a guy would say something like that. Avoid cliches and standard adjectives. Never use words like successful, good looking, attractive, generous, handsome, or wealthy. You get the idea. This is not a hard sell. Let her discover your endearing qualities by herself. Pique her curiosity.

Don't compare yourself to famous people like Tom Cruise, no matter what people have told you. She will be disappointed when she meets you and you will look like an idiot. Keep those annoying acronyms to a minimum. You are not trying to restrict the number of replies by drawing all sorts of boundaries. Never say negative things like "tired of the bar scene" or "hurt but healing."

Next find a few good personals listings in your area. Shoot for the high end. Read through several publications until you find one or two that you like. Now you have to put in some study time, you have to learn the ropes. Of course, you will concentrate on the "Women Seeking Men" section but it is a good idea to look at the competition as well — especially if you plan to place your own ad. By the way, that is a decision you will have to make.

You can just answer ads, place your own ad and let the women come to you or do both. If you have something to offer and are not especially needy, then you may want to try answering ads. If you place an ad and do it well, you will get plenty of responses. Unfortunately, many of them will not be acceptable for any number of reasons. This takes time. Of course, working both sides of the street takes even more time. We recommend that you start by answering ads to get some experience.

You will have to establish some minimum standards and stick to them in order to work your way through the listings. It may cost two to four dollars per minute on your phone bill to listen to the voice ad and leave a response. You want to be sure to eliminate all ads that will not meet your requirements. Some of the categories that you will consider may include:

Age – Figure a minimum and maximum you are willing to accept. If she says "20s", she is 29.

Height – If you are tall or average, you have an advantage. You can date 'em all, short or tall. Establish a height range you will accept.

Weight – We will be blunt here. Many women place ads because they are overweight. Sometimes they reveal this with phrases like queen size, pleasingly plump, rubenesque, medium build, etc. Generally, they will understate their true condition. Sometimes they will mention their actual weight. If a woman is in good shape, she will usually include this as an advantage by using phrases like petite, trim, athletic, thin, or include the poundage. If they say nothing about it, watch out. The odds are that they are overweight and trying to conceal it. Of course, this may not be too much of an issue for you depending on your preferences and your own condition.

Marital Status – Women who are married but separated will place ads. Heck, we've heard of married men and women doing it. What status are you willing to accept — divorced, widowed, estranged (separated) or single (usually this means never married)?

Children – Single/divorced moms have a tough time finding dates and often place ads. You need to decide how you feel about this. See the discussion of this issue in Chapter 3.

Race – Decide what your preferences are. Most ads will reveal the woman's race.

Location – People will often place ads in other cities. How far are you willing to travel for a movie date?

Education – It may not be all that important but you should have some ideas on this issue. If you have a master's degree and she is a high school dropout, is that OK? What about the reverse?

Interests – If the woman is a NASCAR and country music fan and you aren't, it could be a long evening.

Religion –The word "Christian" usually denotes that the person has strong fundamental beliefs and prefers someone who shares them. The same applies to Catholic or Jewish. If it doesn't matter too much to the woman, it's usually not included in the ad.

Non-Smoker – They usually mean it. We warned you.

You have to learn the acronyms. There is a lot of information in those little letters. Try to avoid putting them in your own ad. Here are some tips.

A - Asian	M - Male
B – Black	N/D - Nondrinker
D – Divorced	N/S – Non Smoker
F - Female	NA - Native American
G - Gay	P - Professional
H – Hispanic	S - Single
ISO – In Search Of	W – White
J – Jewish	WW – Widowed
LTR - Long-Term Relationship	

Circle all the ads that meet your requirements. There will probably be a code number with the ad. Set up a notebook page each week. Write down the code, the first few words of the ad (sometimes they are listed alphabetically) and some vital statistics. Leave some space for notes when you hear the voice ad and talk to the lady. You don't want to call the same ad twice or mix up the women (very embarrassing).

Pay careful attention the first time you call the service. They will try all sorts of scams to keep you on the line. Learn to use the menu system so you can get to the ads you want as quickly as possible. Have a brief script ready to leave your message. You can include some basic information that is the same for every ad and then personalize the response based on what she said.

Stock Message: (It should probably be a bit longer than this — write it out.) "Hi, Karen. I liked your ad. My name is Bill. My number is 555-1234. I'm 32, about 5'8" and 160 with brown hair and blue eyes. I'm a systems analyst and I went to Georgia Tech. I love golf, the beach and my dog."

Personalized Additional Message: (You can write this out or do it on the fly.) "Hi, Karen, it appears that we have some things in common. I like honesty, Seinfeld and the Sunday crossword, too. Also, your voice really appealed to me. I'd love to talk to you. How about giving me a call? Again, my name is Bill and the number is 555-1234. I'm usually home after 7. Take care, Karen. Bye now."

Putting your name and number at the beginning and the end is helpful to her. Repeating her name a few times is a nice touch, too. Relax. Be warm and friendly and don't speak too fast. There is usually plenty of time allowed on the service.

Don't let her requirements discourage you, within reason. If you are outside her age limit but have offsetting qualities, she will probably consider you. It's worth a shot. If there is a serious difference, she just won't call.

You have to understand the odds and be prepared for the consequences. We have no hard statistics but the following scenario is not unreasonable.

1. You circle and respond to twenty ads.

2. Five women call you over a three-week period. You must be very patient. People get busy. Many women will not leave messages on voice mail.

3. After a conversation, three of the five agree to meet you.

4. One is not nearly "as advertised" and you gracefully excuse yourself.

5. One gracefully excuses herself because you are "not what she is looking for." Ouch.

6. One fails to show up. Double ouch.

7. Oh well, there's always next week. As we mentioned, this takes patience and thick skin.

Women (bless their hearts) are fond of including phrases in their ads like romantic walks, moonlight, quiet times, nature, quality time, spontaneity, *ad nauseum*. These mean nothing and can be ignored.

Once you start the process you have to be prepared to receive calls at any time. The woman is under the naïve impression that hers is the only ad you answered and you are expecting her call — tricky. She will probably lead with:

"Bill? Hi. My name is Karen and you answered my ad."

The ball is now in your court. Here is where your notes are worth their weight in Microsoft stock. Run for them. In the meantime, make her feel comfortable. (A portable phone can be quite helpful.)

"Hello. I'm really glad you called. Your ad was great. This is a really crazy process isn't it? I'll bet you've received a lot of responses." (Keep things light and breezy — no pressure.)

"You must have some questions about me. Let's have some fun. You ask any question you like and I'll give you an honest answer. Of course, then it's my turn!"

She will be very comfortable because she can fill in some blanks about you. This will buy you some time while you grab your notes. As soon as possible, begin to ask her some questions and jot down some comments. It may be two weeks until you talk to her again. By the way, if the first conversation isn't really going that well, delay asking her out until you have a chance to talk a few more times.

Try to determine if there are any deal killers on the table for you or for her. You don't want to waste each other's time. She will appreciate this. She may have hidden some key facts, like she has four kids. Work some questions into the general conversation from your requirement list. If you hit a show-stopper, be honest and cut it short.

"Wow, Karen, I didn't realize you were still married. I think I would be more comfortable if you were actually divorced." Continue the conversation and keep it as pleasant as possible. You may be able to make her an ally in your quest. If she finds you sincere and interesting, she may actually refer you to a friend.

The subject of a photo may come up. Sooner or later, you will have an occasion to provide one. You're much better off being prepared. Find a friend who is fairly handy with a camera and ask him to shoot a couple rolls of you. You could use a professional but it's expensive and might give the wrong impression. Wait for a really good day when you have some time and the sun is out. Get a good haircut a few days beforehand and buy a few new clothes for the occasion. All this will make you feel better and it will show in the photos. They should be casual and show you at your best. Take some of just your head, from the chest up and full body. Try a variety of relaxed poses. Lean against a fence post. Look for props that say something about you — golf clubs, your dog, or your laptop. Pick a nice local spot such as a college campus or a park. When you get the prints back ask several friends which are the most attractive. Blow up two or three to 5x7 and have some good color copies made. Keep these handy.

Sometimes you may wish to exchange photos with someone before you meet. Also, you may want to give her one to show her friends and family later on.

If things go well, suggest a meeting. The purpose is to meet briefly and see how things go from there. If she agrees, ask her to suggest a time and place convenient for her. She should feel comfortable. You want to meet for an hour, preferably less. If things go well, the two of you can decide to linger.

Ask her how you can recognize her. This is great. She has to describe herself in relative detail. Lots of clues here. Tell her what you will be wearing and be sure to be there early so that she doesn't have to wait. Also, you get to see her first as she arrives. If there is something about her appearance that eliminates her as a possibility, you can make things easy on both of you. After greeting her, make it clear that your time is very limited today. On the other hand, if you find her attractive you can mentally prepare yourself to do your best.

Sample Ads by Women

Here are some examples of ads placed by women for your examination. They were chosen at random. We include some comments for your consideration. We have been very blunt but we are just surmising. Enjoy.

ATTRACTIVE SINGLE WHITE professional Female, blonde/blue, 5'2", no dependents, nonsmoking, loves dancing, traveling, movies, beaches, sincere, seeks attractive Single White Male, 32-42, with similar interests.
Could be a great catch. Probably late thirties. Didn't mention her weight so there may be a surprise there.

ATTRACTIVE, EDUCATED MOM of one, 5', 135 lbs. Seeking handsome white male, 25-45, to share a cup of coffee. Must be educated, professional, financially secure and enjoy children.
Definitely looking for a Dad. Age doesn't matter. Wants security. She might be a terrific partner, if you can accept the whole package.

BLUE-EYED, COMPASSIONATE SINGLE White Female, late 30s, slim, seeks caring, romantic, all-around nice guy, late 30s plus, for long-term relationship and commitment. All calls returned. Children welcome.
She's 39 and a bit desperate (all calls returned). Might have kids.

CAN BE OCCASIONALLY playful as a kitten. Single White Female, 41, 5'3", nonsmoker, nondrinker, sensitive, caring, intelligent, enjoys nature walks, soft rock, movies, conversation, seeks Single Male, 41-46.

If this is your age range, she could be an interesting possibility. Cute lead line.

DIVORCED WHITE FEMALE, 31, mother of two, looking for Single or Divorced White Male for laughs, fun, friendship, loves family, volleyball, the beach, boating, fishing, skiing. Family-oriented and children a plus.
A definite Brady Bunch situation. Sounds like an active, fun person.

EXCEPTIONAL, NEVER-MARRIED, WHITE professional Female, 34, attractive, physically fit, adores animals, beach, travel, music, sports. Seeking well-built, good-looking, Christian White Man, similar interests. Friends, then marriage. Call for more information.
Sounds like she has a lot to offer. Sounds like she has her act together. You had better be in shape and like to go to her church.

HONEST SINGLE WHITE Female, 32, 5'8", full-figured, brown/blue, searching for honest, commitment-minded Single Male, 29-35. No players. Smokers and light drinkers okay. Love children.
An overweight, smoking, drinking Mom looking for a Dad. At least she's honest. "No players" probably means she has been burned a few times.

HUMOR AND HONESTY. Single White Female, 28, blue-eyed blonde, full-figured, loves romantic comedies, NASCAR, walks and Stephen King, looking for Single White Male, 28-38. No games please.
Very specific on interests. Weight problem. "No games please" indicates that she has been hurt.

PROFESSIONAL, EASYGOING, PETITE Single White Female, 33, blonde hair, blue eyes, enjoys sports, traveling, dining out, seeking professional White Male, 28-36, with similar interests, for dating, possible relationship.
Sounds great. Healthy attitude.

SINGLE WHITE FEMALE, 30, 5'8", medium build brown/brown. Enjoys traveling, hiking, camping in the mountains. Professional seeking adventurous, blue-collar worker, 28-35. Must enjoy the outdoors. Those who enjoys country music a plus.
Knows what she wants. "Medium build" is typically an understatement, but perhaps not. If you fit the bill, it could be fun.

VIVACIOUS, PETITE, REDHEAD, professional, attractive, fit Female seeking professional, fit, trim, financially secure man for casual dating, possibly more. Likes music, dancing and more.
Sounds like a fun person with some standards.

Sample Ads by Men

Now, here are some ads from your competition. You can see what to do right and what not to do. These were randomly chosen and include some comments. Good luck.

29-YEAR-OLD WHITE PROFESSIONAL Male, 6'1", 195 lbs, conservative, yet fun-loving and adventurous. Seeks athletic, White professional Female, 23-35, with good values, to enjoy conversation, sports, travel, humor and evenings out.
Starting your lead line with a number sorts you to the top of the list sometimes. Could use some personality, perhaps.

39-YEAR-OLD, NONSMOKING WHITE Male, 5'8", 160 lbs, educator, athletic, honest, easygoing, loves children, seeking Female, 30-45, for friendship.
A teacher looking to settle down and start a family. Nice tone.

ADVENTUROUS SINGLE WHITE Male, 30s, in search of slender, nonsmoking Single White Female, between 18 and 33. Enjoys movies, walks photography, dining and other fun things.
This guy just wants to date. He is going a bit young since he's probably 38.

AFFECTIONATE, CARING, EMOTIONAL, sensitive Male, mid-30s, considered handsome, extreme appreciation for arts and entertainment. Unappreciative of Women playing dating games. Seeking attractive Woman who appreciates Man with aforementioned attributes, for dating.
Sounds a bit needy and desperate. The word choice sounds a bit pretentious.

AFFECTIONATE, VERY HANDSOME, secure Single White Male, 37, brown hair, brown eyes, enjoys music, dining, dancing and cuddling, seeking Single White Female, age open, for dating, possible relationship.
Drop the "very handsome." Say something like "been told I'm attractive" instead, if that's the case.

ATTRACTIVE WHITE MALE, well-built, believes in very healthy lifestyle, financially secure, homeowner, sense of humor, easy to talk to, 39, (looks younger). Would like to meet a healthy, classy, attractive Female.
Lots of qualifications. "Sense of humor" and "easy to talk to" are good comments.

DATING PARTNER WANTED. Single White Female, 25-35, who is adventurous, exciting, charming and cute. To enjoy the company of Single White Male 40, with similar characteristics.
He's going to have a tough time finding a casual dating experience in that age range. Also, he is saying he is adventurous, exciting, charming and cute (similar characteristics).

DEVOTED DAD. SINGLE White Male, 40, 5'8", 190 lbs, father of delightful, well-mannered 7-year-old, seeking good-looking, slender Female, for romance, adventure and long-term relationship.

A bit too much about junior.

GORGEOUS WHITE MALE, 5'6", 135 lbs, 30, seeking Single Female, race open, 20-35, no full-figured Women. Enjoys outdoors, sports, quiet times, for relationship.
Oh, please. Gorgeous?

HARDWORKING SINGLE BLACK Male, trying to make a living, enjoys sports, jazz, concerts, dining out, meeting people, seeking similar Female, 25-40, for friendship, possible relationship.
Solid, honest ad.

HONEST, COMPASSIONATE, FUN-LOVING, affectionate Single White Male believes in companionship, communication, laughter and romance, seeks one very caring, unselfish, honest, loyal, rather feminine, well-built, professional Single White Female, with good values.
Hmmm. How about a bit of personality and some stats?

LONELY SINGLE WHITE Male, 6'8", looking for taller than average Female for dating, possibly more. Likes movies, drag racing, car shows,
Wow. Tough criteria. At least it's all right out front. Good luck.

PHYSICALLY FIT, PROFESSIONAL White Male, 33, 6'1", 195 lbs, easy-going, reliable, cheerful. Interests include traveling, outdoors, sports and dining. Seeking thin, responsive, optimistic, fit White Female, 25-35, for friendship, possible relationship.
Sounds like a real catch. Should do well if it's all true.

WARM, CARING SINGLE White Male, 38, 5'11", 180 lbs, enjoys dining, music, football, feeding and watching the deer, seeking Woman to show my respect to. I'll never take you for granted.
Sounds like a decent guy. Perhaps a bit needy.

Cyber-dating

The Internet offers opportunities for personals but there are some problems. Most Internet users are men. Many of the women who are using it for cyber-dating are less than desirable. This will change over time as Internet usage increases. Also, people will contact you from all over. Internet users prefer to exchange endless e-mails before meeting. They find it entertaining. It preserves anonymity. This does not work to your best interest. You need voice contact as soon as possible. At this time a local personals section is much more useful. If you would like to try it, we recommend a free service called American Singles. You can both place and answer ads for free. They can be found at www.as.org

A glance at the membership on this service, which is one of the largest, demonstrates the inequity in Internet usage between men and women. In October, 1998 there were about 30,000 women listed in the US while there were 111,600 men — a ratio of four to one. A breakdown of selected states follows.

	Men	Women
California	15,311	3,566
Florida	6,369	1,730
New York	6,831	1,900
Ohio	4,674	1,094
Pennsylvania	4,539	1,171
Texas	8,295	2,490

Singles Socials

Singles events are generally not a good idea. They will typically be full of needy folks without a lot to offer. One exception could be "Parents Without Partners," if you are a parent. What you will end up with is a "Brady Bunch" type of situation — her and her kids, you and yours. Your odds of success may be higher under these circumstances. You will be sharing the same challenges and joys as parents. Of course, you will have to deal with ex-spouses and sibling rivalries times two. (See the section on children in Chapter 3.) There are dinner clubs in some cities that can be interesting. They have a gathering at an upscale restaurant once or twice a month. Singles dress up and mingle. They can be pricey but worth exploring.

Religious Institutions

If you have strong religious convictions, you should check into the singles events in your church or synagogue. This presumes that religious convictions are very high on your list of required criteria and that religion is an essential part of your life. The honest truth is that other criteria such as looks will not be a high priority among this crowd — no disrespect, just an observation. Of course, we could easily be wrong in any given case. By the way, if religion is that important to you, this is the right thing to do. You will be happier.

Dating Services

Forget it. These are high-pressure businesses that prey on the unfulfilled dreams of their clients. They will be incredibly interested in you until you fork over one thousand dollars or more of your hard-earned money. After that, they will want to spend as little time on you as possible. A few simple observations:

• They rely on aggressive sales techniques and expensive advertising to attract clients. If they were really effective, word of mouth would do the job.

- They will reveal no statistics on their success. We suspect it is dismal. An interesting number would be the percentage of marriages per contracts signed.
- They will not let you see the merchandise. "Photos and videos don't reveal everything about a person." Right. If they had dozens of women dying to meet a guy like you, why not show you some pictures without names?
- They pick the dates for you anonymously. This is how they fulfill their contract. They guarantee one or two dates per month, so you get a name and number in the mail and you're on your own.
- Try to find some satisfied customers. Ask others who have tried it (if you can get them to admit it). Good luck.
- Unfortunately, the majority of the women in the catalog might not attract your attention on the street. Of course, the agency will tell you that they are just too busy to date and need the service to set up their social schedule.

If you are in a desperate situation, do everything you can by using the ideas in this book before you invest in one of these services. Remember — they have no idea about your value system or character. How can they hope to match you with an appropriate date?

Best places to meet women:

Weddings are great. Everyone is dressed up and looking good. Make sure you are. Women are in the right frame of mind. There is plenty of time to talk to them and ask them to dance. They can't really refuse. Also there is this great tradition where all the single girls have to go out on the floor and catch the bouquet. Any questions? Always accept wedding invitations. Never take a date.

Other people's office Christmas parties — never yours! (See Dating at Work.) They are similar to weddings in that everyone is looking their best and feeling great. Your chances of success are vastly increased here. Your friends can introduce you to lots of women. Don't ignore married/engaged women, they may have single friends. Talk to them. Make them your friends.

Health clubs. You find a good caliber of women here, trying to improve their health and appearance while wearing spandex. Cool.

Bookstore/coffee shops. Culture, cappuccino, cuties abound.

After-work happy hours at upscale lounges. This is not quite the same as singles bars. People are still dressed from work. They are ready to relax. The women are looking for a paradigm shift. Everyone is talking. Talking is good.

Any place selling yummy food. Yogurt shops, gourmet anything, — women love to stuff their faces. They will congregate at the shops with the best goodies, especially at lunchtime.

Upscale shopping areas with women's shops. Make sure you look good and do a bit of shopping yourself. Look and be seen. Stop and chat.

Best of all are worthwhile activities that you truly enjoy. We discussed this earlier but it is worth repeating. Charity events, concerts and art galleries, classes, community organizations and festivals offer excellent opportunities to encounter quality women who share your values and interests. The more value the event has, the better the quality of the attendees. If you plug into this circuit you will be pleasantly surprised at the result. Make a study of your community and see what is out there. When you hear people talking about their participation in an organization or event, ask a lot of questions. Keep attending until you find a few that you enjoy. Besides, it's good for you. You will grow. Your value as a potential partner will increase

There is always the spontaneous encounter in an unlikely spot such as a line at the bank. This is tough. In order to be receptive to your advances, a lady will need to feel secure in her environment, be in a receptive frame of mind and open to the possibility. To understand this, consider the reverse situation. People are often disappointed when they return from a vacation and have had no success meeting someone. A cruise or a week at the beach are ideal settings for romance and expectations are high. The point is that you must choose the right time and place. Timing is essential. However, if an opportunity presents itself in a bookstore, you should go for it. It will just be more difficult and you will have to work harder.

Worst places to meet women

"Wastin' our time on cheap talk and wine . . ."

— *The Eagles*

Bars. Sorry, it doesn't work for a number of reasons. The conditions are horrible, the competition is fierce and the mindset of the women is all wrong. The music is too loud for decent conversation, which is essential. It could happen, but luck is not with you. *NEVER GO TO A BAR BY YOURSELF!* You immediately have the word LOSER tattooed on your forehead. What are you going to do — stand against the wall with a beer and watch the girls walk by? Are you hoping one of them will stop and say, "Hey, you really remind me of Harrison Ford — how about coming back to my place?" Right.

Only go to a bar with a group and for a reason. You can go with some buddies to watch a game or hear a good band or celebrate Jim's promotion. The best situation is to go with a mixed group of couples and singles. You have a crowd to hang with. You can invite a lady to join your group if the opportunity presents itself. You are talking and enjoying yourself and you will appear much more attractive than the collection of single dolts standing by the ladies' room.

While a number of couples have met at bars, they present a plethora of problems. We all understand the effects of alcohol. The buzz changes your perception of reality. It diminishes your ability to think, therefore you use your chemistry more than your brain. You are not yourself. You know the old image of the guy with the lampshade on his head — amusing or pitiful? You may wonder about the quality of the women you are meeting. Why are they there? It seems hypocritical but you will have a bit less respect for them. A lot of boorish behavior takes place in bars — arguments, obnoxious antics, even fights. Is this the place to meet the mother of your children?

If you happen to find yourself at a bar, here are some ideas to increase your odds. Don't sit in a corner. You need to be where you can be seen. The best place is either near the entrance or close to the dance floor. You can observe who is coming and going and increase your opportunities for eye contact. (See flirting.)

If you are with a group of friends (and you should be), spend a lot of time talking to the women — the more attractive and interesting, the better. You may be concerned that other women will think you are "taken" — wrong. The more attractive the woman that you are laughing with — the more desirable you will appear. Think this through. If you are consistently observed around town in the company of attractive women, will this hurt or enhance your image in the eyes of available women? Who knows if it is your sister, cousin, neighbor or co-worker? They don't know that you're not on a date.

Your place of employment. There are many potential problems here. See the discussion to follow.

Business meetings, formal occasions and situations where people are dealing with something serious such as their careers or health are very limited opportunities for romantic contact. People are preoccupied and in the wrong mind set. While this is not always the case, you would do well to simply attempt to meet her on a professional level.

Your mother's house. God bless her, she will never find the perfect girl for you. Her criteria are way out of whack with yours. You'll just tic mom off when it doesn't work out.

Family Reunions. Just kidding. Lighten up. However, make sure you attend your high school and college reunions. They are a lot of fun. It's very interesting to see what life does to your peer set. You may find that your high school obsession is divorced and ready to date. This is a great place to network.

Keep Your Business and Love Life Separate

Dating at work can be extremely risky. In a large corporation it may be possible. Working in different departments or buildings might provide enough separation. In a small company or department, there's no hiding place. It is very natural for people to develop an attraction for one another when they are working toward a common goal. We try to look and act our best at work. There are the advantages of regular contact, the thrill of victory and the agony of defeat. You share common enemies and common objectives. While all this is positive, you must take your career and hers into consideration. People will talk. Under most circumstances it is probably better to resist the temptation. Consider them all to be your sisters in commerce. They are your teammates in your struggle for success. Suppose the relationship doesn't work out? If she is your superior, you lose. If she reports to you, you could be fired. At the very least, the relationship could go south and you will have to bump into her at the water cooler and suffer regular awkward moments and office gossip. You have enough problems there, guy. Look elsewhere and enjoy your hours at work.

However, you may want to become more active in the social framework on the job to increase your networking opportunities. Consider organizing events such as softball leagues or charity functions. There is always a need for someone to take the lead in these cases. You get to talk to just about everyone with a noble purpose. This is an excellent chance to show your better side while working on your social skills.

Once you have identified some likely locations to frequent, you will need to know what to do once you get there. We have some fun ideas that may help.

Chapter 14
You The Man!

"A merry heart doeth good like a medicine ..."
— *Proverbs, 17:22.*

Party Time

If you decide to have a party, select an evening at least two months in advance. Themes are a good idea. The Superbowl, Christmas, Memorial Day, anything will do. It is often very nice to throw a party for someone else. Engagements, promotions, going away or birthdays are good ideas for parties. Send out invitations requesting an RSVP. You can invite people on the fly. It is nice to be in a position to play host and extend invitations to attractive women.

Make sure your place is spotless, especially the bathroom and the kitchen. You really don't need to do a lot of decorating. A few candles and some fresh flowers will help. Clean out your refrigerator and stock it with soft drinks, beer, wine and extra ice. You don't have to go to a great deal of trouble for food. Your supermarket will sell you veggie and cheese trays. Have lots of crackers, chips and salsa around. If you have some close lady friends (and you should), invite them to show off by bringing a covered dish. Be sure to make a fuss when they do. Since you are the host, you get to circulate and see to everyone's comfort and be sure that they have met the other guests. This is just great. Of course, you will make every attempt to attract as many single women as possible to your party. Don't forget to invite some single guys as well. Share the wealth. You can't date them all.

Fred Astaire Always Had Beautiful Partners

Can you dance? Women love it. They love it so much, they are willing to dance with each other if they have to. You don't have to be Fred Astaire. You don't even have to have rhythm. What you need is attitude. In any dancing environment, there will be three to four times more fast songs than slow ones.

Fast dancing is about as unstructured as you can get. Anything goes. You don't have to be great — you just have to be out there. This takes some nerve. (Never be the first couple on the floor — you don't have a prayer.) Observe as many people as possible. It doesn't matter if they are male or female. The moves are the same. Watch the feet. There are several variations of a simple basic shuffle used. Often dancers will plant their feet and move everything else. The real key is in your hips. They have to move or you will look like Al Gore. Of course, you don't want to look like a belly dancer either. Try a side-to-side move. Now for the arms. Lots of variation here. Keep your eyes open and you will observe all sorts of moves. Pick a couple and alternate. A little side-to-side head action can be cool. Back to the attitude. It has to be in your face as well. Do you look scared to death — or bored? Smile, cowboy, smile. Look at the lady, look at your feet, look at the band, look at your friends at the table — but don't look at the other women! She'll know in a second. Oh yeah, don't bite your lower lip while you're dancing. It really looks stupid.

What you need to do is practice. Do this alone at home. Turn on a music channel like MTV or VH1 if you have it. There are dance programs that can help. The secret is to dance often and watch yourself in a mirror. All you need to do is get used to yourself and increase your confidence. When you are ready, see if you can practice with a female relative or close friend. Try it at home and then head out to a club on a Tuesday night when the crowd is light.

Slow dancing is tougher. It requires coordination between you and your partner. Worse yet, you are expected to lead! Don't panic. Here are some basics. It's important to get the body positions right. This is half the battle. Hold her hand and walk her out to the floor. Place your right hand gently around her waist. Keep it there. Anything below her waist is off limits at this point. Leave an inch or two between you unless things are going really well. Put your left hand out as if you are checking for rain and she will place her hand on top. Keep your right foot between her feet and you will avoid stepping on her toes. The simplest thing to do is gently rock back and forth on each foot in time to the music to the best of your ability. Obviously you can't stay in one spot for four and half minutes. The solution is to gradually circle in a clockwise fashion (We really don't know why, it just feels right.) If she pulls you closer or rests her head on your right shoulder, congratulations. These are promising signals. Let her make these moves. Again, attitude really helps. If you are leading, she will follow, if not — disaster. Try not to bump into anyone. Talk to her and smile. When the song ends, thank her and walk her off the floor holding her hand. These simple basics will get you by. You'll need help from a friend, professional instruction or natural talent to improve.

By the way, are you in touch with contemporary music or are you still stuck in the eighties? It's a good idea to stay up to date. Listen to a Top 40 countdown and pick up some trivia about the artists. You'll be more interesting. Women love music.

If you have some capability and a helpful lady friend, learn to do the Electric Slide, Macarena or Achy Breaky. What is great about these dances is that they have become classics, the moves are really very simple and repetitive and the odds on the floor are 20 - 1 in your favor. They can be real icebreakers. You can find yourself dancing next to three or four great-looking women. However, if you don't learn the moves well enough you can look like a geek — just a thought.

If you are a country and western music fan and it is popular in your area get involved with Country line dancing. You don't need a partner and everything we said in the last paragraph will also apply here.

Swing dancing is back big time. This is the style that your grandparents knew as the Jitterbug or Lindy Hop. It was the way to dance to fast songs on American Bandstand when it was still in black and white and in Philadelphia. A recent Gap commercial has given the style a big boost. Groups such as Big Bad Voodoo Daddy and the Brian Setzer Orchestra are reviving and updating the big band style that drives swing dancing. Check with your elder relatives and learn how. If you can find a partner when you are out, you will be an instant hit. *There are always more women looking for partners than guys that know how to cut a rug.* Free lessons are being offered at some clubs to attract crowds. It will take some effort on your part. Swing is a true partner style of dance. This means that both of you must move in sync and you must lead. There are three popular styles: Lindy Hop, East Coast Swing and West Coast Swing. Once you learn the basic foot patterns and a few turns, you can get through an evening just fine. After that, you will be able to build your collection of moves by watching and dancing with different partners. *Trust us. This is a very good thing.*

Learn to play the guitar

Going to a party or gathering? Bring an attention getter that invites participation — a game, a food item or drink that requires group preparation. (Be sure to check with the host first.) Make up your own fortune cookies. Women love astrology/horoscope devices. Buy some tarot cards and learn how to use them. Be proactive. Get the party going without being obnoxious. You might want to consider leaving your gear in the car until the party gets going. See if the scene is conducive first.

Visit a local magic shop and buy a few inexpensive coin or card tricks. Everyone enjoys them if they are done well and with some personality. You also get to pick your assistant from the crowd. Have you ever seen the assistants magicians typically use? If you're really aggressive, learn hypnosis.

Cooking is another idea. If you learn to make tasty dishes, you will always be welcome. Bring something to the party that requires extra preparation there. Now you're the chef and you can appoint assistants. "Megan, would you mind dicing some celery?" Get the idea?

We're serious about the guitar. If you have any musical inclination at all, it is quite easy to learn to play a few chords. Chords are arrangements of notes. You place your fingers in set positions on the strings and strum away. Most popular songs require no more than three to five chords. Check the songbooks of your favorite groups at a local music store. You'll be pleasantly surprised. Keep your eye on the classifieds for a used acoustic guitar. If you have a buddy who plays, ask his advice. See if he's willing to help you a bit. Sitting down at a party and strumming while people sing along is really cool. You don't even have to be able to sing yourself. What you will discover is that the women are more interested in singing than the guys. Good.

You Ought To Be In Pictures

Become an amateur photographer. Enroll in a basic class and purchase some decent equipment. You may meet some interesting women in the class but there is another facet to this new skill. While some women are camera-shy, many love to have their pictures taken. This is especially true at events such as weddings, Christmas parties or community events. Volunteer to take candid shots of everyone and hand out prints. Don't limit yourself to available women when you do this or your motives will be suspect. Your cost will be minimal. After you take an available woman's photo, either by herself or in a group, hand her your card and offer to provide some prints for her. Once she calls, you can suggest meeting for coffee to show her the whole roll in advance. She can have her pick. You have just made a solid acquaintance. Move on to small talk.

Networking

If a relative calls and says, "I know just the girl for you!" — *be very cautious.* The problem is that she has no idea what you are looking for. If you implement the ideas in this book you will develop a clear idea of the type of person you are seeking. She only knows what she *thinks* would be good for you. Women love to do this. They cannot tolerate a salt shaker without a pepper shaker. It's in their genes. Just as nature abhors a vacuum, a woman abhors an available, unmatched male. Beware. You will be set up on a blind date with a minimal chance of success. When the date is over, the "matchmaker" will call and say, "Well, what did you think? Isn't she terrific?" Now what do you say? You will end up hurting Aunt Hilda's feelings and struggling through an uncomfortable cup of coffee with her best friend's daughter who is determined to start a mink farm and have at least seven children.

So how do you handle referrals? In spite of the last paragraph, this is to be encouraged. You see, the example in the previous paragraph was *unsolicited.* On the other hand, if you communicate your interest effectively, you get to be in control. It's called networking. As an example, try to arrange a meeting with a group of people. ("A bunch of us are going to the Arts Festival this weekend. Why don't you and Fred bring Karen and we can meet?" — very safe for both of you.) Avoid spending an evening at the well-meaning couple's home for dinner. It will be the longest night of your life.

Let people know that you are open to meeting available women but be careful how you present the idea. You don't want to sound desperate or needy. Also, you don't want friends and relatives to trot out every dysfunctional cousin in the family tree. You are looking for fun people to date who meet your basic criteria. Don't depend on the standards and opinions of these well-meaning matchmakers. When they ask you some questions, fill them in with a few basics. Then make sure they give you a bit of a description before they talk to the lucky girl. There is no sense getting everyone all excited and hurting someone's feelings if there is no possibility of a future. You can't depend on these matchmakers to consider important details like that. They just want to put you in the win column at any cost.

Revisit old friends and contacts. Old address books, friends from school or previous jobs can be gold mines. Make contact to catch up. If she is available and you have some history, try to get together. If not, mention that you are dating. You do want to encourage referrals, so don't be too tough on them. Also remember that even though Cousin Susie may not work out for you she could have a friend who would. Never burn a bridge.

Networking Dos and Don'ts

Do:
- Keep it light.
- Make it easy on your friend by doing most of the work yourself.
- Show them that there is something in it for them such as fun, "going along on the honeymoon", etc.
- Promise to follow through and protect their friendship with the lady.

Don't:
- Give the impression that you are needy.
- Present unrealistic requirements.
- Bore them with stories of all your failed blind dates.
- Appear incapable of helping yourself.

If you are still uncomfortable asking friends for referrals, try this. *Make it clear that you are just looking for friends to round out your social schedule.* Be specific. "Do you know any women who like to play golf? I'm tired of playing with the same guys all the time." While you may find yourself in the company of a woman that lacks potential as a dating partner, she may have a friend.

The old adage about men being hesitant to ask for help is germane here. If we refuse to even stop and ask for directions, how are we going to ask a friend for a date? You may have to make some adjustments. Think of the process as advertising the availability of a really great guy for a limited time (until you find someone to start dating) and you will sound secure and desirable.

Don't forget to properly thank friends for referrals. They don't need every detail of the evening but let them know how things went in general. Be vague about future plans. Assume a "we'll see" posture. Encourage them to continue looking, if that's what you want. Never give any negative feedback. Remember, you asked them for a favor and you want to keep them as friends.

Blind Dates

If you are going to have a blind date, here's some help. Call her first and spend some time getting know her on the phone. You need to cover some basic criteria. For example, if you are not interested in a ready-made family and she has two kids . . . you get the idea. Issues like age, height, education, life circumstances, religion and interests are fair to discuss. Why waste each other's time if there is a deal-killer on the table? If everything seems to be OK, you will still need to know what she looks like to recognize her when you meet. Here you get to ask some good questions. What color is your hair? How do you wear it? Eye color, height, clothing are all valid topics. Unfortunately, one place you cannot go is weight. The best you can do is portray yourself as very active and fit. (It better be true.) She can draw her own conclusions. If you decide to meet, make it lunch or a cup of coffee after work. The meeting should be less than an hour in a convenient public place where she will be comfortable. Arrive before she does so she doesn't have to sit by herself and wait for you. Keep it light. Ask a lot of questions. It is always better to listen than to talk. You learn so much more. That's why you have two ears and one mouth.

One of four things will happen at the end of this encounter.
1. Neither of you will be interested in each other — no problem.
2. She will be interested in you (you'll know) and you will not be interested. This will require some diplomacy. If you feel that it isn't going to work, simply glance at your watch, rise and shake her hand and say, "It was very nice to meet you. Thanks for taking the time to meet me. I'm going to run back to work now. Take care." She'll get the idea. Her dignity is still intact and you are free to go.
3. You will be interested in her but she will not be interested in you (you'll know). Suck it up, buddy. Be gracious and friendly. She may have a friend.
4. Both of you are interested. Cool. Ask for the date. At least ask if you can call her soon. Then be sure to do it.

The Possibilities

Let's explore this a bit deeper. Be honest. If she is not going to make it in the looks department, you will know right away. If there are serious mismatches in other areas, they will be revealed early in your conversation. *She may be interested while you are not.* What you want to do is be gracious and give her the courtesy of a pleasant cup of coffee. Can you remember being turned down for a job on a first interview? If the recruiter was a decent person, you at least got the respect of a few questions and some conversation. After a few minutes, let her know that you must be somewhere in half an hour or so. Then enjoy her company and practice networking. You never know. Even if it isn't going to work, she may find you so charming that she'll tell her roommate. When it's time to go, pay the check, ask if you can walk her to her car. Tell her it was nice to meet her and wish her luck. Don't feel guilty. You met your obligation and behaved like a gentleman. You have nothing to apologize for. The next time it could be your turn.

Never burn a bridge. We know of situations where a woman has called back after a year to reconnect. Of course, you have to keep your radar up for whackos. They are out there. See the movie, *Fatal Attraction* for research. Some women can be very persistent and have no pride. Easy, bud. It's not that you're so special. They just want a guy in their lives — anyone will do. You need a good "shut-down" line for these situations. *The best thing to say is that you are seeing someone exclusively right now.* This does not hurt her self-esteem and allows you an innocent exit. If that doesn't work, you will have to get a bit tougher. Say that you are not interested and would appreciate it if she didn't call again. Say goodbye and hang up. Learn how to use the Call Block feature on your phone. After that, check the local penal code on stalking. (We think it should work both ways.)

By the way, make sure you have a good answering machine or preferably, voice-mail service. Record a pleasant, clever message. Change it about once a month. Also consider caller ID. It is really helpful to know who is calling before you pick up the line. You can see who called without leaving a message (and how many times she has called).

The odds are one in ten million, but your dream girl could walk in the door. She's stunning. You're stunned. Based purely on physical appearance, she will evaluate you. If you're not a Tom Cruise stunt double, she may be looking at her watch. *So your pulse is up twenty points and she is underwhelmed.* If you're good enough, you may be able to salvage the situation during conversation. You will have to use all your skills to do this. You're playing catch-up ball. Here is where you have an advantage as a man. You can ask her out. Wait until close to the "end" of your meeting and say, "**We should get together again sometime.**" This is a great statement. Memorize it. It suggests the possibility without actually calling for a response on her part. See what her reaction is. You just might land a date. If she doesn't seem interested, recover your pride and make a cool exit. At least she will respect you for that. You never know, your paths may cross again.

The third possibility is that neither one of you is particularly interested. If this is abundantly obvious, follow the first strategy. Show her a brief but pleasant time and allow both of you to make a gracious exit.

Unfortunately, the least likely possibility is that both of you are interested. She will let you know with body language and attitude. You lucky dog. *Carpe diem.* Stay as long as it feels right to stir up as much interest as possible. Ask for her number or ask for a date about a week from now. It would be a good idea to talk on the phone in a few days to reassure her and get to know her a bit better. Set up the specifics for the date and proceed to our section on the first date. Way to go.

Do You Have a Conversation Piece?

Usually this refers to something on a coffee table. However, you could consider a number of ideas using your body. Baseball caps, shirt logos, rings, distinctive watches (Mickey Mouse makes you seem safe and childlike — not bad) are all good possibilities. While conversation pieces may not initiate conversation, they can sustain it. If there is a gap in the chatter, the lady can ask you about your favorite team, college or the unusual ring you're wearing. Remember, women were born to shop. To them it is an art. They love the story behind a purchase. Be sure you have one.

Carry a good book with an intriguing title if you will be waiting for an appointment or a plane. It could be a good conversation piece if a woman catches the title. This also works well in cafes or places of leisure like the beach. It shows that you are interesting and trying to improve yourself. Titles can also reveal a bit about you and your interests. You can look at the best-seller list or browse for intriguing titles. Smaller volumes are more convenient. As much as it pains us, *A Man's Field Guide to Dating* is probably not your best choice. Some suggestions are:
• Exercise and Health
• Self-help, motivational
• Zen, Eastern philosophy
• Art, photography
• Biographies
• Classics such as *To Kill a Mockingbird*

Things to Carry

• Several business cards (print the classiest ones you can afford).
• A very nice pen so you can write your home number on your card with something cute like "Call me!" Better yet, write down hers.
• A roll of mints. Women will usually say yes to your offer of one and they will keep your breath fresh.

- A lighter. I know this seems strange because we don't think that you should smoke and you probably don't want to date a smoker. However, lighting a woman's cigarette is so suave. They love it. If she touches your hand while you do it — heavy signal. Also, you may need to light a candle. . .
- Tissues. You can blow your nose (out of earshot), lend her one or clean up a spill.
- A bit more money than you think you will need.
- Don't carry a cell phone or a beeper unless you absolutely have to. It's sort of pretentious and can be intrusive.

Keep a Log of Your Activity

Make it a goal to talk to at least five (or insert your own number) women a day. When you get home at night, jot down how you did. You can analyze this log to see how you can improve. Every guy's environment is different. What works in Rochester may not work in Atlanta. Which approaches seem to work well for you? What doesn't work?

Carefully analyze your non-working time for a period of at least two weeks. Everyone is entitled to kick back and relax in front of the tube. However, you need to remember that you are on a mission to change your life for the better. It will take energy and it will take time. That time is going to have to come from somewhere in your current schedule. You will have to make sacrifices. Create a table for yourself like the one below and put it on your bathroom mirror (a great place for motivational stuff — you start and end your day there).

	M	T	W	TH	F	S	S
TV							
Reading							
Drinking							
Exercise							
Golf							
Chores							
Shopping							
Dating							
Volunteer							
Parties							

Of course, you will customize this and add more rows. Just be sure to include all your current activities at the top and desirable date-increasing activities at the bottom. Include these even if you aren't doing much about them now. At the end of two weeks, total the rows and calculate a percentage for each. Your goal is to shift time away from the top of the chart to the bottom. Of course, only you can set the priorities. If this is too complicated for you, perhaps you could just think through the process and make a commitment to yourself to add several hours a week to your dating life.

Make a list of where or how you met any dates you have had in the last few years. Go back as far as you can. This is a positive indication of what can work for you. It doesn't really matter how the dates turned out since there is little correlation. What is important it that you should consider what went right with the initial process and how it can be improved or increased.

Remember Sam, the handsome bachelor, from the TV show, *Cheers?* He had a famous "black book." It was supposedly crammed with the names, numbers and data of dozens of attractive women he had dated. Wouldn't it be great if you had the same problem as Sam? It could happen. Don't run the risk of losing a number written on a scrap of paper, confusing two women or forgetting a birthday. Here is a sample format you can use. You can download a handy Microsoft Excel version from our website at www.dating-guide.com.

Last	Adams	Last Contact	12/31/99
First	Karen	City	Yourtown
Home Phone	(111) 555-1212	State	PA
Work Phone	(111) 555-1212	ZIP	17111-1111
email Address	kadams@email.com	Notes	Skier, knows Bill, has a cat

Keep it on a diskette, not on your hard drive at work. Make a backup and keep a printout handy but not where others can see it. Keep it up to date.

Failing to Plan Is Planning to Fail

Make your plans for the weekend in advance or stay home. When you ask for a date you should be specific, otherwise how can she decide? (This does not refer to the opener discussed earlier — you have decided to ask her out.) Give her several days lead time. You would do the same for your boss. Three or four days is good. This means you need to start lining up the coming weekend early in the week. Monday or Tuesday is not too early. Most guys don't think this way. Keep a date calendar. Perhaps you already have one, but use it only for business. Begin to identify coming occasions such as parties, concerts or special events and put them down. You will always have a number of opportunities available when you meet someone interesting.

If you have an empty weekend because of luck or poor planning, do not make the mistake of cruising the bars alone. Never do this — never. You can see them standing around at any singles bar in town. They show up alone, drink too much and go home alone — night after night. People will see you and tag you. Instead, do something constructive. Go work out, get a healthy dinner, and read. Don't dwell on the fact that it's Saturday night. Use the time wisely. People have no idea where you are. (You might want to consider not answering the phone!) You could be out with a super model for all they know. The key is not to appear desperate. If you don't have a date and it's early enough in the week, invite a few friends over. (See Entertaining.)

If you want to do something constructive with a weekend evening, conduct a nightspot survey. Bring a notepad and visit as many nightclubs, restaurants and coffee shops as you can. If you live in a metropolitan area this could take several evenings. You are scouting for likely places to take dates. You only need to spend fifteen to thirty minutes in each place, so you can visit quite a few.

For each establishment take notes on the following questions.
What is the best route to get there?
How is the clientele?
What is the price range?
What are the hours?
What about parking and the safety of the neighborhood?
What is the expected dress?
Is there entertainment, music or dancing?

After you have completed a general survey, select a few places you like and patronize them. Get to know the hostess, servers and bartenders. Tip well. When you show up with your date, you will be right at home and very welcome. You always know where to go. You have backup plans three deep.

The next issue to address is actually initiating an encounter with a woman who has captured your interest. We have some ideas and techniques to help.

Chapter 15
Busting a Move

"The only way to have a friend is to be one."
— *Ralph Waldo Emerson, Essays, First Series: "Friendship," 1841.*

Tactics — Tried and True

You will probably be in neutral territory when you first meet a woman. This could be a club, lounge, party, bookstore, festival, art gallery, dance, grocery store or even on the street. It is neutral because you both went there voluntarily for your own reasons. The surroundings are not likely to be conducive to private, quiet conversation. You can't really function as host. You need to move. If she is even mildly interested, you have a good chance to persuade her to join you for a cup of coffee. Of course, she may have solid reasons why it is not possible right now. You need to be aware of this before you extend the invitation. She may have commitments or be in a hurry.

If you see an attractive woman headed toward you on the street, try to check her left hand for jewelry. When she gets close enough, smile, excuse yourself and ask for directions. A nice touch is to ask about a place in the direction she is headed. This gives you a chance to walk with her for a while and strike up a conversation. In this case, introduce yourself immediately to increase her comfort level. If things go well, write your home number on the back of your business card and give it to her. Be honest and say you really wanted to meet her. Ask her to call after she has thought about it. Quickly wish her a pleasant day and walk away. You have a fifty-fifty chance, or maybe less. Just be sure you remember her name. It could be two weeks before she calls.

Look at your watch, wrinkle your brow and ask for the time. Compliment her watch and launch a conversation about getting batteries for the darned things or how hard some watch faces are to read, etc.

115

Keep a few simple, blank greeting cards handy in your car or briefcase. You can jot down a message and your phone number. Hand it to her, smile and walk away. Alternatively, you could stand there while she opens it and strike up a conversation depending on her perceived reaction. Just be prepared for rejection. She could be in a relationship.

Know the location of flower shops in your area. Often supermarkets will sell them. If you really want to make an impact you can leave a party, bar, meeting, or concert where you have spotted someone special and fetch a single flower to surprise her. Try to get a rose or an unusual blossom. Choose yellow or white as it is not as laden with meaning as red. Don't give carnations — they look cheap. This is a very bold move. Very few women have had the experience. It would be best if you had some positive indication of interest first. You will be remembered. Announce that you felt compelled to do this when you saw her. There is something about her that attracted you to her. Of course, you can't put your finger on it. The mystery will be pleasantly irritating to her. Was it her hair, eyes, laugh, what? Follow up with your card.

Here is a really wild idea. If you spot an attractive woman while driving and you both have cell phones, try to position yourself near her car safely. Hold up a sign with your mobile number and give her a big smile. She might call. Be ready with your small talk. You might want to keep a sign like this ready for this purpose — another reason to keep your car clean.

Buy a really cute dog. Walk him often. Pause and stop when you encounter an interesting lady. Women typically can't resist petting and cooing over your canine buddy. Have plenty of small talk ready about him/her. (By the way, if you decide to get a dog you are assuming responsibility for the little guy. Dogs will live fifteen years or longer and need to visit the vet regularly. Be sure to get Fido spayed or neutered. She will notice if you aren't taking good care of your pets.)

Is she with a group at a bar or restaurant? Write a pleasant note on the back of your card with your home number and hand it to her on your way out. Just say, "Excuse me, I'd like you to have this." This is important. You need to be a fleeting image. If you hang around afterwards, the situation becomes awkward for her. Rest assured you will be the topic of conversation for the rest of the night at her table. She might call. Be ready with your small talk.

Is she sitting by herself? Send over a drink, (tell the waiter to send another of whatever she is having), wait until she receives it, smile and hold up your glass as a toast. If you get a positive reaction such as a smile, walk over and say, "Hi, my name is Jeff. May I join you for a little while?" She may have a reason why not. However, since she knows your name (and you don't know hers) and you said a little while, your odds are good. Be ready with your small talk.

A Few Great Tips

Learn some jokes. Especially clean ones. The dirty ones are usually funnier but you need to play it safe. *Be extremely cautious about the topic. Jokes that are derogatory of ethnic groups or gays can make you appear thoughtless and insensitive.* Tape some top comedians. Write the jokes down if you have to. People often say they can't remember jokes. That is because they don't immediately tell them. Practice at the office or with your relatives or anyone who will listen. You only need two or three good ones. Don't drag them out. Get to the punch line quickly. Tell it with animation. Watch the pros and learn. You should be aware that good jokes travel around very quickly. You may want to preface them with something like, "I heard a good one the other day" or "Stop me if you've heard this."

You need to be familiar with popular culture. It provides useful small talk. It makes you appear informed and hip. Pay attention to current phrases. There is always a set of terms out there. Some current examples include What's up with that?, Hellooo, Work with me here, and Yada, yada. There's a bunch of them and they go in and then out of style. Sometimes they can be juvenile but it is a good idea to sprinkle some in your conversation at the right time. Be sure you get the context and meaning right.

Try to get familiar with as many current subjects as possible. It would be helpful if you knew three or four of the most popular songs, shows, artists, etc. in each category. You don't have to be a fan of rap music or computers but it is helpful to be able to converse or at least recognize some important artists or terms. It's simply a matter of being informed. This does not require a lot of effort. Read a variety of magazines such as *People, Time, Rolling Stone, U.S. News and World Report, Wired, Cosmopolitan* (Yes, you want to know what *they* are into) and your local paper. Listen to several radio stations. Make it a point to know the top three artists in each music genre, top current films, actors, news stories, etc.

The broader your perspective, the more interesting you become as a conversationalist. It builds your confidence to be able to participate in a conversation rather than stand on the sidelines with a confused look on your face. Try to learn something about these and other topics:

* Music
* Books
* Movies
* TV Shows
* Current Events

* Popular Trends
* Fashion
* Local Events
* Sports
* The Internet and computers

Some Approach Strategies

Don't flirt with 70 percent of the women in the room in sequence. Pick one and take your best shot. If that fails, wait a decent amount of time before trying someone else, preferably after she leaves. You can't really flirt with more than three or four women in an evening without looking like a jerk.

Don't flirt with women who are overtly sexual. Heavy makeup, seductive clothing, aggressive behavior are the signs. The quality women in the room are looking at her with disdain. What chance will you have with any of them after you're seen coming on to little Miss Bimbo? Zilch.

Always check her left hand first. You don't want to walk up to engaged or married women you don't know. No sense wasting time. Do your best to make sure that she is not with anyone. This may take some time and subtle observation. Flirting with someone else's date or significant other can result in bodily harm.

Observe her from afar for a few minutes. Does she seem like your type? Is she loud and obnoxious? Is she hanging over other guys? Is she drinking too much? Is she smoking? Are other guys making attempts? What is happening when they do? Pick your prospects carefully.

If she is with a large group of friends it could be difficult to get an opening. *Wait until she is standing alone or with just one friend.* Your odds are better. If you approach in a crowd, your move becomes their entertainment. She may dismiss you just to avoid embarrassment.

Busting a Move

It is the general nature of things that the man is expected to make the first move. That's just the way it is. Although women will occasionally speak first, it is rare. You have to learn to initiate conversations with women who look interesting to you. If you don't, nothing will happen. This is a learned skill. While some guys seem to approach women easily, most of us are afraid of getting shot down. Well, obviously it's going to happen some of the time. You just have to accept this. What you need is an exit line to gracefully withdraw and preserve your cool. This is more difficult than the initial approach. So practice it and have it ready. Here's an example

You: "Hi there. My name's Bill. Are you having a good time this evening?" (or something like this, more openers later).

Her: "Oh. Hi. I'm waiting for my boyfriend to come back. I'm sorry."

You: (Hold up both hands and smile big.) "Hey, no problem. You can't blame a guy for trying. You two enjoy yourselves. Ciao." (An Italian phrase for goodbye or hello pronounced "chow.") Then walk away with your head held high, still smiling.

That wasn't so hard, was it? Once you have an exit move, how can you get hurt? If she's rude, you don't want to meet her anyway. Just say something like, "Whoa. My mistake. Bye."

You will probably be able to get a conversation started less than 50 percent of the time. Once you accept those odds, it gets easy. So you approach two women with no result and start talking to the third — not bad. Just don't be too obvious. You can't hit them like ducks in an arcade. They'll notice and you will look like a loser. Be cool. Take your time. Wait fifteen or thirty minutes between each attempt and move to another part of the room.

If you are out with a bunch of buddies, you are going to have to cut out of the herd to have any chance at all. Women are very intimidated by a group of men. There is no way she will engage in a conversation with you while six of your buddies nudge each other and snicker.

It is possible to approach two women as long as you do not focus on one or the other. If you do, one will be miffed because she was ignored and the other will want to compensate for her hurt feelings. You will be the loser in this situation. Greet them simultaneously. Be charming and hand out compliments. Split your attention and eye contact and see what develops. One of them may withdraw by stating that she is involved with someone. Alternatively, you can very gradually shift your attention to the one that interests you. If you were pleasant and a gentleman her friend may even assist you.

The same is true if you want to approach a woman who is in a larger group. Step up and introduce yourself. Go around the table and get everyone's name. Play a game and see if you can repeat them all. Share yourself with the whole table equally. If you can involve a friend or two in the effort, that helps. Make it a party. Order up some appetizers and a round of drinks. You can split the tab with your friends. Just make sure to keep everything equal — no special attention to any one woman. After a while you can attempt to focus a bit on the woman who has your interest as long as it is subtle. People will come and go and you may have a chance to have some one-on-one conversation with her.

Sometimes a simple direct approach works well. We don't really recommend it, but if the spirit moves you and you love to dance — go for it. Your chances are better if it's a hot song (lots of couples will be headed for the dance floor). Choose a fast song rather than a slow one. Asking a lady to dance could be as simple as walking up to her slowly while looking directly in her eyes with a nice smile and saying: "Hello. My name is Bill and I would love to dance with you." If you have enough nerve, hold her hand while you say it, then you can lead her out on the floor. Did she hesitate? Add: "I'll even let you lead."

Never walk up to one woman in a group and ask for a dance. Women have a code about this and the odds are against you. They don't want to leave their sisters standing alone. One possibility is to ask if anyone in the group would like to dance. Of course, you're taking your chances. The one you like may not be the one who says yes, but at least you have something going. When you escort her back to the group, you can strike up some conversation. It is better, of course, to talk first and dance later. Be sure to check out the group dynamics first. If they appear to be cliquish or isolated, you may not have a prayer. If they are in high spirits, looking around and laughing a lot — it could work.

You cannot know in advance whether a lady will meet your criteria or expectations when you approach her. She may be involved with someone. She may be visiting from a city 3,000 miles away and returning tomorrow. She may be a smoker (and you are not). Lighten up, guy. Enjoy the ride. There is nothing wrong with spending a few minutes chatting with someone, even if it doesn't pan out. Of course, you can enhance your capabilities by limiting your approaches to those who meet essential physical criteria.

Our natural resistance to making initial contact is a huge impediment. Once you start chatting you have to be prepared for the possibility that nothing much will happen — that's OK. You met someone. You have a new acquaintance. The next time you see her, you can say hello like old friends. You can introduce her to your friends, have her sit at your table, ask her to dance, etc. Don't be so narrow-minded that every woman you meet has to be a future date or forget it. Be willing to make a lady friend. It's excellent practice and you never know.

It has been observed that Joe Dimaggio's glove always seemed to be positioned exactly where the batter directed his hit — funny how that works. Was he lucky? Hardly. He had a sense for all the elements of the game and made sure he was in the right place at the right time. You can do the same. Supermarkets and stores offer several checkout lines. The best one is not always the shortest. You may be better off standing in a longer line behind an interesting looking lady. More time to chat. Get the idea?

Who Is That Guy?

Here is an interesting tactic you can employ at any gathering. We assume that there is a woman you would like to approach. Simply select any other person in the room who is *not* an available female. A guy would be best. It would be ideal if you vaguely know or have a slight interest in meeting him/her. Walk up to the woman and say, "Excuse me, could you help me out? I'm sure I know that guy over there but I can't remember from where. Do you happen to know his name?"

Most people are more than willing to help. It really doesn't matter much about the result with the guy in question. If she does know him — fine. If she doesn't, just say thanks and walk over to him. Have a brief conversation. She will probably be watching. Pass by her afterwards, thank her again and give her a report. Women love a story.

Look and Learn

Begin to pay attention to the behavior of known romantic actors like Tom Cruise. How do they talk, walk and flirt? Listen to the pattern and tone in their voices. Gestures can be very effective. These guys are the masters. They study hard and are directed by the best. They get to deliver great dialogue. You could learn a lot.

Working the Room

Before you arrive at a party or gathering, go through a visualization exercise. See yourself entering the room. You are pleased to be there. You can't wait to start working the room. Who is the first lucky person you will chat with? You don't hesitate. You walk right in and go to the bar to get a drink. (A drink is a great prop even if it's mineral water.) While you are getting the drink you chat with the bartender or the person standing next to you. It doesn't take much. "Great crowd. I don't think we've met. My name is Bill." Never hesitate. You are always busy talking to someone. Your biggest problem is how to get around and talk to everyone in the room. When the conversation lulls, excuse yourself and move on. If you know someone — that's great. Walk right over to them and say hello. Go through this in your mind. You now have a program. You have a script. You know what to do. By the time you actually walk into that room, you are ready.

Remember names. Get in the habit of introducing others. Did you ever consider assuming the role of helping out the poor souls lining the walls by themselves? It's a start. Even if you just met someone, you can introduce him to someone else. Do this a lot. Try to include as many people as possible in your little group. It will grow. Guess what? Before long you are the center of attention on that side of the room. You are attracting attention from other parts of the room. Who *is* that guy? He sure is popular. All this can happen in less than thirty minutes if you work it right. After you get the group going, move on. You have work to do. You have people to meet. Don't worry about the women. Talk to everyone — married couples, single guys and women that are not candidates for one reason or another. It really doesn't matter. The single women will notice. Why isn't he talking to me? What are they talking about?

If you don't believe this is the way it works, stand back and watch the social lions operate. We have just described the behavior patterns you will see in the elite. It is not nearly enough to be attractive. Women want to hang with someone who is fun. They want to be part of the life of the party. They will drift away from a good-looking but boring date and want to hang out with you because you are happening.

Men frequently make the mistake of walking in to a party or gathering with a false assumption. They think that they will attract a lady who will find him quite enchanting. She will then spend the rest of the evening with only him, hanging on his every word. It rarely works out this way. You will be more successful if you properly set your expectations. Make it your goal to meet and converse with a number of women and have a great time. Increase your skills and confidence. View it more as a scrimmage than the Super Bowl. Take the pressure off and enjoy yourself.

Some guys don't know what to do with their hands. Don't fold them behind your back. Don't put both of them in your pants pockets. One is OK. It may be alright to fold your arms across your chest, but it does appear defensive simply because people often do that in negative situations.

This is a lot to carry off but it is the right stuff. Imagine a movie star like Kevin Costner walking into a room. How would he carry himself? What would he do? Would he be loud and boorish? Would he talk incessantly about himself and his many accomplishments? Would he brag about the many conquests he enjoyed? Would he stand quietly in a corner hoping someone would talk to him? How would he walk?

Remember to always carry some business cards and a nice pen. If you don't have business cards, get some printed right away. It's quite inexpensive. If things are going well with a lady, jot your home phone on the back and hand it to her. She now knows a lot about you and is sure you aren't married or involved. Otherwise you wouldn't risk giving her all this data and asking her to call. Say something like, "I wouldn't presume to ask you for your number, but if you are interested in finding out more about the music festival (or whatever), feel free to give me a call. I'd enjoy that." Do this right before you excuse yourself. It is very rare that a woman will refuse to take it. The odds are 50/50 that she will call, but she may actually offer hers. Also, women like to look at handwriting. Go figure.

You should try not to feel tense or nervous when entering a party, dinner, bar or gathering. It will show and identify you as weak or needy. You must appear cool, even if you don't feel that way. However, you can persuade yourself that you are cool. Having a plan helps. Here are some tips.

- When you first walk in stop, look around and smile. People will be looking. Everyone is always curious about who just arrived because they have already scoped out the existing crowd. Your entrance is news.
- Plan to take about fifteen minutes to check things out. Find the bar, food, restrooms, fire exits (you never know), dance floor, etc.
- Identify as many unattached women as you can. Wedding or engagement rings? Plan to talk to your top four selections before the night is over. Keep your eye on their comings and goings (a kick-boxing boyfriend may be in the men's room at the moment).
- Visualize yourself approaching these women. What will you open with? How will you keep the conversation going? Is there anything in the environment you can use — music, food, the crowd, the occasion?

- It's better to make an entrance with a friend than alone. By the way, be "fashionably late" unless you are meeting someone at a specific time. A party or gathering rarely gets going precisely at the stated time. If the party starts at 8, show up around 8:30 unless it's a surprise party.
- You are at the gathering to make new friends, not find your one and only. You can never have too many friends.

You need to put yourself in the right frame of mind before you arrive. Pump yourself up as you are driving by visualizing yourself meeting at least five new women. Think about some of the successful moments of your life. Games you have won, great dates you have had, promotions, etc. Play your favorite upbeat music. You can persuade yourself that you are going to have a good time. Strangely enough, it will happen. You must continue to reaffirm this during the course of the evening. Every hour or two find an opportunity to renew your attitude, especially if you have had a bit of success.

Try to identify someone who could use a bit of encouragement to join the party. By focusing on her, you can take the pressure off you. There are a number of ways you can "get busy." Offer to refill drinks. Fill a plate with snacks and bring it over for others. Become a spark plug for a small group. You can create a party within the party.

You need to circulate and make yourself busy. Never stand or sit by yourself. Don't look away when others attempt eye contact. Gatherings usually last only a few hours and you probably only attend a few each month. Therefore, you need to take total advantage of these opportunities. You can be shy the rest of the week.

In the old days, a lady at a formal dance would carry a dance card and write in the names of the gentlemen she wished to meet. It was a schedule. Think of a party along these lines. Have your own mental dance card. Of course, you will make it up as you go along. It's great practice. When you spot someone interesting, walk up, smile and deliver an opener. Chat for ten or fifteen minutes, close and move on. You will seem like the life of the party and meet many women in the course of an evening. You are relaxed, casual and enjoying yourself. It's actually very entertaining.

The same technique applies to dancing. We don't recommend asking a girl to dance cold. Your odds are reduced. You will be judged purely on your looks. Chat for a while first. Ask if she likes to dance. Make sure it's a good song. Did you ever notice how some songs fill up a dance floor and others clear it? The right music can be a great motivator. (See the section on dancing.) When the song is over, you are at an awkward point. Another song will start. Unless she indicates she wants to keep dancing, let her off the hook by escorting her back to her spot. Having successfully spent a few minutes on the dance floor is not an invitation to occupy her for the rest of the evening. As in conversation, unless she is sending you major signals of interest, simply thank her, excuse yourself and move on. It's OK. Let her think about you a bit. If you stand around mumbling, it can get very uncomfortable.

Because you visualize yourself moving from person to person and actually behave this way, you can easily move on. Don't make the mistake of dwelling on a woman if you don't think there is a point in continuing. Remember you are wasting her time also. Plan on spending only fifteen minutes or so, then move on. You will need to get smooth at this. If you set the premise up front it helps. "I'd love to talk to you for a while" or "I really wanted to chat with you before I have to go."

Let her know that you enjoyed talking to her by thanking her. "Thanks for chatting with me. I hope I catch up with you later" or "I see an old friend over there. Enjoy the rest of the evening."

(Remember not to let the evening's activities constitute a validation of your worth. That comes from inside you and not from the way strangers treat you at a party.)

When you put food on your plate, take small portions so you have to return. No one will notice how many times you use the men's room. It allows you to move across the room and exit a situation. Offer to help out in the kitchen if you are at a home.

Wedding and engagement rings are usually easy to identify. However, it is possible that a married or engaged woman may have removed them or she wears a very unusual design. Also, some women will wear a decorative ring on the third finger of their left hand just for style or to divert attention from themselves. Also, how do you know if a woman without a ring is in a relationship? After a bit of conversation say something like, "You're quite a lady. I hope your boyfriend (husband, fiancée) appreciates you." Don't be crushed if she is involved — make her your friend. You never know.

Women scope out a crowd just as much as guys do. They are probably more skilled than you. By the time you get from the front door to your first spot, you have been evaluated and categorized by many of the women. They will watch how you carry yourself, how you interact with others and if you are putting moves on every woman in the room.

Remember that *you* have body language as well. Are you standing with your arms crossed? Are you scoping out every woman's anatomy and elbowing the guy next to you? You can't possibly keep track of the focus of every woman in the room simultaneously. Assume you are being watched. In a larger sense, this really shouldn't be much of a problem for you. You should be conducting yourself like the gentleman you are. If you are a jerk, there is no way to hide it. The truth will come out when you think nobody is looking. By the way, be careful who you hang out with. Take a good look around. Would you send your sister over to the crowd around you? Although you may not even know them, if you are standing near losers, guess what the women will assume?

Try to match your body language with your best attitude. You are positive, friendly, confident and sincere. Do you look that way? Is your head up? Are you smiling? Is your body position open? Observe talk show guests and actors for tips. What kind of body language would you have if you were up for an Academy Award?

Be humorously self-deprecating. It actually shows confidence and sincerity. On the other hand, don't dwell on every flaw you have. Use humor to take the edge off your obvious ones and move on to other things.

You have to look around the room. We know that. You just have to be cool about it. One hint is to keep your gaze traveling and only stop at safe points such as the food, a window or a painting. Then you can scan on to something else while taking in the available women on the way. What really annoys women and marks you as a "player" (a negative term for a man who dates only for sex) is applying a once-over to each woman in the room as if you're browsing sports coats. You can easily observe your competition engaging in this behavior. Good. Women definitely notice and it turns them off.

How Do You Determine If a Woman is Available?

Dress and make-up are generally not a good indicator of availability. This is because women are expected to dress fashionably. Madison Avenue and mass media have equated fashion to sex. This means that married, engaged and involved women will look very sexy but are obviously not available. Body language is a much more reliable indication of availability. Women do this by displaying their advantages.

- Crossing her legs and slightly lifting the top leg while pointing the toe.
- Preening — hair stroking, fussing with clothing, moistening lips.
- A woman will often tilt her head when she is receptive. This is a very heavy flirting maneuver. Many women flirt while doing it unconsciously.
- Exaggerated posture — shoulders back, displaying her assets.
- General body position (feet, shoulders) pointed in your direction.

Lack of these signals — or worse yet — negative signals are your key to take your leave. It may be possible to recover by delivering an effective line of conversation but it is not likely. Cut your losses and move on — more on this later.

Be a Nice Shark

What we mean is that although they have a fierce reputation, sharks are excellent predators. They are persistent, fearless and always on the hunt. It is our understanding that sharks must keep moving constantly to keep their gills full of oxygen. However, while they are doing what is required to stay alive they always have a beady eye scanning the waters for their next meal. No opportunity is passed up. Heck, they will attack a steel cage containing a diver!

Now, let's remove the negative connotations and see what you can learn from these creatures. Of course, you do not intend to hurt anyone. Also, you sleep, work and wax your car. We are suggesting that you consider every occasion where you find yourself in public as a flirting opportunity — *every single one*. Trips to the bank, bookstore, post office, bakery, gym, ATM or yogurt stand are chances to meet available women. If you look at it this way, you will begin to look forward to chores. Make sure you are looking your casual best, then put on your shark attitude.

You should be flirting at every opportunity. Flirting is all about *conversation*. *The way to a woman's heart is through her ear*. Hence, you need to speak to as many women as possible every day. You are not rude, aggressive or threatening — just friendly. After all, you have no idea of the lady's status. She may be in a long-term relationship. (You *did* check her left hand, didn't you?) A bit of friendly small talk never hurt anyone. People usually welcome it because they are bored with the same chore you are performing. What else are you going to do in a line at the deli?

Once you have a woman's attention, you must be able to flirt with her. Guys are usually not too experienced with flirting but it is essential. With some good advice, it is a skill you can learn.

Chapter 16
Be a Flirt

"All mankind love a lover."
— Ralph Waldo Emerson, Essays, First Series: "Love," 1841.

Flirting

Flirting is essential. It must be done innocently and sincerely. You must be proactive. It is much easier to do if you have no expected outcomes. Indeed, this is the best way to practice. You can flirt with friends, relatives and co-workers (making certain not to cross any boundaries or taboos). You will discover that when there is no pressure you can get quite good at it.

When you flirt you are sending out strong positive messages about your feelings and opinions concerning the other person. You are pleased to be in her company. You exude warmth. You wish her well. You appreciate her qualities. Flirting is an end in itself. It is offered free to the recipient. Who can refuse?

A flirtatious encounter might last ten seconds and consist of nothing more than a simple compliment or greeting accompanied by a very warm smile and direct gaze. This being the case, you could flirt with dozens of women in a given day. The secret is that you must sincerely mean what you say. If you walk around indiscriminately handing out insincere or false compliments and act like a jerk the rest of the day, you are dead meat. Your reputation will be shot. Study successful flirting whenever you can. Become a connoisseur. Movies, TV, and best of all, real life, offer opportunities to learn.

Notice things. Be observant. Women constantly make changes to their appearance. Hairstyles, make-up, nails and clothing are a huge part of their identity. Most men are typically oblivious to all of this. Here is an opportunity for an advantage.

If there is a lady who has caught your eye that you see on a regular basis, begin a subtle flirting campaign. Light up when you see her and greet her warmly. Always do this. Make a brief sincere comment on her appearance and breeze on by. Mix it up. You don't want to engage her with compliments on every occasion. Watch for a response on her part. If you get the sense that she would like you to linger a while and continue chatting, you have been invited. Seize the opportunity. Delve a bit deeper into the area you have complimented. "Where did you get the great tan?" or "What is the name of that book you are so absorbed in?"

After an initial encounter in the flirting game, it is time to tentatively move forward. This is done through touch. You must be very careful. You can touch safe areas such as the hand, arm, back or shoulder. It is best to have a flimsy excuse for this such as escorting her to a table, helping her out of a car or handing her a menu. Take the chance with a light touch accompanied by a smile and then wait for her to respond. It may take a while but once you have taken the initiative she may find a reason to touch you back. This could be a touch on the arm during a laugh or perhaps something more aggressive. If there is no response, wait a while and try again. It is a dance. A total lack of response is, of course, not good. She may be unsure of you or, worse, not interested. Here you will have to weigh your options. Some people are not particularly "touchy-feely." She may be mildly interested, but wants to take some time to think about you. Who knows? The bottom line is that you should make the attempt to keep the flirting ritual moving forward.

So the process of flirting, while not pure, goes something like this:
- Eye contact
- Body language signs (tilted head, deep smile, touching hair, open body position)
- Light conversation (openers, introductions, small talk)
- More intimate conversation (anything on an emotional level)
- Mutual laughter (relieves tension and indicates comfort level)
- Touching

During these phases (that may not occur in this order), you and the lady could gradually move closer until you are sharing intimate space. Other signals such as eye messages and increased breathing may be present.

Are You a Shy Guy?

This is even tougher than nervousness. You will have to do some preparatory work before you get out on the playing field. You need to learn to block and tackle. You need to scrimmage. Here are some suggestions to help you gradually build your confidence.

You must recognize that you will not be able to successfully date without conversing. *Make it a priority goal.* You must learn to approach and speak to people.

Start with e-mail. If you don't have e-mail, get it. You can use the Internet at libraries and get free email accounts through services such as Yahoo, Hotmail or geocities.com. Start e-mail exchanges with friends, relatives and associates. It's a safe and easy way to put thoughts together and get some conversational experience.

Record Yourself. Buy an inexpensive cassette recorder and practice. Begin by reading the newspaper. Play it back and listen. Get used to the sound of your voice. Try to improve. Learn to like it. Borrow a book of poetry from the library and record some poems. Try to speak lower and slower. Do this until you are comfortable that your voice and style of speech are pleasing.

Talk on the phone. Call stores and ask about merchandise or services. You don't have to identify yourself or buy. Just talk. Call 800 numbers for just about anything. Be very friendly when you are talking to these folks. It will brighten their day a bit. Perhaps you could volunteer to work the phones for a charity or fundraiser. You will have a purpose and a script and be talking for hours. It's great practice.

Bug Customer Service. Take every opportunity to talk to clerks, sales associates, information-desk personnel and customer service. Don't be annoying or trivial. Don't do it when there are three people in line behind you. Have a reason to do so. Try to extend the conversation. See if they are willing to share a bit of themselves. You will find that if they are not busy, they will welcome some idle chit-chat. For example, visit a ski shop and ask the salesperson about local slopes and conditions.

Get involved in group discussions. It could be at work or really anywhere people you know (or don't) gather. Listen and learn from the more skilled participants and take a few opportunities to say something. It doesn't have to be lengthy, just well said. Go over what you are going to say several times in your mind, then jump in there.

(There was an ancient Greek orator named Demosthenes who honed his skills by speaking to the crashing waves before moving on to humans. He eventually became renowned as the greatest speaker of his time. Good lesson.)

Pull Yourself Together

So what's a guy to do? Here's how to put stomach butterflies in their proper place.

- Set your sights as high as possible. There is more room at the top. Most guys won't have the nerve to approach a woman of obvious quality.
- Recognize that she is not *better* than you as a human being. She has the same internal frailties, life challenges and need for love as anyone else.
- Welcome the rush of pursuit. It's like sky-diving and horror flicks. That edge is required to ignite the passion you will need to sustain a good relationship.
- Accept the fact that you are going to experience *a certain level of anxiety*. Acknowledge it, expect it, deal with it, make it your friend.

- Realize that women will think much more of a man who has the courage to take the initiative in spite of his internal uncertainties. Women will pity a man who is controlled by his own self-doubts and doesn't act.
- This sense of intimidation is an excellent indicator that you are making progress toward your goal of building a great relationship with an exciting, interesting, worthwhile woman. You should be worried if you are not experiencing it.

Do you remember junior-high or middle-school dances? Typically all the boys huddled on one side of the gym and the girls on the other. You would have to walk all the way across the floor in front of everyone and ask a girl to dance. The floor seemed two miles wide. Your palms were sweating and your throat was dry. You could feel your friends' eyes on your back. Naturally you were going to ask the prettiest girl you could find. Then when you got up the courage to ask — she said no. Now you had to walk all the way back in front of everyone while they laughed and snickered. Talk about trauma!

Perhaps it wasn't that bad for you. Here is the point. As adult men, what has really changed? Aren't those childhood memories still in place in your subconscious? We still have to work up our nerve to approach a woman and put our pride and self-esteem on the line. However, there is a difference. This fear of rejection is all in your mind. Twenty of your buddies are not standing around watching and waiting to make fun of you, although you may harbor subconscious memories of that. Also, you don't have to face the woman who declined for the rest of the school year! What training or counseling have you had to show you a better way?

If you are resolute and approach a woman immediately after she sends positive signals through eye contact you have a lot of advantage. She is expecting to have to make some choices once she meets you. Your bold approach will make any alternatives that may be at hand fade for a moment. You will have her attention. You need to convince her that chatting with you is her best choice for now. She wants to talk to a nice guy. She knows what she wants. You have to be that guy. As you are chatting with her you need to look for signals that indicate her preferences and frame yourself in that way. This doesn't mean you have to be a chameleon. However, perhaps you can discover what she likes in a man and emphasize your strengths in those areas. This is tricky and requires some skill. Remember, you can practice on other women such as friends and colleagues. Learn to get women to open up about themselves.

Even though a woman may look quite attractive to you, she often does not feel that way. *Don't make the mistake of believing that she considers herself above you.* In general, women are never satisfied with their looks. They have created a multi-billion dollar industry as evidence. They spend hours at home preparing themselves to go out. Then they spend more time in the ladies' room after they arrive. If you could listen to them chatting among themselves, you would hear them complain about their imperfections.

We often make the mistake of associating an attractive woman with the image presented on television or in the movies. You may think that because she looks like Meg Ryan she has the same star power and mystique. No, she has the same mundane problems as anyone else. She is no better or worse than you. She has doubts and insecurities. She wants to be happy. She craves attention and compliments as the rest of us do. You could very well be the best thing that has ever happened to her.

Personal space

We maintain several zones of personal space depending on our comfort level.

- We will let anyone, other than terrorists, to remain more than *five feet* out of range. We are effectively ignoring these people. Of course, this range may be used for distance flirting.
- In a business or social setting we expect people to remain *two to four* feet away to maintain a comfort level. In the initial stages of flirting, this is where you need to be.
- When signs of success are obvious and you think you are invited, you can move into the intimate zone — an *arm's length* or less. In general, women will not allow anyone this close unless they are very comfortable and very interested. If you get to this point it is a very good sign. Do your best to stay here as long as possible.

Eye Contact

Eye contact is usually the initial stage of flirting. It is the definitive means of getting someone's attention. It must be deliberate and sincere. Remember, flirting is similar to acting. The best actors can convince you with their behavior that they have become their characters. You must deliver your good intentions and complimentary thoughts with only your eyes — not easy. Of course, if you are truly sincere, much of the work is already done. You shouldn't initiate a conversation until you have made some eye contact.

Eye contact is usually delivered and received simultaneously. If you are receiving it — congratulations. Always acknowledge and return it with a smile or a nod, unless you are definitely not interested. If you are delivering it, things get more complicated.

As you scan your environment, look for an opportunity to catch her eye. Lock on for a few seconds, look elsewhere and return to her eyes — the classic second look. If it doesn't work at first, try again. She may be uncertain of your intentions or think that you are looking at someone behind her. This is a critical point. If she gets the message, she will react in some way. Perhaps she will smile or fiddle with her hair or drink. If she is interested, she will hardly be able to disguise it. You must look for these signs. Let's put it this way: if she is not interested, you will know by her aloofness, disdain or indifference. Anything warmer than that should be considered positive.

If you are reasonably certain that you have connected with her, you need to confirm it with a big smile, nod of your head or toast of your glass. Watch her reaction. Does she still seem interested? You must act — now. You can wimp out and send over a drink but we suggest that you get off your duff, walk over and introduce yourself. Your odds are very high for at least a bit of conversation and maybe a lot more. Of course, this is up to you. Are you ready with several threads of good small talk? You will need them.

Eye contact is critical. It is similar to radar. Let's consider it in more detail. You can glance around a room even from a distance and look for a reaction from any lady that meets your fancy. Women will telegraph their interest (or lack of it) with their eyes. It goes something like this:

You see an interesting lady across the room. You glance her way every once in awhile until you catch her eye. The message you are sending is "I find you attractive." Once she has received this message, she can decide to do three things with the information:

She can quickly decide that she is not interested for any one of a hundred reasons. She will look away and not look back. She may even turn her body and talk to someone else. This will happen very quickly. Move on.

She can decide that she is interested. She may smile slightly and look away, but *she will look at you again.* This is the key. The second glance will come because she wants reassurance that you are not just idly staring at her or someone behind her. You must acknowledge this with a smile, a tip of your glass, or some gesture of interest. See how she reacts. If she smiles, you've been invited. She may look away again but you have just been given permission to move to the next step. You need to find an opportunity to speak to her as soon as possible. Walk over and say hello. There is an outside chance that you are wrong but we doubt it. Of course, once you start talking, you could blow it, but that's another program.

She may give you the second glance and look away without smiling back at you. She may exhibit some stalling body language. She is saying that she is not sure. While you have not been invited, there is some chance that she would be open to a chat. Proceed with caution. Give her a chance to think about it. Maybe she just doesn't feel well. Maybe she doesn't like your haircut. Who knows what she is thinking? Some women are very shy about this sort of thing. Keep sending glances and smiles her way and watch closely.

The trick is not to turn a glance into a stare. That will make her feel creepy. Try this little mind game. When you glance, say something brief to her in your head like, "I think you're cute," then look away. It will ensure your timing and you will project the right non-verbal message.

You would do well to learn to read eyes. We have all heard the old phrase "the eyes are the windows of the soul." When we are emotionally absorbed, we display much with our eyes unconsciously. The issue is rather complex. Not everyone will display these characteristics. Levels of emotion and psychological factors will heavily influence these displays. On the other hand, if you detect some of these characteristics it is cause to rejoice.

There are several factors here:

You can't flirt with a woman if she can't see you. Move into her field of vision and adjust your position so your eyes can meet. If there are people or plants in the way, move. Sit down or stand up, but be subtle. Gradually improve your location until she can't help but see you. Now you have a chance.

Once you have some positive eye contact and/or body language you must act without hesitation. Think of it as a basketball tip-off. Will either of the centers hesitate once that ball is in the air? Try to develop a knee-jerk reaction to positive flirting signals. Interpret them as a message that says, "You look interesting. Please come over and talk to me. Now." Then put one foot in front of the other and compose your opener while you walk. By the way, you can take your time as you approach. It adds a bit of drama. Just don't delay your move. She knows you're coming and her pulse rate will be rising. If you rush over like a cocker spaniel it will turn her off. Use the time to visualize and put yourself in the right frame of mind.

Never look away or look down when you have made eye contact with a woman. Of course, if you are not interested in her at all, that is exactly what you should do. You have probably done this many times without realizing it. When you pass a hassled mom herding her three kids down the supermarket aisle you might make eye contact briefly but you very quickly look away. What's the point? Now, if you do the same thing after some positive eye contact with an interesting woman, you're finished.

Hold her gaze as long as possible. The longer she gazes, the more interested she is. It can get very uncomfortable, but think of it as a staring contest like you had when you were a kid. See who blinks first. Keep smiling and emoting warmth. Have fun with it. If she looks down, it is a sign of submission. You should go over. If she looks away, wait to see if she looks back. As soon as she does, make your move. If she turns away or starts looking at someone else, well . . . you may be able to revisit the situation later.

If a woman is interested, she will make that abundantly clear with her eyes and body language. What else can she do? She is punting and you are a receiver. You had better run that ball back and make some yardage.

Focus and length of stare

If a woman seems focused on you and gazes for extended periods it is an obvious indication of interest. Of course, she will need a break from time to time. She will direct her gaze elsewhere to relieve tension or collect her thoughts. This is good as long as her focus returns to you. If she gazes downward, she may be dealing with some powerful emotional feelings. If she gazes upwards she is likely to be collecting some thoughts to continue the conversation. This may be accompanied by a head tilt. All of these movements are positive.

If her gaze lingers with you only briefly and her eyes are darting from place to place (especially around the room), you are in trouble. You don't have her interest. You may notice fidgeting behavior along with this lack of focus. You have to decide if the situation is worth pursuing. The odds are not with you.

Watch for the ideal combination of these factors, although it may take awhile for it to occur. Narrow eyes, pupil dilation, and perhaps a bit of moisture in a glazed-over, almost hypnotic stare are the best possible signs. If you are fortunate enough to be the object of this intensity, the next move is yours.

Pupil Dilation

This is a change in the size of the dark center of our eyes. Usually, this is an automatic reaction to the amount of light around us. As the light decreases the pupil increases (dilates) to optimize our vision. (Alcohol and drugs can have a significant effect on pupil dilation.) Under normal, steady light conditions you may observe dilation for other reasons. In general, dilation means interest as she relaxes and attempts to take in as much of you as possible. Of course, it could mean that the sun is going down!

Width

This refers to how wide the eyes are open. Wide eyes mean surprise or anger — not good. Narrow eyes (as long as they are not combined with furrowing of the brow and between the eyebrows) are very good. She is relaxing and zeroing in on you.

Moisture

Obviously this is the initial stage of tears. However, if she is not upset, it may mean that she has some intense feelings that are unfolding. The term often used is "misty." Even sports stars are subject to this when announcing their retirement or accepting an honor. This is a very strong signal.

Eyebrow Furrowing

Lines between the brows. This is generally not a good sign. It indicates intense concentration or anger. This is the wrong posture for flirting, of course. Remember, a high level academic discussion is not where you want to be. However, she may be thinking carefully about something you have said or making a decision. Conversely, you will observe this expression during intense lovemaking.

Here are some behaviors that you may (or may not) notice when a woman is interested.
- Eyes are open a bit wider than normal
- Blinking or "batting her eyelashes"
- A wink (sort of rare)
- Posture becomes more erect, muscles tighten up
- Touching ears or jewelry
- Preening her hair in the back
- Palms or wrists are open towards you
- Rubbing her wrists, thighs or edge of her blouse
- Leaning toward you
- Pointing the foot of a crossed leg toward you or rocking the leg
- Bumps into you or brushes by you when passing
- Fingers moving on her glass suggestively
- An "I really like you" smile which shows some teeth and is relaxed
- Mouth slightly open
- Moistening lips
- Kicking her shoe off and on from a crossed leg
- Arms at her side or on her hips and legs apart while standing
- Leaning slightly in to you
- While seated an arm over the back of the chair and turning toward you
- If a woman delivers extended eye contact *and* a smile, it is a very strong signal. You must act immediately.

Bad signs:
- Turning away from you
- Loss of eye contact
- Folding her arms
- Fidgeting, glancing at watch
- "Fake smile" with lips tight and drawn
- Touching her nose (Weird, but true)
- Arms folded
- Hands folded in lap
- Ankles crossed while seated

You would do well to study the body language that women display in a variety of situations. Observe women when there are no available males around. What body language do they display when they are bored, irritated or absorbed in something? See if you can spot a couple involved in an encounter. Park yourself at a singles bar and watch as men approach women. Learn to detect the eye contact and body language. You will be very surprised at the consistency of this behavior. Watch for these signs when you are out. Study body language very carefully.

If You Don't Talk - She'll Walk

If you're not talking to a woman, you're getting nowhere fast. You must talk to succeed. Standing there looking cool will accomplish next to nothing. No matter how attractive you are, a woman wants to hear your voice and thoughts. Good conversation is the only path to a date/relationship. *The path to a woman's heart is through her ear.*

Do this simple test. Go to a local singles bar, sit down and observe. You will see any number of men, either by themselves or in groups, standing around staring at the crowd acting like roosters. They will posture, flex, suck in their stomachs and do their level best to look cool — all to no avail. Women will ignore them, in general.

You may also observe a few men having some measure of success. These men will be TALKING to women. You will not see women hanging on the arms of *silent* men, gazing at them in awe. That only happens in rock videos. Find the conversations and you will find the success. Now — what do you think *you* should be working on?

Become a good conversationalist. Learn to listen and ask good questions. Practice all you can. Talk to your female colleagues, friends and family members. Become as comfortable as you can in the company of women. If you practice this in the relative comfort of familiar people, without expected outcomes you will increase your self-confidence.

From our perspective there is a mysterious "disconnect point" or a brick wall that we hit when attempting to approach a woman. You may smile, wave, wink or send over a drink. For some reason too many men stop there. Obviously it is fear of rejection. Beware of this sticking point. It is like stopping a golf swing with the club overhead. You have to hit the ball and follow through. The strange thing is that after you talk to women for awhile, you will be surprised how often they express insecurities about themselves. If only you could get over your fear of rejection, you may discover that they are more nervous than you are!

Girls are raised differently from boys. The women's movement bemoans this as prejudicial, but it remains the case for most children. Our culture encourages girls to become nurturing, loving, maternal and protective of their dolls, pets and siblings. They are being prepared to provide for the needs and comfort of their own children and their husband. They are encouraged to be free and open with their emotions. They are not comfortable with aggression. Boys, on the other hand, are drawn to violence and aggression. They play with toy weapons, watch the WWF and hide their sensitive side. Boys are not supposed to cry. So traditional child-rearing and mass media have pre-programmed our dating roles. In general, women will wait for the right suitor to approach her. In general, men are expected to select a woman and approach her with self-confidence and determination. If she detects weakness or hesitation, she will reject the suitor. This is not social commentary. We just want you to understand the probable circumstances you will encounter. Most people are still predisposed to these roles.

The strange thing is that once you have boldly approached her and demonstrated your strength, she will be looking for something entirely different. You must be an understanding, open, honest guy with lots of romantic potential. All this must be delivered in a matter of minutes. She will look into her heart and use her intuition and feelings to determine whether you have the potential to be her next relationship. If you can convince her that you might be, you will succeed.

You have to be prepared for a "thanks but no thanks." It is going to happen more often than you would prefer. Salespeople know this and accept it. Imagine what it is like for telemarketers. How many of these folks have you hung up on in the last few months? They depend on the percentages. If they can make one or two sales per shift, that's fine. They learn to accept dozens of rejections as part of the game.

Look at it this way. How many dates can you handle each month? Probably between four and eight would be just fine. Heck, you might be happy with two. Now, assume that some percentage of approaches will be dead-ends. If you bat .200 (not bad), that means you have to make five approaches to land one date. Multiply this factor times the number of dates you would like. For example, if you want four dates (one per week), you may have to have enough nerve to talk to twenty women and get rejected sixteen times. Are four dates worth sixteen polite apologies? We think so. As you get better at qualifying prospects and improving your style, you will increase your success factor. You will increase the number of dates and decrease the number of rejections. Do you think Val Kilmer was ever turned down? Of course. Guys like that just have so much confidence, it rolls right off them. Try to work on that attitude.

You have to initiate some conversation with a lady who interests you. It should be as natural as calling a good friend. It's no big deal. It's what you do as a single guy. It is expected. As a matter of fact, one of the most frequent complaints and frustrations that women voice is that men are too hesitant to make the first move. After all, it is a great deal more difficult for them to approach a man without looking sleazy. If you make the first move, all they have to do is say yes or no! So the kickoff is all in our hands. No kickoff — no game. In a given year you should approach dozens, possibly hundreds, of women. That is a great New Year's resolution for you.

You should completely abandon the idea of "picking-up" a woman. They hate the concept. Do everything you can to avoid the impression and behavior. She needs to feel that she is meeting an interesting man with relationship potential. In general, women are not happy being alone (without a date). Assume that the woman you are attracted to would much rather spend time with a nice guy like you than gabbing with her girlfriends or staring at her drink. Although women have experienced numerous attempts at pick-ups, they typically remain optimistic that the right guy could come along. That is what they are waiting for. That is who you need to be. We can take it a step further. We hate to use the word "desperate," but . . . there is a lot of pressure on women after they reach their mid to late twenties. This pressure comes from their families, their married friends and their biological clocks. They also create their own. While many women thoroughly enjoy being single, most would prefer to be in a relationship with a nice guy who is headed somewhere. You could be that guy. At least that is what she will initially think.

If you get the sense that a woman is very smooth when you are chatting, be careful. Women who are very experienced with flirting and dating may be superficial or worse. While this is not always true, there may be a mismatch in your motives. She may be looking for entertainment or amusing herself at your expense. There is also the possibility that she is playing in another league. If you are looking for quality women who would be good candidates as partners, don't attempt to play in that league. It's not that she is above you. She is just in another place. Move on.

For years men have labored under the misconception that the right combination of words will open any woman's heart. Sorry — it is simply not true. However, your first few words are very important. Let's separate myth from reality.

Chapter 17
The Myth of the Line

"Whoso loves / Believes the Impossible."
— *Elizabeth Barrett Browning, "Aurora Leigh", 1856.*

Openers

We don't like the term "line." It has a negative connotation. It implies that the comment is insincere or contrived. If your purpose is honorable (you just want to meet her), an opener is an acceptable means to a desirable end. You will need an opener and an exit line just in case. Beyond that you will need some "rap" after the opener, if it is successful. Your opener should be very natural and suited to your personality. You don't want a mismatch between the first words you utter and everything else you ever say to the woman.

The purpose of your opener is to get permission to spend a few minutes chatting with her. Also, the opener should put her in a receptive and positive frame of mind. You will do better if you can raise her pulse a few points. She knows *why* — unless you screw it up by coming on like a pimp. *Never use sexual innuendo as an opener,* e.g., "If I told you that you had a beautiful body would you hold it against me?"

Let's assume that you have had some positive eye contact and decided to approach a woman. You are fairly sure that you have been invited because of her body language and glances in your direction. Do not hesitate. Why would you want to? Are you trying to work up some courage? The longer you wait, the worse it will get. She will wonder what you are waiting for. Be decisive. Put on your warmest, most sincere smile and walk over as if you are going to meet a friend you haven't seen for years. When she tells you her name, ask what her family calls her. If her name is Elizabeth, they may call her Liz or Beth. Ask if you can call her that. Say her name as often as possible from that point on. Start your questions and statements with it. Shake her hand as warmly as you can while you look in her eyes. This is very important because it may be awhile until you can touch her again. Try to put as much into that handshake as you can. It should be strong and comforting. Try placing your left hand on top. Accompany the shake with your best smile and warmest eye contact. Then release and let her make herself comfortable.

You must be prepared to field a less-than-interested response to your opener. Never worry about the one that got away. Do you remember the statistics you reviewed earlier? There are thousands and thousands of terrific women with lots of potential available if you take the time and energy to meet them. Don't make the mistake of waiting for the right escalator step. The time to act is at your next opportunity. Otherwise you'll still be standing there when they close the store.

Humor, surprise, outrageousness, warmth, wit and friendliness are great characteristics to describe an effective opener. The openers that you hear in the movies will rarely work. Remember that it's a script. The actor and actress already have their next twenty lines memorized. You need something natural for you that will be effective. You will have to work on it — hard.

- Practice mentally for a while when you encounter opportunities. You are in an elevator with an attractive woman. Look the situation over and see if you can come up with something that would be appropriate and effective. Try it out in your mind. Review it after she's gone. Would it have worked? Try to think of better ones.
- Try out your openers on your female friends. (You are working on getting a few, aren't you?)
- Keep your ears open for good openers when you are out and about. A little eavesdropping is OK. See if they work. Would they work for you?
- Try developing a few for candidates whom you have seen in your daily routine (that cutie at the gym, the girl next door, etc.)
- Try saying them aloud in front of a mirror, in a tape recorder or on videotape.
- Memorize them and make them second nature.

I know it seems like we are making a big deal of this, but it is a big deal. Do you remember the tense feeling you had the first time you stood on a diving board or stared down a ski slope? That's the fear you have to overcome. You have to do this to succeed. Make it a priority. It's not just the opener, it's the courage to use it.

Some tips:
- Say hello instead of hi — it has more warmth.
- Mention your name first. She will probably follow with hers.
- Repeat her name as often as possible.
- Shake her hand firmly. When you do place your other hand on top of hers and just hold it for a moment while you look her right in the eye. You release first.

- Give her reassuring information. Let her know where you work, play and live. Point out friends who are close by. Don't make it sound like a resume — just blend it in with the conversation.
- Extend a gentle compliment. Be careful. It must sound sincere and be true. It should be about her and her alone. Don't tell her she has the most beautiful eyes you've ever seen. Don't tell her she's the best looking woman in the room. Tell her she looks great in black. It sets off her hair.

A few samples:

"Hello. You seem to be familiar with (this type of book, music, magazine, video, blender, whatever). What do you recommend for a guy like me? By the way, my name is Jeff. And you are . . .?"

"Hello. Is this seat taken? (pause for permission) Thanks. I just love the espresso here. What are you having? You seem to be enjoying it."

"I hope you don't mind but I was watching you from across the room. You have such a great laugh, I just had to meet you. My name is Jeff."

"Can I share a bit of this fresh air with you? I promise not to use much. It sure is hot in there. My name is Jeff."

"So this guy walks into a bar with a frog and a tiny piano . . . (she will let you finish the joke). Hope I didn't bore you. My name is Jeff."

"That step machine is a real pain to program. I don't mean to intrude but can I help?" (We are assuming she is having trouble.)

Turn it around — "You seem to know how to program this darned thing, would you mind giving me the benefit of your expertise. . . Thanks, my name is Jeff"

You will have to come up with some that are truly your own. You will also have to develop the ability to make them up on the spot. The goal is to break the ice, introduce yourself, and have a bit of conversation. As long as there is no pressure and you don't move too fast, you should have lots of success.

Remember, never use an invitation to dance as your opener. Your odds are dismal. She will decide based solely on your looks and how she feels at the moment. Talk first.

If you think that you will see her again (she's a member of your gym, etc.), you can afford to just say goodbye and build up a connection over time. If it's a chance meeting, you will have to be more aggressive.

She may let you know right away that she isn't interested. Let this bounce right off you, be polite and excuse yourself with your exit line.

She may let the conversation continue for a while (ten minutes or so), then send some "no sale" signals. She is just being polite and doesn't want to hurt your feelings. Again, pull out your exit line and move on.

If the conversation goes well, hand her a card right before you excuse yourself. If things go very well you may be able to get her number or land a date right there. Use "we should get together sometime" to do this.

Never use overt, sexual openers. You've heard them before.

"How'd you like to do the breaststroke in my waterbed?"

"Sit on my lap and we'll talk about the first thing that pops up."

"Nice hooters."

We'll spare you any other examples.

Stay away from trite openers. Women hate this. Think about it. If you've heard it before, so has she. She hears a lot more lines than you do.

"What's a nice girl like you doing in a place like this?"

"Do you come here often?"

"Do you live around here?"

Worse yet — "Do you live around here often?" (Just kidding.)

"Haven't we met before?"

"Where have you been all my life?"

"Can I buy you a drink?"

"What's happening?"

"What's up?"

"What's your sign?"

"Wanna dance?"

"Your place or mine?"

The Best Line Is No Line At All

In general, if you have heard an opener a few times before, don't use it. The best opener is spontaneous. Here is some guidance to help you compose your own.

- Your words need to make her feel special and important. If you deliver the right phrase in a sincere way you will trigger chemical reactions in her brain that will link her feelings to you — at least for the moment.
- A woman has spent hours trying to look appealing and hoping someone nice will notice. It happens too rarely.
- Remember, your words are not as important as the sincerity and feeling behind them.
- No matter what happens, a woman will always remember the first thing you said to her.

- Your opener should be simple and direct.
- *It should have two thoughts — a sincere compliment and permission to join her.* Tell her that you think she is beautiful. If you don't think so, why are you approaching her?

The permission is easy. Simply say "May I join you?" or "Would you mind if I joined you?"

Your compliment can include an explanation for your approach. Here are some examples.

"I know we haven't met, but I just had to tell you how beautiful you look tonight."

"A woman as beautiful as you should have a beautiful evening."

"Hello, I'm hoping a beautiful woman would enjoy some pleasant company."

"I heard you laughing from across the room and I had to come over and tell you how beautiful you are."

"That outfit is stunning and so are you."

We are using the word "beautiful." You may wish to soften this a bit by selecting pretty, attractive, very nice, lovely, wonderful or great instead.

Here is the whole formula.

1. SMILE, be sincere and warm and speak smoothly without hesitation.
2. Deliver the compliment followed immediately by the request to join her.
3. Introduce yourself in order to make her comfortable while shaking her hand.
4. Ask her name. Repeat it immediately in your next statement.
5. Express your sincerity and tell her how you were compelled to come over and meet her.
6. If she speaks, let her continue without interruption. If not, don't hesitate. Launch right into some conversation focused on her.
7. Do your best to draw her out and show warmth and feeling. Maintain eye contact.

All this will take less than one minute. Very few women will not allow you continue the conversation. If it should happen, there will be a solid reason. Express your regrets and excuse yourself with a smile.

You need to be aware that women will typically make up their minds about you very quickly. We may sit and ponder things but they will give you a narrow window of opportunity to deliver your best shot. Hesitation and stumbling will close the door. Of course, she will be polite and you may not even know that it has happened.

Here is an example you can use to develop your own spontaneous openers.

You have made eye contact with a woman across the room and observed some positive body language. You do not hesitate. You smile warmly and immediately stroll over while maintaining eye contact.

You: "Hello. I was intrigued by your beauty and just had to meet you. May I join you?"

(Shake her hand warmly.) "My name is Bill. You are . . .?"

Her: "Well, hi. The name is Kelli. Thanks for the sweet thought."

You: "You're more than welcome, Kelli. I was quite sincere about what I said."

"Kelli, do you mind if I ask you about that necklace? It's very distinctive. Where did you find it?"

Her: "Thanks, Bill. I'm really fond of it. A friend of mine makes jewelry. I try to buy something from her every time I visit."

You: "Cool. Does she live far away? I'm always looking for unique presents for my sister and my mom."

As you continue to converse remember to keep the topic focused on her and her feelings. Maintain eye contact, project warmth, keep smiling and try to mirror her body language.

Using openers is perfectly acceptable if you bear a few principles in mind.

- *Approaching a woman respectfully is a compliment.* You were attracted by her appearance and behavior and are recognizing it.

- If you are coming from the right place (your values and priorities are in order) you will be perceived as the nice guy you are and not some slimeball. *Trust your self-image to deliver the right message.*

- *An opener is delivered without any expected outcome.* It is a spontaneous gift. If it leads somewhere, great. If not, no problem. You just smile and move on. If you are expecting something in return, you will telegraph it and kill the opportunity.

The nerve required to make an approach shows that you are a take-charge guy and would make an interesting date at the very least, maybe more. Pity the poor slob standing in the corner who doesn't have the nerve to say a word. He'll still be standing there a year from now. The more attractive the woman is, the harder she has worked at it. She is even more appreciative of compliments. If a woman is not particularly attractive, compliments are difficult to compose and will be suspect. In this case, compliment her on something other than a physical aspect such as her laugh.

How to Handle a "Pass-by" or Chance Encounter

Under these circumstances you will not have the luxury of flirting, eye contact and body language. There is no time. It is very probable that the woman is involved in something like shopping, running errands or eating lunch. She is busy and not in a receptive mood as compared to, say, a party or other social gathering. You will have to apologize, represent yourself as respectful and make her feel safe before you can make any progress. You will have to say more and project even more warmth than usual. Possibly the best you can hope for under these circumstances is to give her a positive first impression and get her phone number or give her yours. You may get fortunate and have an extended conversation, but don't push your luck. At the very least, she may accept your card and home number.

Keep your distance, smile and maintain eye contact. Speak slowly and warmly. The pattern consists of an apology, a compliment, recognition of her possible discomfort and an explanation of your motives. It seems like a lot but you have no choice. An insincere creep would not go to all this trouble. If you are warm and sincere, she will at least listen. Here is an example to use when composing your own opener.

You: "Hello. Please forgive me. I don't want you to think of me as disrespectful or rude, but I was so impressed with your beauty that I just had to tell you. I realize that we don't know each other and that may make you uncomfortable, but I couldn't think of any other way to let you know. At the risk of appearing forward, I'm not the type of guy who lets an opportunity pass me by. If you're not involved with anyone, I'd love it if you would spend a few minutes with me."

(You have apologized, complimented her, recognized her possible discomfort and explained yourself — all this in less than a minute. Keep things moving. Don't leave her time to compose doubts about you. Give her a very brief opportunity to reply. Introduce yourself as soon as possible and shake her hand warmly.)

Her: "Oh, no, well, that's fine . . .I guess."

You: "Thanks. My name is Jeff. And you are . . .?" (Shake her hand.)

Her: "My name is Carol."

You: "Hi Carol. It's nice to meet you. I can't believe how crowded it is in here today. You were lucky to get this table."

Her: "Please. Sit down. I know. I guess everyone likes the food here and wants to eat at the same time."

You: "Do you work close by, Carol?"

Continue to focus the conversation on her as much as possible. Be respectful of her time. Look for signals and body language that she wants to leave or continue with what she is doing. Offer your card with your home number on the back and ask for hers. If she gives it to you, tell her exactly when you would like to call and be sure to do it.

You: "Thanks for trusting me enough to give me your number, Carol. Would it be convenient for me to call early Tuesday evening?"

Her: "Sure. I should be back from the gym by 7:30 or so. Well, I really have to run now . . ."

You: "Of course. I'm looking forward to getting to know you better. Take care, Carol." (Give her a big smile and stroll away.)

Of course, it may not all go this smoothly. If she is willing to talk with you, just accept whatever she is willing to give and be gracious — no pressure. The odds of success under these circumstances are minimal. We are assuming that there is something compelling about her and the effort is justified. Realize that you could acquire a reputation as a "masher" if you approach strange women too frequently.

Handling "No"

Ouch. "No" can really hurt. It used to hurt when your mom or your teacher said it. When it's the object of your affection, it's even worse. So what can you do about it? First, you need to understand that *hurt is an internal event.* This does not mean that it isn't real. It is. It is your *emotional reaction to a set of circumstances beyond your control.* When you think about it, being hurt by a "no" is illogical, as Mr. Spock would say. Of course, we are not Vulcans.

"No" cannot be avoided unless you stop trying. That is unacceptable. Therefore, the harder you try the more you are likely to hear "no." This will stop the faint of heart and cause them to retreat to the safety of their room, where nobody will reject them. The problem is that they are saying "no" to themselves. No — you may not have a social life. No — you may not date interesting women. No — you may not have a satisfying relationship. Does this make sense to you? — of course not. *The first step in handling "no" is to accept and expect it.* It happens to everyone, even movie stars. Why shouldn't it happen to you?

Accepting "no" is a simply an outcome of your control over your environment. You can be reactive or proactive. The more willing you are to take chances, the higher the odds that "no" will become "yes". If you are truly self-confident in your worth as a person another person's "no" can not have an effect on you. Things happen for a reason. Her no may be sparing you further embarrassment or hurt.

What can you do after "no?" Well, you can smile, wish her well and walk away with your head held high. If you think there is a bit of room for a second chance you may want to attempt to leave a door open.

- Give her your number anyway and ask her to call if she changes her mind. Although the odds are not good, you would be surprised how often it it successful.
- If appropriate, suggest an un-date. You will need some information about her interests. Help her pick out a new dishwasher. Agree to pick her up at the airport.
- Suggest that she join you and some of your friends at a restaurant or event. Alternatively, invite her to a party, then plan it later. This relieves some of the conversational pressure of a one-on-one.
- Throw some empathy her way if you sense that it's appropriate. Is she hassled by something? Is the party noisy and smoky? Tell her you feel the same way. Make an emotional deposit. It may eventually yield dividends. You may be able to keep the conversation going and make some progress later.
- If someone's "no" does get to you, there are options to offset its effect. Don't internalize. Tell a friend about it without whining. Turn it into an interesting story about the crazy world of dating. Go to the gym and work out.

In the movie *Wag the Dog*, Dustin Hoffman's character continually responds to every adversity by saying, "This is nothing!" He would then relate a situation from the past that was much worse. You can use the same technique. Is her "no" worse than an IRS audit? Tell yourself that you can live with this and that the emotional reaction will be over soon. You don't want to hand over a big slice of influence to the source of the "no." It's her loss. She could have had a relationship with a really great, caring guy. Instead she judged him on some superficial criteria. It doesn't sound like you lost much.

You must be realistic and recognize that there are unhappy, disenchanted women out there who delight in putting guys down. Mean people suck. Fortunately, they are a very small minority. Who knows what is driving them to behave this way? Perhaps they have been in abusive relationships. You will hear them say, "all men are pigs." Regardless of how physically attractive they appear, they are just waiting for some poor slob to approach them. They will then delight in destroying them in front of everyone. We call them barracudas. There is another "b" word used sometimes. You cannot defend yourself against them because they will blindside you. Sooner or later it happens to all of us. The best you can do is to be aware that they exist and excuse yourself as soon as you recognize the species. Keep your cool and remain a gentleman. You are a quality guy and above her on the food chain.

On the other hand, in today's world it is possible for a woman to be interested in a man for purely physical reasons. Sometimes, this will occur between a younger man and a woman who is his senior. Some women will joke about the idea of having a "boy toy." If you are a sincere young man and have your priorities in order, it would be easy to be hurt in a situation like this. The lure of an easy sexual encounter is very compelling to most men. If you find yourself in the sack most of the time and experiencing very few of the traditional dating behaviors — watch out. You could become attached and be very disappointed. It's not as attractive as it might sound.

Rejection

We believe that the fear of rejection is the single biggest obstacle men face in the dating process. It is similar to the fear you face when you have to speak in front of an audience. Do you remember how you dealt with that problem? You over-prepared by memorizing your speech and rehearsing it over and over. Perhaps you tried it out on your friends or family. Once you were in total control of the content, you played some mind games with yourself to get over your stage fright. You know — the old solution of imaging the audience in their underwear. We suggest that you use the same strategy to conquer your fear of rejection by women. Work hard on the suggestions and ideas in this book. Your preparation and understanding will give you control and lessen your fear.

If you want to know exactly what *not* to do, see the movie *A Night at the Roxbury*. The two characters from *Saturday Night Live*, Will Ferrell and Chris Kattan, do everything wrong. It is a study in guaranteed rejection. What is interesting is that although these guys are clueless that no woman is interested in them, they refuse to even recognize the rejection and forge ahead blindly. There is a perverse lesson in this.

All a woman can control is her own actions and words. Everything else is in your mind. You have to will the positive outcome of the encounter. You must have confidence and be convinced of your eventual success. Accept the adrenaline you will feel as a natural side effect of doing something adventurous. Let it pump you up, not hold you back. Anxiety is chemical and irrational. It defies logic. You are letting something unreasonable cloud your judgment, blur your speech and stall your progress. It's like going to work drunk. You can control drinking and you can control anxiety. You are in control of what you feel and think after she says no.

Some fear of rejection may extend from childhood experiences and low self-esteem. Perhaps your parents were very critical. You may have been teased or criticized by classmates, teachers or siblings. As an adult, you can look back on these memories and realize that the hurt was based on poor treatment by others, not your true self-worth. Use the power of this knowledge to rationalize any hurt feelings you are anticipating.

A woman will not usually tell a guy to get lost in the first fifteen seconds. If she does, she may be a barracuda and you have lost nothing. Consider yourself lucky. Most women will deliver gentle hints and body language and hope you get the message. They don't want to hurt anyone. If you are perceptive enough to notice them, you can gracefully move on. You are in control and your pride is intact. You get to say "see you later." How could that hurt? At least you don't have to walk across the junior high gym floor while your friends laugh at you. Believe us, no one else in the room is interested in what just happened. They are all working their own agendas.

Don't make the mistake of convincing yourself that the people around you are reviewing how you look and how you are behaving. Others are too busy concentrating on their own performances to spend time and effort judging your social skills or lack thereof. Imagine you are skiing down a challenging slope with a group. You are concentrating on every turn and bump. Do you think those around you are staring at you and how you are doing? Hardly — they would soon be eating snow if they did. Don't assume that everyone else is a master of social interaction. They have the same insecurities as you. They may, however, have more practice than you do. That is something that you can easily change.

Don't sit there and stare at a woman while you ponder every reason why she wouldn't talk to you. Don't assume that she is with another guy. Don't assume that she is programmed to turn down every guy who approaches her. It ain't necessarily so. Assume instead that she will be friendly and happy to talk to you if you approach her with warmth and sincerity and deliver an irresistible compliment as explained in this chapter.

Reasons A Woman Might Say "No Thank You"

- She's married
- She's engaged
- She's in love
- She's gay
- She was fired today
- She was turned down for a raise, got a D on a term paper or flunked a test
- Her car died
- Her grandfather died
- Her cat died
- She just got her period
- She has diarrhea, constipation or gas
- She just got a huge runner in her new pantyhose
- She has a toothache, headache, cold, flu, dirty contact, etc.
- She just had a fight with her girlfriend, mother, boss, roommate, etc.
- She just saw her ex-boyfriend dancing with her best friend
- She has to be home in fifteen minutes
- Her new shoes hurt
- She is having a bad hair day

Now we could continue with this list but you get the point. What does any of this stuff have to do with you as a person? Have a little respect for her life circumstance and frame of mind. Have you ever just wanted to sit down, have a drink and be left alone? Of course you have. Perhaps you have even rejected the approach of someone yourself. Give her some space. Don't be so sensitive.

You need to measure the potential benefit of approaching a woman against the risk. The risk is very small. She may say, "thanks but no thanks." You may feel hurt for a few minutes. On the other hand, consider how great you will feel if you persuade her to go out with you. Which situation has more impact on your life? How does fifteen minutes of sulking stack up against an evening with an attractive woman or more? It's similar to buying a lottery ticket for a penny with 100-to-1 odds and a $1,000 payoff. Would you take it?

Don't be put off if she doesn't immediately accept your first invitation. An attempt to get together with a woman is not that different from the way you handle your business calendar. You make appointments all the time with doctors, repairmen, clients and friends. Don't you normally find yourself negotiating and juggling times and dates? Does the following conversation with your friend Joe make any sense to you?

You: "Hey Joe, I was wondering if you'd like to come over and see the new deck I built on Monday night."

Joe: "Gee, Ken I don't think I can make it."

You: "Oh, I see . . ." (looking down with a hurt expression.) "Well, I guess I'll be going now."

Joe: "What the hell is the matter with you, Ken? Are you sick or something? Jeez. Get a grip."

Sounds ridiculous, doesn't it? However, that is exactly what a lot of guys will do if a woman says she can't accept your first suggestion for getting together. Treat it like any other appointment. Try alternatives. Work it out in a friendly relaxed way just as you would with a friend or a colleague. It really is no different. Give the woman a break. She has a life beyond you.

If you manage to initiate a conversation with her you will face a larger problem. What do you say next? Here is where a lot of guys freeze up and lose it. You need to be prepared with some techniques to keep things rolling. Let's consider your rap.

Chapter 18
Your Rap

"If your rap is strong, you can't go wrong"

— Anonymous

Keep it Going

There is a crucial period between your opener and your close (asking for the date or her number). You will have to fill this with entertaining flirtatious conversation. If things are going well, she will help you. It doesn't matter too much what you talk about. It's all part of the dance. She needs a chance to see how she feels around you. *She wants to listen to the sound of your voice and get a sense for the kind of guy you are.* So, you will be yourself. That has to be enough or it isn't going to happen. Of course, you are going to be at your best.

When you start your conversation after your opener you will have to ask a question. You will have to ask many questions. Remember Oprah, Leno and Letterman. Use what is available and try to establish a connection. Possibilities include her attire, your surroundings, whatever she is doing, whatever you are doing, the season or current events. Whatever you choose should give her a reasonable chance to respond and move you into a conversation about her feelings and emotions. Use your broken field running (later in this chapter).

- When you talk to her, look her straight in the eyes. Nowhere else. A lot of guys will be gazing around the room for their next mark. Give her your undivided attention. Also, keep your gaze above her neck, no matter how tempting the scenery below might be.
- If you have the opportunity, reveal that you have a romantic side. Be careful. You must show *potential*, but do not express romantic gestures now. It is much too early. She should just know that if things work out between the two of you, she has a lot to look forward to.

151

- Keep the conversation light and focused on her as much as possible. Ask lots of open-ended questions. This keeps the pressure off you and you will learn more.
- Only continue the conversation as long as things are working. If there are too many awkward silences or she is delivering negative body language, move on.
- Don't say "I" too much. Reveal only the information she asks for.
- If you can include a friend of yours or hers, she may be more comfortable.
- Repeat her name often during the conversation. People love to hear their name.
- Don't invade her space. A foot or two apart is good. Keep your hands to yourself.

Ask a lot of questions. Give her plenty of time to answer. Follow up with other questions. Observe the interview technique of stars like Oprah, Letterman or Leno. They have the ability to make a wide spectrum of personalities comfortable and interesting. You could learn a lot. When she asks you a question, answer briefly and throw the ball right back in her court. Why? It takes the pressure off you. You get to listen and learn. Have you ever observed some poor trapped woman forced to listen to a guy running at the mouth about how terrific he is? It is not necessary to impress her with information. Make her comfortable first. What you want to project is understated strength. Think about Clint Eastwood, Chuck Norris, John Wayne or James Bond. Calm, cool, confident men of few words. Women find this intriguing. You have an air of mystery about you. Women are naturally curious. Make her work to get any information.

Remember that your initial interest or infatuation is an emotional response to the appearance of the woman and your desire to fulfill your psychological needs. It is important to rise above this when you begin talking to her for the first time. You would be surprised at how much information you deliver with those first few sentences. It is not the words, but the way you say them and the way you behave that sets the tone for what happens next.

Observe her body language. If she is fidgeting and gazing around or looking at her watch, you are about to be dismissed. Pre-empt her. Excuse yourself. Tell her you enjoyed talking with her and hope to see her again. Save her the trouble and preserve your cool.

On the other hand, you may be fortunate enough to observe some positive signs. Is she laughing a lot at what you say? Women will play with their hair and tilt their heads when they are interested in you. It may be contrived or it may be second nature. Either way, you are in good shape. Is she leaning into your space? Is she touching your arm or playfully nudging you? These are very strong signs. She is inviting you to make the next move. What you want is the opportunity for a date. If everything is going well, we remind you of the useful statement, *"you and I should get together sometime."*

Remember, the reason this is so effective is that she can't really shoot you down. You haven't asked her out. On the other hand, she has to respond. If she agrees, ask for the date right then and there. If she hesitates, immediately agree and say, "Yeah, I guess you're right, it might not be such a good idea after all." Your dignity is intact and you can excuse yourself.

You need to have an idea or two for a date in your back pocket at all times. A movie you'd like to see or a restaurant you want to try will do nicely. Give her a general time frame at least three or four days later. Let her respond. If she can't make it because she has plans, she will probably suggest another night if she's really interested.

"You know, Kelly, there's this really cool Mexican restaurant I've been dying to try. The food is very authentic. Would like to go sometime next weekend?"

"Hey, I have an idea. My friend Jim is having some people over to watch the Grammy Awards on his big screen next week — no big deal, just some nice people and great food. What do you think?"

Small Talk Ain't (Small, That Is)

Have some respect for this much-maligned process. In daily life, it can be meaningless — e.g., discussions about the weather with cab drivers. In an initial encounter, it's life and death. *Small talk is not about the topic or words, it's about the whole experience.* She is much more interested in the sound of your voice and how you carry yourself than how witty you are. Don't try too hard — you will sound desperate. The simple exchange permits both of you to relax a bit while you experience some of each other's personality.

If you find yourself in a group, ask questions when people seem to show some expertise in something. You are naturally curious. You are always willing to learn. This shows intelligence. People make the mistake of believing that this makes you look stupid or uninformed. Wrong. You are now fifty percent of an interesting conversation. Put on your David Letterman hat. People will notice. Some of these people are available women. Get the picture?

The best strategy is to break in with an informed question. Of course, you have to know enough to ask. People love to help others out with their opinions. It doesn't matter too much if they are right or wrong. Ask open-ended questions. The point is to get in the game. You will appear more attractive if you are participating.

Examples: (Assuming there is an existing conversation going on.)

"Bill, you seem to know a lot about guitar. I always wondered if guitarists like Clapton tune differently when they use a slide."

"What do you think will be the result of China's takeover in Hong Kong?"

"Do you think Web TV will catch on?"

"Have you tried snow-boarding? I was wondering if it is harder than skiing."

"Do you prefer investing in stocks or mutual funds?"

"What is your favorite beach on the East coast? I love Dewey Beach myself."

The key is to show some interest and appear somewhat informed. Interesting people are always curious about everything. They love to hear about experiences they have not had. What did it feel like to sky-dive? Observe good interviewers and adapt their techniques. One question follows another. It is rare that the interviewee asks a question. If they do, the answer is very brief and the ball is passed right back. Just be careful not to pry.

There is nothing small about small talk. Get good at it — *very* good. You will need it. Have about four or five little stories or conversations that you can pull up at a moment's notice. It doesn't really matter what they are, but here are a few tips:

- The topic should be of general interest to just about anyone.
- It should not be controversial in any way — you never know.
- It's nice if the story reveals a bit about you, just don't brag. It would be better if it revealed a positive side of you.
- It should be short — one or two minutes or less.
- It should invite a response and initiate an exchange.
- Keep it light and humorous if possible.

Often guests on talk shows will have these stories ready to go. Of course, they are usually much longer. Most Jerry Seinfeld episodes are loaded with this banter about nothing special. Be ready to switch gears. That's why you need several. Segue from one to another if the first one is not catching fire. This is a critical skill and it can be practiced with anyone — relatives, friends, co-workers or people you meet in line. Because the topic will not be romantic and very general, you can easily get in the habit of doing this. It will serve you well. The point is to keep the conversation going — very much like a tennis volley. Silence during small talk is not golden — it is certain death. If the conversation is over, your chances are over.

Small talk should last no more than five to fifteen minutes. You will begin to sound like an idiot after a while. She will expect you to engage her on another level by then or end the conversation. Make sure you do.

You must be able to end a conversation as well as start one. This is a major mistake many people make. You are at a party or gathering and manage to strike up a conversation with someone interesting. You are doing well. Remember — it is a long evening. She will want to mix and so should you. Unless you are getting major signs of interest, you would do well to end the conversation first and move on. If she is interested, she will remember you. You can always come back later. Excuse yourself gracefully. "Well, good luck with the new job, Linda. It was fun talking to you. I'm going to see if I can find my friends. Bye."

It is awkward to force her to dismiss you. It will also hurt a bit. You will recognize the uncomfortable silence and body language when it's time to move on. She will gaze around the room, shift from foot to foot, glance at her watch, etc. As soon as you detect this, get outta there. You can turn things around. "Well, Linda, I don't want to deprive the rest of the party of your company. It was fun talking to you. I hope to catch up with you later."

Broken Field Running

All great halfbacks are good at this. They zig and zag, picking their options as they go. They don't know where they're going to end up except that it's going to be down the field. It depends on what the defense presents. *After small talk you need to find something to talk about that lights her fire.* She needs to feel that the two of you are together on this topic and could discuss it for quite a while. Naturally, you have no idea what that might be, so you have to jump around until you can see daylight. Be persistent in trying different topics until something clicks. Be prepared to be blocked. Just roll off it and try something else.

An example:

You: "This band is just great. Ever heard them before?"

Her: "Nope."

You: "They played at the beach last summer. Do you like the beach?"

Her: "No. I prefer rock climbing and mountain biking. The sand bugs me."

You: "I know what you mean. It gets everywhere. Where do like to go to climb and bike. I've always wanted to try that."

Her: "Oh, I really like Carson's Gap. It's so cool up there. You get these great views and the trails are really challenging but not too dangerous. You have to be in good shape, though. Do you work out?"

Bingo. You now are talking about her favorite pastime and *your* physical condition! She can ramble for hours. You are the newbie. She wants to know if you work out. This is very good. Remember where you started? You went from a band to the beach to the sand to the mountains and your physical condition. That's broken field running.

Conversation

Conversations consist of statements, questions and answers. Although the percentages are approximate, your side of the conversation should be 70 percent questions, 20 percent answers and 10 percent statements. Blowhards will switch the percentages on questions and statements. All conversations have a life cycle of their own. They start high and plateau for a while then gradually decline as interest wanes. You need to get a sense for this. How long does the typical talk show guest visit last? Fifteen minutes? You need to end the conversation first. You need to end it before it deteriorates. You need to leave her hungry for more. Of course, she may beat you to it for one reason or another — not the least of which is that you are not all that charming to her. You should know that she is probably aware of these principles as well. Be cool. If you sense that you about to be dismissed (watch for the signs), gracefully excuse yourself if possible.

"Carol, it was nice talking to you but I'd don't want to tie you up all night. Catch you later."

You do not appear needy. You are safe company. You have style and grace. She may want to talk to you again later when she discovers that the rest of the room is full of jerks (the odds are high). Besides, she will notice that you simply moved on to talk to someone else and you are showing those pearly whites and just having the best time — very effective.

If you are consistently talented at being personable and a highlight of any gathering, your reputation will grow. You will be invited to more parties. Your circle of friends and acquaintances will increase. This is the best of all possible worlds. This is where you want to be. It is surprisingly easy.

Someone needs to speak first. Equal rights aside, society generally expects the man to take that role. If she speaks first — congratulations. It is rare but not impossible. By the way, always return an invitation to chat, no matter what the woman looks like. It is a nice thing to do, improves your confidence and conditions you to automatically go into conversational mode at every opportunity.

If a woman speaks first by asking the time or directions or by making a general comment, consider this an advance. It could be a rare, golden chance at romance. You may be wrong but it is worth exploring if you think you are interested. It takes a lot for a woman to do this, so either she is interested in you or really needs to know the time and you just happen to have a watch. If she appeals to you, follow up immediately with a question. This will take some creativity because you will be caught off guard. Do your best to initiate a conversation and keep it going. In the process, you can watch her body language and determine if there is a real opportunity here. If you wimp out, she will drop the issue immediately and the opportunity will have passed. Pity.

What do you say? Anything. It really doesn't matter too much. It could be centered around what you are mutually experiencing. The line is long, you don't know where the books about physical fitness are located, she has Virginia plates on her car, whatever. *Just say something.* You will get an immediate indication as to her receptiveness. She will reply or mumble or ignore you. At least you will know. If she seems completely uninterested, simply smile and say "have a great day." No harm done. You dropped a line in the water, got a nibble and the fish swam away. So what? It's good practice. It toughens your resolve and makes it easier the next time.

With some luck, she may reply with a question of her own or an acknowledging smile. That is enough signal to continue. Center the next comment or question around her. "Have you ever tried Smith's Deli?" She has a chance to participate easily and perhaps develop the conversation herself. Just keep chatting and smiling. After two or three exchanges — *introduce yourself*. This is key. She needs a comfort level. Once she knows your name, she can drop her guard a bit. You are no longer a total stranger, you are a guy she met at the deli. That's progress.

Steer the conversation to value matching when you can. Since you have your list memorized, start asking about her ambitions, dreams and values. Don't be too intrusive. It is just as important to make her feel like you are an old friend she can trust as it is to gather information. You must be sincere and truthful at all times. You want to entice her with your potential as a romantic partner. Do this by revealing what you like and then observing her reaction. Make her curious to find out more. The price for that information is spending more time with you.

If you are in a setting where she is having a drink, look for an opportunity to buy her another. Don't be pushy about it. Make her feel like your guest. When you sense that she is very comfortable with you, and not before, ask if she would like to accompany you to a nice café for coffee and more chatting. Identify the place and say how nice it is. Say that she could follow you in her car and head home from there since it is very close. Of course, you have done your research and know a few appropriate places in the area, right?

If she hesitates because she is not quite comfortable, lead her to believe that she could be missing out on something very nice — a possible date with you! Since a great relationship is exactly what she's looking for, it could turn the tide. Keep things light, not threatening. It takes a certain amount of self-confidence, but a conversation like this might be appropriate.

Her: "I don't think I want to get that involved right now, thanks."

You: "You know, Karen, opportunity is a funny thing. I see the possibility of us having the best time getting to know each other better. I see us out at a nice restaurant laughing and enjoying a great meal. I'm the kind of guy who can't let a good thing pass me by. Don't you think it's exciting to do something a bit adventurous? How about investing an hour and finding out?"

By the way, one of the biggest mistakes we make is to let our eyes wander around the room while we are talking to a woman. *They hate that.* If you think about it, so would you. Summon all your concentration and maintain eye contact while you follow every word she says. Study the section on active listening very carefully. Play mind games with yourself if you must. Pretend she holds the secrets of the universe and will be revealing them soon. She can tell you who will win next year's Superbowl. That should help. By the way, if it's really this difficult for you to listen to her now, maybe this isn't the gal for you. If you end up in a relationship with her, you will be listening a lot. It should be pleasant.

Guess My Gig

When the topic of your job comes up, and it will early on, tell the simple truth. Be proud but don't embellish beyond the truth. It is not as important as you may think. If she is after money, let her go. You probably don't have the kind of cash she's looking for anyway. Have a plan for the future and share a bit of it with her. If you are honest, direct and self-assured, that is more than enough.

Her: "So what do you do for a living, Ken?"

You: "Well, Kathy, I'm an administrative assistant at the Department of Education at the moment. I've been on some very encouraging interviews lately, though. I'd like to move on to something that puts my degree to better use. How long have you been at Smith & Jenkins?"

You looked her right in the eye and told the whole truth. She doesn't need to pull any more out of you about your present job. You don't sound like you are satisfied with it. However, you have shown initiative and you sound like you have a future. You didn't drone on or brag about it. She might ask you about your degree and your dream. That's fine. You also turned the conversation around to her. It's OK to have a dream about your future and your career but be careful about anything else. Spinning wild tales about how you'd like to try out for the NFL or own a Ferrari someday will get you nowhere.

Compliments

Women don't hear enough compliments. Just ask them. The compliments that they do hear are often lame or off color. This presents an opportunity for you to set yourself apart from your competition. A compliment must be freely offered from the heart with no expected outcome. You must project this with your demeanor. What to say? Look at the lady. What has attracted you? Anything other than her body is fair game. Consider aspects other than her appearance as well. Here are some ideas:

- Smile
- Hair
- Eyes
- Jewelry
- Clothes
- Style

- Laugh
- Intelligence
- Personality
- Sensitivity
- Elegance
- Sophistication

Deliver your compliment warmly and simply. She will probably thank you. Move on to something else. Don't gush. Limit your compliments to two or three at the most and spread them out. They will begin to lose their meaning if there are too many.

Why Do People Love Oprah ?

Watch her carefully. She is a master of conversation. Ever notice how little you learn about *her* while she interviews guests? Is there a lot of laughter? Is the guest relaxed? How does she do it? She *asks simple open-ended questions* and lets the guest roll. She shows *sincere interest* in what they are saying and participates without going off topic. The conversation rarely shifts to her. She is carefully processing what the guest is saying and preparing her next question. Look at her body language. Posture, eye contact and gestures all contribute to the guest's comfort level.

If a good conversationalist speaks, it will be to encourage the partner to continue or move to another topic when the current one is exhausted. Maintain a pleasant smile and warm eye contact. From time to time use simple phrases like:

"Yes. . ."

"Oh, I see . . ."

"Uh, huh. . ."

"Then what?"

Learn to rephrase what she has just said. This shows interest and ensures that you understand. Take the last event or idea and summarize it in one sentence.

"So, you booked this ski trip on a whim? Right out of the blue?"

"Let me get this straight. You have three jobs? One full time and two part time?"

"You mean you just walked up to your roommate and said you were moving out that night?"

You get the idea. Another variation is to ask for verification of your understanding. You could ask her to repeat part of what she said or ask if your rephrasing is correct. This is a very powerful and useful conversational technique. By the way, a side benefit is that is takes a lot of pressure off of you.

Put Yourself in Her Shoes

A big part of successful conversation is delivering a sincere, caring feeling. This is not easy if it isn't real, so *don't try to fake it.* If you're not interested enough in her to empathize with her life issues, move on. Remember that friendship is the first requirement of a successful relationship. Listen to the way that women talk to each other. You will hear lots of genuine concern for the welfare of the other. They aren't judgmental or full of advice. They are there to listen.

You will have to use your own words in your own way. It has to come from your heart and have the ring of truth. Here is some guidance for your conversation. Above all, you are a decent, honest guy with values who knows what he wants — a nice relationship with a quality woman. Spending some time with you is the best alternative she has tonight. None of the other men around are going to offer a better alternative. Focus on her life and her problems — never your own. Has she had a lousy experience with another guy? Take her side and empathize. Tell her you always admired the way your parents got along and solved their problems. (You may have to stretch a bit here.) It is rare that a great opportunity presents itself. She should take the plunge and enjoy the ride. She will be kicking herself later if she lets this chance go by.

Every Woman is Unique

Avoid comparing a woman to any other woman, even famous and beautiful ones. You just never know. Your idea of someone gorgeous may be her idea of a tinseltown slime ball. As soon as you say "You remind me of . . ." or "You look just like . . .", her radar is immediately up. You are dead meat. You cannot win. Don't go there. Once a guy we know compared a very attractive woman to Carly Simon. It turned out that she was very sensitive about her wide smile, although it was beautiful. Go figure. Concentrate compliments on safe aspects of her behavior, personality or character. "You have a great laugh." "You sure do seem to have a lot of friends." "I wish I had your patience." She can't reject comments like that.

Is Silence Always Golden?

What if neither of you talks for a while? Yikes. It can seem like years. When people know each other well, this is not a problem. Think about the times you have spent with friends or family in complete silence. In early conversations, it's deadly. It can be very awkward. You have to take control. It's up to you to keep things rolling. Here are some ideas:

Call it what it is. Say, "Uh-oh, here's the part where neither of us knows what to say next and we both get embarrassed. You know in Russia they say a policeman dies when there's a gap in the conversation (true saying, by the way). We can't let that happen!" Acknowledging it takes the edge off. Try to make it amusing.

Hello! Are you there? Make sure you're not the cause of the gap. Are you busy looking around? Are you looking over her shoulder at the game on TV? Are you talking to everyone that walks by? You had better refocus.

Share the pain. Sometimes encouraging her to talk is not enough. You have to be willing to share some of yourself. Just keep it in balance. If there's a gap and she seems hesitant to step to the plate, pull out something completely different. "I really love James Taylor. I have every one of his CDs. Did you ever catch him in concert? No? Wow, he's amazing. . ." Go on to describe a concert you saw. Then pass the ball back to her. She may tell you about her favorite artist.

Can't get a word in edgewise? It's possible that you could find yourself face-to-face with a major chatterbox. It's OK if she's excited and has a long story to tell but if she cuts you off and doesn't want to give up the floor — look out. This ain't healthy. Make a few humorous attempts to contribute. Make the "time-out" sign with your hands or raise your hand as in school. It may just be nervous energy. See if she can sit still for a few minutes while you share something. If not, make it a short evening.

Maintain an air of mystery. Don't be an open book. Don't incessantly talk about yourself or reveal too much. Women are naturally curious. She needs to use her feminine skills. Don't make it too easy for her.

After you are involved in a conversation and things are going smoothly, an incidental touch can be effective. You have to be *very* careful. It has to be subtle. Avoid using your hands. Let your shoulders brush briefly. If you are sitting next to each other, let your legs touch occasionally. Just be sure it is not overt and that it is almost unconscious.

Your conversation is a way to move toward an emotional connection. As soon as possible move away from mundane topics to emotions and feelings. As a matter of fact, use the word "feel" as often as possible. Be constantly searching for matching values.

Mirroring

Mirroring is a very effective way to increase the comfort level of the object of your interest. Ideally you would do this during conversation. *People are most comfortable with people like themselves.* Observe her body language. Is she leaning forward in her chair and leaning on the table? Do likewise. Is she sitting back and crossing her legs? You get the idea. Now, be careful you don't act like a chimpanzee and get caught. Be very casual about it. You can do the same with speech. Try to mimic the style and speed of her chatter. Is she animated or easy-going? She will be more relaxed and open to you if you seem like an old friend. Hypnotists will even mirror the subject's breathing patterns until they match precisely. This isn't deceitful; actually, it is a form of flattery. A significant portion of communication is transmitted non-verbally. Take advantage of it. Try to establish rapport by mirroring, avoiding confrontation and nurturing similarities.

Over time study the style and dress of the women that you find attractive. What would a suitable date for these ladies look like? How would they be dressed. How would they behave? Try to model your appearance and style to more closely match that of the women you seek.

Mirror her vocal patterns.
• Mood
• Tone
• Speed
• Volume
• Phrases and cliches

Mirror her body language
• Body movements
• Facial expressions
• Hand gestures

Be sure to be subtle about this. Try to find a natural rhythm that compliments her movements — similar to defending in basketball. If she moves left, so do you. If she jumps, you jump. This has to be so smooth that she is totally unaware of your pattern. It will make her feel very comfortable and close to you. It is a matter of getting in sync with her. Mirroring is very easy to practice, even with other guys. It is a great sales and negotiating tool. How would you make a child feel comfortable with you? Have you ever seen full-grown adults making meaningless noises to infants or getting down on the floor to color with a young child? This is just an extension of the same principle. Her body language, facial and speech expressions are manifestations of her inner feelings. If you can get in touch with that, you have made a powerful connection on an emotional level.

What Are You Trying To Accomplish?

The primary goal of an encounter should be to persuade the woman to accompany you to another location where you can quietly talk and get to know each other better. The secondary goal is to persuade her to give you her phone number so that you can call her and ask her out. The last goal is to have her accept your card and phone number and hope that she will call you.

When you invite a woman to "go someplace nice and comfortable where we can talk," make it easy for her to say yes. Have her follow you in her car to a safe, clean place that is close and easy to find. This is where your night spot survey will help a great deal. Give her a time frame so she can get home at a decent hour. NEVER invite her to your place. Extend your invitation at the high point of your conversation — when things are going very well. If it is too early and she is not comfortable that you are a nice guy with lots of potential, she will decline. If you drone on and on, it will get too late and she may become bored. It takes some delicate timing.

Some Positive Signs

Here are a few behaviors to watch for. Sometimes guys don't even realize that they are doing well. These indicators are an invitation to move ahead in the process.

- If a woman asks you to pose as her date to fend off a jerk, smile and co-operate. It is only one step from the role to reality.
- If she offers any compliment at all, you are blessed. It is a solid sign of interest on her part.
- If she playfully laughs while disagreeing with you, that's good. "Oh sure, come on. Who are you trying to kid?"
- Is she asking you to repeat yourself? Do you have to lean in and talk directly in her ear? She's interested in your thoughts and doesn't want to miss anything.
- Does she find you extremely amusing? Is she laughing a bit hard at your lame jokes? She's trying.
- If she is still waiting for you when you leave for a moment or returns to you after visiting the ladies' room, she's definitely interested.
- If she doesn't pull back or stiffen if you have to reach across her or invade her space for an acceptable reason such as reaching for something, it's a good sign.
- If she says, "Oh, do you have to go?" as you make your exit, it means "please stay."

At last it is time to address the heart of the matter — the date. How do you ask for one? How do you make plans? All this and more is revealed in the next chapter.

Chapter 19
The Dating Process

"As I grow older, I pay less attention to what men say. I just watch what they do."

— Andrew Carnegie

The Process

There is a pattern that has evolved in our society for dating. It may be helpful to step back and look at the big picture before you jump in to the game. We don't mean to scare you, but this is generally what society, including your mom, expects to happen. You may as well recognize it now while your head is clear. It goes something like this:

• *Encounter* – You meet her casually and feel things out. Your approach is enough to express interest. You look for signs of interest while you entertain her with your charming conversation. Keep it short — no pressure. Repeat as required, or perhaps . . .

• *Ask for the date* – You are decisive and prepared for a negative response. If she agrees and your plans are solid, the conversation is over. You have what you need; get out of her face and let her think about it.

• *Deliver a great evening* – Not too much, not too little. Light conversation, a cool and breezy upbeat attitude and no dead spots. Two stimulating, pleasant hours are vastly superior to four mediocre, gradually declining ones. As the show biz saying goes, "Leave 'em laughing."

• *Move on to the next date, and the next, and the next* – *one date at a time*. More of the same style, different program. Mix it up. Be creative. Surprise her. Ask and listen. Tap into her emotional needs without being intrusive. Keep frequency down to once or twice a week. Let her up the ante. This should go on for several months.

• *Get exclusive* – When everything is right, you will know. She will bring it up. If you both agree that dating other people is not what you both want — it's time to test the trust factor. Be open, honest and communicative without scaring her off. Remember, if you say no, it's over. Don't surrender your whole life. You are simply restricting your dating to one special girl.

- *Stay exclusive for an extended period* – This time (several months to one year) is required to build trust and emotional commitment. Learn as much as you can. Continue to maintain some independence. Let her take the lead. She will give you strong signs when she is ready for the next step . . .

- *Visit your friendly local jeweler* – You had better be damn sure, pal. Broken engagements are nearly as bad as divorces. Never make this move unless you thoroughly intend to change her last name. The link between engagement and marriage is extremely strong. Once she has that ring, she believes it's over. The rest is just logistics. It will take a lot of time and planning to put together a wedding and set up house. Use this time (again, several months) to complete the emotional bond and be sure enough that you are willing to bet your life. That's exactly what you are doing. Of course, you know what's next. This is where we get off. Best of luck to you both. Life is risky, but is better to share it with the right woman. Ask an old bachelor.

Asking for her Number

It is very important that you get a woman's phone number. In an initial encounter, it's really the best you can hope for. You want to succeed at the end of the encounter. If things have gone well, she will be dying to give it to you. Why is it so important? If she gives it to you she wants things to continue. She *expects* you to call. You had *better* do it. A big pet peeve for women is when they give men their numbers and they don't call. It's almost a slap in the face.

It is not the same as when you meet a guy on a plane and talk for awhile, then exchange business cards. It's no big deal if neither of you calls. The exchange of cards was more of a courtesy. Not so with a woman's phone number. Remember, they guard their home number with their life. They don't want creeps and geeks calling them at home. They are scared and for good reason. If she gives you her number it is a sign of interest and trust. What more could you want?

Be confident, sincere and warm when you ask for her number. It is better to ask after you have handed her your card and jotted your home number on the back. A creep or a guy with something to hide will not likely hand out so much information. You are worthy of her trust.

"Susan, I have to get going now but I have really enjoying meeting you. I'd love to see you again. May I call you?"

"Before you go, I just want to let you know how much I have enjoyed this. Would you be interested in exchanging phone numbers?" Hand her your card.

If she hesitates, hand her your card anyway and hope that she calls. By the way, be certain you have a nice pen with you at all times. If she turns down your request for her number with a lame excuse such as "I don't have a phone" or "I *never* give my number out," that's not good. You can probably tell when you are hearing a lie. Are you interested in more of the same?

Speak for Yourself, John

Do you remember the story of John Alden? Henry Wadsworth Longfellow wrote the poem "The Courtship of Miles Standish" in which John Alden, deeply in love with Priscilla Mullens, proposes to her on behalf of his shy friend Miles Standish. Her response? "Why don't you speak for yourself, John?" In 1623, John Alden married Priscilla Mullens.

And you thought dating was a contemporary issue. Always do your own work. Don't test the waters by telling her friends that you are interested. That's high school stuff. The dating process should be between two people only. Keep others out of it as much as possible.

When to Call

So, everything went well in your first meeting and you have her phone number. You didn't ask for the date or you have agreed to get together sometime soon. When should you call? It would probably be better to wait a day or two in order to give her time to think about you and build up a bit of anticipation. She may talk to her friends about you and it adds a bit of drama to her week. The best time to call is between seven and ten PM. This gives her time to eat dinner and relax a bit. It is impolite in general to call people after ten PM.

There is a *"rule"* floating around out there that says you should wait three days before calling a woman after first meeting her. Bull. First of all, everyone knows about it. Therefore, if you call *exactly* three days later you look like a boob. Second, it makes no sense. Anticipation does not increase with time, frustration does. These are "mind games." It's not honest and no one likes it. If you have a good feeling about the first encounter and want to give her a quick call in the next day or two — do it. However, you have to be wary of appearing desperate or needy. Keep it light and breezy. Tell her you enjoyed meeting her and are interested in seeing her again. *Give her a chance to reply.* You can quickly tell where you stand.

Cold: If she doesn't remember who you are or starts to stammer about how busy she is these days, you're dead in the water. Remain cool and say that you understand — no problem. What you want to do is preserve the possibility that she may be more interested next month. Wish her well and make a note to call her after the air clears. Your odds are not good, but you never know.

Lukewarm: You're not sure what her feelings are. Who knows what is going on? She may be having a bad day. Don't jump right into an invitation. Chat for a while. Feel her out. Go back to whatever might be familiar to both of you — maybe the place that you met. If she still seems hesitant, ask if you may call again in a few days. Do your best to make a connection and pique her interest. When you think things have warmed up enough, ask for the date. Patience.

Warm/Hot: Make the date. Remember to have a specific plan and timeframe in mind. Enjoy the moment and the adrenaline.

Being Cool on the Phone

Everyone loves that blinking red light on their answering machine. However, try not to leave messages initially. Be aware that many women have Caller ID. She will be able to tell if you called sixteen times on Wednesday. If you have tried one or two evenings in a row, leave a very brief message to keep the process going. The problem is that many of us sound like dorks on a machine. You need to speak to her directly to best represent yourself. If you decide to leave a message, write it out. Identify yourself and give her a day and time when you will call again. When you call, spend some time making small talk. Get to know her. Encourage her to open up. What has her week been like so far? Did she get her hair cut like she mentioned?

If you were paying close attention during your last meeting and encouraging her to talk, you will have no problem. Ask her to join you for specific plans on a specific night sometime the next weekend or several (three or four) days ahead. This is important. If you ask for a date tomorrow night, you appear too anxious and you are not respecting her schedule. What makes you think she would be available on such short notice? Don't you think she has a life? ("Hey Megan, would you like to see the new James Bond flick that's opening next Friday? I can get tickets ahead of time. Later we can go to this nice club I know. A few of my friends might show up.") Give her a chance to respond. She may be busy that night. Don't let this discourage you. She may ask if you can make it another night. Be cooperative. Of course you can. Have a back-up plan. ("Hey, no problem. How about going to the Arts Festival on Sunday afternoon?") Nail down the time. Give her some hint about the dress if you need to. Then don't call her again. If you do you will appear needy and it will make her uncomfortable.

Ask for the Order (Date)

Asking for the order is a time-honored salesperson's golden rule. Sometimes they get so wrapped up in their pitch, they neglect to ask the prospect to buy. If all the circumstances look good — go for it. So how do you ask for a date? The biggest mistake guys make is to appear wishy-washy. Avoid sounding like the guys below.

Date-Killers

"I don't know, what would you like to do?"

"We could go to a movie or a ball game or grab a bite or, or, or. . ."

"How about going dancing. What clubs do you like?"

You are doing the inviting. She is your intended "guest." Be specific and in control. A great idea is to keep potential events lined up on your calendar. Pencil in favorite restaurants, movies you'd like to see or parties. Then you always have an idea for a date. You also have a backup if your first suggestion isn't going to work. Suggest a day. Be prepared with an alternate day.

You: "Would you like have dinner with me at Ambrosia?"

Her: "Ooo. That sounds nice, except I was just there last week."

You: "It's great, isn't it? Well, I'd like to try Casa Luna. . ."

Her: "I'd love to try that place. My roommate says it's really different."

You: "I'm free Friday evening. . .?"

Her: "Darn, that's my sister's birthday. . ."

You: "No problem. Would Saturday work for you? Say around 7?"

Her: "Great. How about if I meet you there?"

You: "Fine. It's a date then."

You extended a specific invitation. She had an objection. You immediately countered with an alternative. It would be good to have a third. Notice that you said you were *free* Friday, which makes you sound busy. She had a conflict. You came right back with another day *and a time* — very decisive. She wants to meet at the restaurant because she feels safer. You don't mind. You nail it by identifying it as a *date*.

Things can get a bit awkward at this point. She may want to continue chatting, but it would be best to let her go. You might want to suggest that you call to confirm and ask for her number. Don't be put off if she prefers to decline.

What to Say

Make sure you are relaxed and alone in a quiet place. Make a few notes about what you want to say. If you are going to invite her out, have two or three suggestions and your calendar handy. Don't accept a call-waiting interruption.

1. Identify yourself in a friendly, upbeat way.

2. Ask if this is a good time for her to talk. If not, ask when you can call back.

3. Try to re-establish your connection by recalling some of the topics you discussed or the place you met. This is to make her comfortable and let her listen to the sound of your voice.

4. Extend your invitation. Tell her what you would like to do, not when.

5. When she accepts the invitation, negotiate a day and time.

6. Maintain a lively pace and a light, fun-filled tone.

7. Reiterate your plans to clarify.

8. Keep the call short — about ten minutes. End the call first.

Here is a sample conversation to help you with that first call:

You: "Sharon? Hi, this is Mark. I hope you remember me from Carla's party last week."

Her: "Sure. Hi, Mark. What's up?"

You: "Is this a good time to call?"

Her: "No problem. I just finished eating. I'm glad you called."

You: "Great. That party was a lot of fun. Of course, meeting you was the best part." (laugh.)

Her: "Oh sure. You say that to all the girls."

(More chit-chat here)

You: "Seriously, I would enjoy continuing our conversation about Europe over some great French food sometime soon."

Her: "That might be fun."

You: "Good. I was thinking of Pierre's on the West Side. What do you think?"

Her: "OK, I've never been there."

You: "Well, Sharon, it will be the first time for both of us then. We can tell them we're critics from the *Times*! How does next week look for you?"

(Continue to discuss a day and time.)

You: "Well, I predict a great evening for two people I know, but I've taken enough of your time tonight. I will see you at Pierre's at 7:30 next Thursday. I'll arrive a bit early to check on the reservation. I'm really looking forward to it, Sharon."

Her: "Me too, Mark."

You: "Have a good night. Take care."

Her: "Bye, Mark."

Obviously, your conversation will be spontaneous. What is important is that you accomplish your goals. What are your goals? First, you hope to land the date. Second, you want to rekindle any attraction the two of you experienced. Third, you want to leave her with a good impression of you and a bit of anticipation. Don't expect to accomplish more. Keep your love chemicals under control. The telephone is not the best medium for an intimate conversation at this point. She needs to see your smile and the sincerity in your eyes. Wait until you see her.

By the way, it might be best to avoid suggesting a Friday or Saturday night date at first. These are heavy nights that are loaded with romantic meaning. Try an early weeknight plan or perhaps a Sunday afternoon. The purpose of the first date is to leave her with a very positive impression and feeling about you, and to land a second date. A Friday or Saturday night date will probably cloud this purpose. Save the big night on the town for the third or fourth date.

Date Behavior

The purpose of a first date is to get a second date. When you invite a woman out for an evening it is like throwing a small party where she is the only guest. You are responsible for everything. She is only expected to show up and be ready to enjoy herself. Be a man of decision. Think James Bond. While you don't have every minute planned, there is a definite flow to the evening. You don't have to reveal everything, you just need to act as though you have everything under control.

Make Careful Plans and Execute

Always make reservations. Are you eating at a place that doesn't take them? Eat somewhere else. Do you know exactly what time that movie starts? Will there be a line because it's opening night? Pick up tickets ahead of time, if possible. How long does it take to drive to that party? She needs to know exactly what time you will pick her up. SHOW UP ON THE DOT. If you are too early, she will not be ready. If you show up late, she is all dressed up with nowhere to go and nothing to do and you're an idiot — bad start.

If you are presented with any situation where choices must be made — make them. Ask her approval after the fact. One great trick as the hostess is escorting you to your table is to ask for another one that is more to your liking (better view, closer to the dance floor, quieter, whatever). Attend to her every need. Hold her chair when she sits. Learn to do this gracefully. If you are having wine, you select it but consider her opinion. Generally, she will be agreeable. Ask questions about the menu. How is the fish prepared? Don't appear arrogant. Know what you want and don't settle for less.

Problems

What if she's late — or worse, doesn't show? Be very patient about this. Things happen. She will make explanations. You will be able to tell if she is putting you on. If her car broke down, OK. If she forgot — that's unacceptable. Tell her you are disappointed that the occasion meant so little to her. Wish her well and say goodbye.

Expect her to be a bit late, then you won't be disappointed. She may be a really terrific date, just not too punctual. Wait at least thirty minutes, then try to call. If she doesn't show within another thirty — leave. Something must have happened. Wait a couple of days to see if she calls. If not, it's up to you whether you want to call her again.

Pace Saves Face

In this day and age everything is compressed. Information attacks us from every direction. In this environment it is easy to see how the beauty of a slowly evolving relationship can be lost. Women are as guilty of this as we are. They can begin to make assumptions after a few dates. They will sometimes turn first encounters into job interviews. Comedians have a good time with this. If you have the right job, drive the right car and have a recent blood test, they will consider a date. Both genders engage in this destructive behavior. Here is a question for you. *How long does it take to make a friend? Shouldn't it take at least as long if not longer to build a long-term relationship?* Keep your perspective. Keep personal questions to a minimum at first, both yours and hers. *Stay in the moment.* Enjoy the present — the food, the music, her smile.

At first, you should pace your dates no more frequently than once a week, perhaps less. Mix it up. Be a bit unpredictable. If you go to the movies and the same restaurant every Friday for three weeks in a row, well . . .

Try to keep yourself under control. *If you are really interested in her, there will be a natural inclination to rush things. You need to resist this urge.* It will weaken your position. Try to read her feelings, never ask. She will give you signs if she wants to turn up the heat. She may even begin to make suggestions or ask you out. Perhaps her girlfriend is having a party next week. There may be a restaurant she's dying to try. Great. This makes it easy on you.

Don't make the mistake of looking for feedback. This is a killer. What is she supposed to say? Why do you need this information? Are you so insecure that you need to be told that you are a great guy? When you say things like the following, you are asking for trouble.

"Jean, we've had three dates now. I was just wondering how you feel about things. Are you really interested in me?"

"Hey, babe. Are you having a good time tonight? Isn't this place great? I sure do know how to treat a lady, don't I?"

"So. What do you think? Is this working for you?"

Keep your big mouth shut. If you need to wallow in this dumb stuff, do it alone at home. Also, do not ask her friends for input. This is even worse. Don't be dense. Her friend is going to tell her you were looking for a "date report card?" This is a real relationship killer.

You need a bit of mystery about you to keep the interest high, especially in the early stages of a relationship. You want to be a great guy who is a fun date. When you show up, it's a big treat. She doesn't really know if there will be another date after this one. *She may work a bit harder to keep you interested. This is the "zone," man.* It is better for you and better for her that you are pursuing her. It has to be that way; you have to ask her out. That is your advantage. You get to extend the invitations and set the pace. She gets to say yes or no. If you are an open book, what challenge is there for her? She can treat you like the clerk at the grocery store, wear whatever she feels like and only accept the dates she wants. You're not going to complain because you have shown her all your cards — "I'm crazy about you. I'm going to keep calling you. I'm totally enchanted by your presence." This is an invitation to disaster. If she is interested, she needs to use her charms to keep your calls coming.

This does not mean that you shouldn't compliment her and show interest in her when she is with you. Sparingly use comments and signs of interest, in the same way as spices are used in cooking. Look for the right moment. *When you first pick her up, take a good look.* She has just finished spending a lot of time trying to look appealing. She may have purchased a new outfit or done something special with her hair. Your compliment will go a long way to making the evening a success. Two or three comments during one date will do nicely. If you say too much, it waters down your compliments and makes you appear too eager. If you say nothing, she will be disappointed and think that you are not interested. Be genuine. If you're attracted enough to her to ask her out, you will find a few positive things to mention.

What Do Women Want?

They prefer a respectful man with a nice personality. They want to be treated gently and with sensitivity.

They expect you to have good manners. You should know how to conduct yourself in society. It should be natural and second nature, therefore you must always be practicing. You should be sociable and relate well to people in general.

You must be honest and have integrity. Don't lie. They will know. They have heard a ton of BS in their time. The truth will set you apart.

You should be friendly and "on her side." She wants to feel that you are in her corner.

Your appearance must be neat and clean to a fault. Details count. Don't overdress. It makes you seem elitist. It is better to be more casual. Try to match your surroundings. She would prefer that you did not stick out. Make sure your clothes fit well. The way to distinguish your dress is to be coordinated, neat and clean. For example, have your slacks and shirts done at a cleaners if at all possible. A professionally pressed shirt is very crisp and sends a nice message. It costs about $1.50. If not, learn how to iron and do it well.

A woman wants strength and reason in a man. She expects that he will not always agree with her. In case you haven't noticed, a woman will readily express her own opinion and let you know when her opinion varies with yours. Don't start an argument. Differences of opinion are interesting. Some things do not require a resolution. Do you prefer the east or the west coast? Avoid sensitive areas such as religion or politics at first as they are too emotional and deeply rooted. Stick to safer ground such as popular culture (music, movies, sports), food or travel. If you have opinions, you are interesting. If you don't, you're a bore who doesn't think, or worse, a wimp.

The more intelligent you seem, the better. Remember Marilyn Monroe and Arthur Miller, the playwright? If not, find an old photo. Women are enchanted by a man who can conduct an intelligent conversation. You do not have to be a college professor. You just have to hold your own. If you didn't do well in school you can compensate by being well informed. Simply read a variety of newspapers and magazines and watch CNN. Of course, reading a worthwhile book now and then will also help. Oh yeah, there's nothing wrong with taking a course a year at the local college. Education should be a lifelong process. Learning for learning's sake can be very compelling to women.

Familiarity breeds contempt. Sorry, but it's true. This is tricky. You want to be reliable and responsible. You just don't want to be too predictable. Pick her up on time. You call when you say you will. You remember her birthday. BUT, you mix things up a bit. Some weekends you make plans with your friends and go without telling her. Maybe you don't call for a week, then a small gift shows up on her doorstep. You are such a rascal! She never knows what you're going to do next. Women love a mystery. They can't wait to see what will happen next in their favorite show. Wouldn't it be great if you were writing the script? That's the advantage of the man's position. You get to lead when you dance. Of course, she can say no. You can't have everything.

Many women are carrying around a dream similar to the romance novels you see in bookstores. By the way, it might be a good idea to read one, if you can stand it. It will shed a lot of light on the type of fantasies women harbor. If you can "become" or behave similar to the hero in these novels, you will be fulfilling a dream. They want an exciting, interesting encounter that will develop into a relationship — something out of the ordinary that will make them feel very special. When you see an interesting attractive woman out alone or with friends, you can assume that this is the case. The odds are that you are correct. Men of course, naturally seek something a bit more immediate. You must suppress this urge and exercise patience.

NO:

Old Lines – They've heard them all.

BS – Don't lie, brag, boast, exaggerate or show off. Sincerity counts.

Mushiness – Lose the little lost puppy look. Romantic men can be strong.

Turn-offs – We listed them for you. Pay attention. Clean up your act.

Fear of Rejection – Get over it. It's not personal. You can't be all things to all people.

Immediate Gratification – You can't have her tonight. She wants a nice relationship down the road.

YES:

Sincerity – It is critical and it must be real. You've got to feel it. It can't be faked.

Romantic Potential – She needs to know that you could sweep her off her feet when the time is right.

Neat and Clean – Details, details — pay attention.

Turn-ons – Make all the improvements you can in your behavior and appearance. We listed them for you. Pay attention.

Safe and Protective – You are a gentleman and have her best interests at heart. She can trust you.

How are your manners? Dating can be a real showcase for your upbringing or a disaster. We haven't included everything here, but there are some sound basics just ahead.

Chapter 20
Be Civil in Your Suit

"Civility costs nothing and buys everything."
— Lady Mary Wortly Monagu, letter to the Countess of Bute, May 30, 1756.

"Mister Manners" Scores Points

One of the hallmarks of our gender is the ability to descend to the lowest common denominator when we gather in groups at bars or hunting camps. The grossest guy gets the most laughs. While there is nothing wrong with this, you need to be able to switch modes when you are out on a date. You probably have heard most of this before. It is a matter of keeping it in mind when you are in her presence. It takes practice and concentration until it becomes second nature. You will rise quickly above your competition. Women preserve many of the finer, nobler aspects of society. Remember what your mom taught you.

Please and thank you. Be very liberal with these two phrases. Your mom was right. Be consistently polite to everyone and it will come naturally. Waiters, valets and cab drivers are all people just like you. She will notice.

Open doors. You would be surprised how much women appreciate this. Most of your competition won't bother. Good. Get out of the car, walk around and open her door. (Don't be staring at her legs as she gets out.) Always extend an arm to help her in or out of a car or a chair. On the way back, unlock her door and let her in first. Walk ahead to doors and hold them open for her as she enters or exits. Always hold doors for her when possible, but in any case NEVER enter ahead of her. Get in the habit of always doing this. It really sets you apart.

Push her chair in. A gentleman always stands when a lady enters or leaves a room. This is especially true at a table. Rise and pull her chair out as she stands up. When she returns, rise again and push her chair in as she sits. If you have to leave, excuse yourself. When being escorted to a table or a seat by an usher or hostess, the man follows the woman. If there is no assistance, the man leads and escorts the lady into the room. If the two of you are walking in together she should be on your right. If it's a formal occasion let her take your right arm. Always offer to help her with her coat. Always offer to walk her to her door at the end of the evening.

When walking down the street with a woman, the appropriate etiquette is for the man to always position himself closest to the street. This means walking on the left at times — and walking on the right at others. The chivalrous origin of this custom is that the street side is more dangerous. She could be swept away by a runaway carriage or such. The man is responsible for the couple's safety — particularly hers. The man watches and guides. The person walking on the street side is also more likely to be splashed by a passing vehicle.

When making introductions give her the advantage by introducing the other person first. "Jane, this is Bill Evans. He's in my volleyball league. Bill, this is Jane, she's stuck with me for the evening." There is a bit of reverse psychology here. It can be very effective. First of all, you seem humble — how charming. She will feel obliged to protest a bit by giving you a bit of a compliment. She will want to rescue your reputation in front of your friend. Besides, she doesn't want to be out with a loser. She will more than likely say something like, "Don't listen to him, Bill. I'm having a great time." It also gives her an easy retort right off the bat. Bill knows nothing about her and she has at least one piece of information to start some conversation if she wishes.

This is the proper way to introduce a lady. The exception is if you are introducing her to an important woman who is her senior such as your mom or your boss. In that case, reverse the order. "Mom, I'd like you to meet Jane. Jane went to Penn State. Jane, this is my mother." Now your mom has the advantage and can follow up with a question or comment. While this may seem like too much formality, it really helps. Guys often fumble with introductions and look clumsy. If you consistently put this in practice, you will always look smooth and put your date at ease.

Stable at the Table

A date at a restaurant is an excellent idea. It is quiet enough for good conversation. The food and the setting can be good topics. The meal can be as short or as long as you require. It makes a great second date. Here are a few ideas to help you be an ideal dining partner. If your experience is limited to eating cheese fries with your fingers at the local bar, you may have some work to do.

Let her order first. After she has ordered, make your choice. It is a good idea to order a bit more than her. Women are sensitive to this. She doesn't want to feel that she is eating more than you. Also, a robust appetite is a masculine sign. Order healthy food — another good sign. Don't eat too much or too fast. Take small bites. Don't talk with your mouth full.

Never be afraid to return something if it is not exactly right. Good food is expensive and the kitchen is obliged to provide a perfect meal. If you asked for French dressing and you received Italian or if your chicken is not thoroughly cooked, politely but firmly ask your server to accommodate you. Be aware of your date's order as well. It is your responsibility to make her happy. "Kathy, I see that you didn't get the asparagus you ordered. Let me get the waiter." She may protest, but insist. If she continues to say that it doesn't matter, respect her wishes. You don't want to create an issue or look like a dictator. The upside is that you show strength and decisiveness. You are concerned about her comfort. You are in control.

Keep your elbows off the table. Keep your left hand (or your right if you eat southpaw) in your lap. We don't know why but that's the way it's done. Use utensils from the outside in. A proper place setting is designed for the convenience of the diner. Use your knife and fork to cut a few pieces of food on your plate, then lean the knife on the plate and eat with the fork. Place the fork on the plate, tines down when not it use and when you are finished. Place bread and rolls on your bread plate. Break off a piece and take small bites. It's OK to use the bread to push some food onto your fork.

Use your napkin frequently. Place your napkin in your lap when not in use and hang onto it. The darn things have a way of ending up on the floor. A good tip is to tuck a corner of the napkin under your belt.

When eating soup, move the spoon through the soup away from you, wipe the bottom of the spoon against the rim and bring it up to your mouth. Don't hunch over the soup bowl. Don't slurp.

Chew with your mouth shut. Take small bites. While eating, if you run into something bad, such as a piece of bone, remove the bite from your mouth immediately with the same utensil and lay the mess on your plate. Don't say anything unless asked.

Don't drink with a straw. You will look like a weenie. Set it aside and drink from the glass. Don't drink anything from a can or a bottle. Ask for a glass. Putting a wedge of lemon or lime in your water or tea is a nice touch. If you are not sure what to order, get a glass of "designer water" like Perrier or Pellegrino.

Many restaurants offer toothpicks at the counter. Don't bother. You will look stupid. Also, the whole process is a bit gross. It's similar to flossing in front of someone. Take advantage of the mints, though. Be sure to offer her one.

Forget "Dutch Treat" Unless You Live in Amsterdam

The man should almost always pay for all expenses on a date. The woman is your guest. You asked *her* out. If you can't afford to date now, wait until you can. Set up a dating budget. Be sure that you are comfortable spending the sum before you ask her out. Consider it part of your expendable income. That way you will never suffer from buyer's remorse. This is the feeling a person gets after they have made a purchase and decided that the purchase was not worth the cost. Never put yourself in this position. If you are completely comfortable with the amount you are spending and your expectations are properly focused, the evening will go much better. So what are your expectations? Be careful here. There is a school of thought that believes there is an implicit dating *quid pro quo* (this for that). I buy you dinner — we go to bed. Sorry, Romeo. That's called prostitution and it's illegal. What you get is the pleasure of the lady's company. If you don't think that's enough, or you think it is not worth the cost of a date — don't ask her out. If you happen to end up the beneficiary of some "huggy-bear, kissy-face" — enjoy. Consider it an unexpected windfall.

There is some psychology behind all this. If you have unrealistic expectations, you will telegraph them to the lady during the evening and make her uncomfortable. When it doesn't turn out the way you had hoped at the end of the evening, you will look like a jerk in her eyes and you will be frustrated. You won't be too thrilled about moving on to your next date, especially not with her — bad scene, your fault. On other hand, if you treat her like a lady and just say goodnight at the door, you appear cool, confident and desirable. Providing you didn't screw up anything else, she'll look forward to the next date. Heck, if she halfway likes you she'll spend the next week waiting by the phone for your call! Six points for you.

Always tip at least 15 percent, preferably 20 percent. Good service deserves it and you will get great service next time. She will probably notice. If you don't tip or tip lightly, she will think you are cheap and thoughtless. What can she expect from you in the future? Romantic dinners of beans and franks? A flashlight for her birthday? It's not that it's all about money but women are going to prefer someone a bit more elegant. Remember — if you can't afford to date, wait.

On a deeper level, women appreciate a man of resources who takes care of things. It's in the genes. This prehistoric programming whispers in her subconscious that she needs to seek a mate who will go out and kill game and keep the cave safe for her and her offspring. If all this sounds sexist, well . . . There is plenty of current research that indicates that a great deal of our dating behavior is based on mating rituals from our distant past. You would do well to understand your own behavior and what you are looking for in this context. More later.

Whistling, Humming, Singing, Finger Snapping and Bopping Your Head

Restaurants often have music playing in the background. You should have some music in your car low enough to carry on a conversation. You may be tempted to join in when you hear a favorite song. All these activities seem innocent enough, but there are problems.

First of all, your exuberance can be annoying to other people. We know that you are just one happy guy and you're expressing yourself but not everyone appreciates it. It could be embarrassing to your date. The problem is that the people in your immediate vicinity have no choice but to listen to you (head bopping aside). Maybe you are quite talented but you are eliminating their choice. How would you feel if they joined in or competed with you?

Second, these are isolating activities. Typically when you sing, whistle or hum, your mind is somewhere else. You are bored with the situation and you are shutting out everyone around you. What is your date supposed to do while you sing along with Sarah McLachlan?

Finally, guys often do this to look cool and impress their dates. It has the opposite effect. Remember, conversation is the key. All these behaviors are conversation killers. *Conversation is the lifeblood of dating.*

Finger snapping will make you look a bit dated — sort of like a beatnik, man. That head bop thing you do when you hear your favorite Metallica tune can make you look like a teenager. Also try to avoid pretending you are a drummer with your hands or the silverware.

If you happen to be at a concert, the rules change dramatically. This is a situation where you want to be full of life. When the band asks you to clap along, do it. At the end of a song or performance you particularly enjoyed, feel free to clap, whistle, hoot and holler as appropriate. However, you will want to watch your date's reaction to avoid making her too uncomfortable.

Music is a wonderful thing. It should be a big part of your persona. Use it to set the mood and for dancing. If the two of you find a song you really like and you both decide to sing along spontaneously while you are driving, that's a beautiful thing. The key is to be in sync with her. When you go off on a solo musical journey, you leave her behind along with your opportunities.

Should you kiss on the first date? What about flowers and presents? Should you talk about former girlfriends? We can help. Read on.

Chapter 21

The Fate of Your Date

"The hunger for love is much more difficult to remove than the hunger for bread."
— Mother Teresa, in *Time*, December 4, 1989.

Double Dating

This is usually an excellent idea. It can be a landmine as well. Don't suggest it until you have been out with her a few times. You need to gel just a bit as a couple first. You'll be less likely to embarrass yourself or make her feel uncomfortable. Choose the other couple carefully and prep them. You want a relaxed, enjoyable evening. Hopefully, she will bond a bit with the other woman. This is a big help. Don't worry too much about the other guy. The main thing is that he doesn't entertain himself at your expense. You don't need this.

Make all the arrangements yourself with the other couple's cooperation. You are inviting them to join you and your date for whatever. This way you can control the evening's events and exhibit some leadership — a sign of strength. Keep the time frame reasonable and allow some time at the end of the evening for the two of you. She may have some things to say and you want her to be thinking about you when you end the evening, not Fred's stupid jokes. If she suggests a double date with friends of hers — fine. You will have a very easy evening. She'll do all the work. You just have to be charming and get along with the other guy.

Beware

Some *bad* ideas for the first few dates:
- A family gathering (yours or hers). Too much, too soon.
- A reunion or work gathering. Ditto.
- Any plans that take longer than three to four hours. It could be the longest night of your life.
- The wrong movie. If it's an action flick you like, she could be bored. If it's too sexy, she'll be embarrassed. Also, you can't talk.

180

- A sport where you excel. She won't be impressed if you kick her butt at pool. Also, she doesn't want either of you to get all sweaty on a date.
- Any plans where you are alone at your place. You'll scare her off.

When Is a Bouquet OK?

Flowers are very powerful and loaded with meaning. They send the same message as a gift — "I'm interested." You need to be sure they will be favorably accepted before you send them. Roses are the most powerful flowers you can send. A single red rose traditionally means, "I love you." The heaviest artillery is a dozen long-stemmed American Beauties (they're dark red). Start with a small bouquet of fresh flowers. Cost? About fifteen dollars or so. This should be saved until you are convinced that there is something going on. A nice touch is to send them to her workplace. The other women will make a big fuss over her. Of course, it could backfire if you misread your status. She will have to explain why this guy she just met is coming on so strong, so soon — bad news for you.

Use flowers as an encouraging sign of interest after a few dates. If you're going to do it, send them as soon as possible after seeing her. Include a simple, light note. Don't use familiar affectionate terms like "love" just yet. The term is loaded with meaning. Something like "thanks for a memorable evening" is just fine. Don't overwhelm her after every date. Save flowers for recognition of something special. Flowers need to be unexpected to maximize their effect. Don't mention them after sending them. You are fishing for compliments or reactions — bad form. If she wants to say something, she will. Don't worry if she doesn't.

When to Present a Present

Gifts have a great deal of meaning associated with them. They speak volumes about your intentions and feelings. They are a message in themselves. First, decide if a gift is appropriate. It should not be given too early. Wait until you have dated a few times. A gift says, "I like you and I want to see you more often. I want to move the relationship along." When a woman receives a gift, she calls her friends and announces it. It's a big deal. Make sure you know what you're doing. If you give a gift too early, it may make her uncomfortable. Too much, too soon. There are three critical days that must be recognized with gifts if you are dating someone — her birthday, Valentine's Day and Christmas. Put a note on your calendar *three days before* each and be sure to come through. Although she may not complain or dump you, you will definitely pay a price. A late gift is not acceptable.

If you want to give her something on the first or second date it must be cheap, simple, creative and humorous. Something like a balloon, a key chain or a card. It should somehow relate to her, where you met, etc. Even after dating a few times, gifts should not be too expensive. Women can become uncomfortable with pricey gifts because there is the appearance that you are buying her affection. What is important is that you spend some time and put some thought into the selection. Listen for clues.

Women will often reveal their preferences. Of course, you can ask. "What is name of that fragrance you're wearing? It's really nice." Women often have a signature fragrance. What could be simpler? Often, there will be a variety of products available for the lady's favorite scent. You can't go wrong. It doesn't matter that she already has it. If she likes dolphins or teddy bears or whatever, look for a little crystal piece she can put in a special spot. Every time she looks at it, she'll think of you. Fancy picture frames are really nice, especially if she puts your picture in it (you may get beat out by her cat). Of course, as the relationship grows more serious, the ante goes up. The ultimate gift is a diamond ring. However, that is the point at which you and this book part company. Congratulations.

By the way, you may find yourself on the receiving end of a gift. It does happen. Be very gracious and grateful no matter what the gift is. *Follow up immediately with a small thank you card.* This is very important. It is an excellent opportunity to show some class.

Flattery Works

Everyone loves compliments, regardless of what they are. Don't you? A compliment should be spontaneous and genuine. Don't gush. Make a simple observation about an aspect of her appearance or better yet, her character or personality. As we noted, one or two compliments over the course of the evening are plenty.

Other Women

When you first begin to date someone there are a few basic unspoken assumptions. *She assumes that you date other women.* Whether you do or not, this is good. It increases your value in her eyes. Neither confirm nor deny. It is not a polite topic of conversation. A gentleman never tells. If you are blabbing about all the success you have had, what will you be saying about her?

Hold on to your ego. *It is very likely that she is dating other guys.* Surprise. Don't worry about it. Certainly don't ask her about it. It's none of your business at this point. You are confident. You're not worried about competition. Let the chips fall where they may. There's nothing you can do about it anyway. Keep things light. The more fun you are, the more interested she will be in seeing you again. This is something that you will get to address later if the relationship continues to develop. Patience.

Your History

You may have to answer questions about your dating past, especially if you have been married or engaged. Answer simply and factually without embellishment. She should get the idea and respect your privacy. These are not really appropriate topics for extended conversation on a first or second date.

She is either searching for fatal flaws or exhibiting some unhealthy behavior. Watch out. Change the subject. Whatever you do, don't reciprocate by asking about her past. Let her reveal it at her own pace. Be very hesitant to discuss the details. Again, this shows confidence, a very good thing.

After a few dates you should both be comfortable revealing some information. It's sort of like "you show me yours and I'll show you mine." If you reveal too much, you will feel vulnerable. If she reveals too much you will feel voyeuristic. Find a balance. The process should be like peeling away the layers of an onion. Move too fast and you'll sting your eyes.

PDAs - Public Displays of Affection

In general, PDAs are bad form. It's embarrassing to her and the folks around you. Of course, there are degrees of PDAs. We assume you're not stupid enough to grope your date. Kissing is next. Keep that act special by saving it for the right time and place in private. It is loaded with meaning. After you have dated a few times you may wish to hold hands or put your arm around her waist while you walk. There are two problems here. It may make walking any distance a bit difficult. Also, at some point you have to disengage. This can be awkward. Who makes the first move? Will anyone's feelings be hurt? This may seem trivial, but it can be an issue. We're just trying to cover the bases, guy. By the way, the same is true of the arm around her shoulders at the movies — a great way to get a cramp. We recommend you let her make the moves on PDAs. Be reactive. If she snuggles up, congratulations. It is an excellent sign.

To Osculate or To Wait?

Make the assumption that you will not be kissing on your first date. This will take some of the pressure off. Also, *you* are in control. You see, typically the man kisses the woman, although it could possibly be the reverse. The trick is to know if she would like you to do it. So, only plant one on her if she is *"asking"* you to. She will do this non-verbally. The strongest signals are touches. Your hair, face, arm and hands are prime targets. If she is stalling her departure at the car or her door she may be interested. Look for the flirting signals discussed earlier such as head tilting and preening. If you decide to go for it, keep it brief and in control.

How to Kiss

Make sure the time is right. For example, you are saying goodnight after your third successful date and things are going well. You will know if your display of affection is going to be welcome. If the time is not right, wait. If could be very awkward if she doesn't want to lock lips just yet.

Everyone will have their own way of smooching. Forget kisses anywhere but on the lips. Foreheads and hands send the wrong message. Women love to talk about this, by the way. They will rate guys on their skill. They will make assumptions about your lovemaking ability based on this first kiss. Make it count. Most of the criteria come from the movies — a great place to pick up tips. Of course, we don't want to spoil the natural dynamics of the moment but here are some ideas.

- When the moment is right, telegraph your intentions by smiling and looking deep into her eyes.
- Hold her hand with your left. Gently place your right hand along the side of her face and slowly pull her towards you.
- Slightly tilt your head so you don't bump noses.
- Close your eyes. There is a big debate about this. *Close your eyes.*
- Kiss her lips once as gently and softly as possible. Do it with feeling and warmth. Don't press into her face. *Keep your lips closed but very soft.*
- Keep it brief. *Pull back*, smile and look deeply into her eyes again.
- Tell her you had a wonderful time, *say goodnight and get out of there.* Let that kiss and that moment be the last thing she remembers as she goes to bed.

After a few dates your kissing behavior will evolve naturally. The kisses will be longer. Disengaging is always an issue. Use your judgement. If you think about taking a break, it's probably time. Better that you do it than her. Caution — women are very aware of this principle as well. After a kiss give her a smile or a hug. Kissing, of course, can become much more intimate. French, or open mouth, kissing is the obvious example. Don't neglect kissing her ears, other parts of her face and neck.

Ending a date

This can be awkward. If it is your first date, it is really quite simple. We presume that you planned the date well. You may have picked her up or met her. She knew generally what time she would be coming home. If you are driving home in the car, you are going to keep a light conversation going about anything at all. Do not start evaluating the evening. Do not ask for feedback. Simply talk to her as you would anyone else. Talk about the movie you saw, the meal, your next vacation, anything. When you arrive at her place, open the car door for her and casually walk up to her front door. Now, you have a decision to make. Be honest. Do you want a second date? *If the answer is no, tell her you had a great time, thank her for joining you, smile and say good night.* You might want to shake hands, your choice. Make sure she gets safely in her house. Turn and casually walk back to the car. Don't babble about maybe calling her or getting together sometime if it isn't going to happen. This is one of the biggest pet peeves women have. When you say you are going to call her, make sure you mean it and make sure you do. Since that's not the case here, don't even hint at it.

If you are interested in a second date, you can ask now or ask later. Remember the purpose of a first date is to get a second date. At least you want to let her know that you're interested. Of course, you had better make sure she is interested as well. The way to do that is to ask. "Would you like to do this again sometime?" She may hesitate or say maybe or flat-out "I don't think so." If that's the case be gracious and say you understand, take care and head home. It is her responsibility to give you some hint of encouragement if she wants to see you again. If not, that's that. Don't take it personally. It just didn't work out. You had a pleasant evening, you had a chance to practice your dating skills, you had a successful date. It's just that you won't be having another one with this particular woman. Don't call. Move on.

"You Said You Would Call"

On the other hand, if she indicates that she would be interested, be very specific about what you are going to do. This is not the best time to try to make plans for next weekend. She needs to think about you a bit. This is to your advantage. You don't want to appear desperate. Give her an exact day when you will call with a suggestion. *Put it on your calendar and make absolutely certain that you come through.* "Karen, that's great. I will call you early Tuesday evening and we can talk about it. Is that a good time?" Now she has a chance to be sure she can take the call. If you are not going to able to call, (and there better be a good reason) call earlier and tell her so. Seriously. If you blow the call, you will either lose the date or have a less-than-warm welcome when you pick her up. *Women make a big deal about this.* Many of them have had the experience where a guy drops them off and says he will call, then doesn't. They hate that. It's one of their biggest complaints about dating. You can really shine if you handle this right.

Don't Hang Around

It would be a big mistake to spoil a perfectly good evening by overstaying your welcome. It would be much better if you left before she was ready to let you go (within reason). *Go home.* If you feel some compulsion to extend things, send her a little something in the next day or two. A card or a very simple bouquet is more than enough. Make certain that it is light and fun.

Obsessive-Compulsive?

If things went very well on your first date or two, here is a recipe for disaster.
• Call her two or three times a day
• Visit her at work
• Show up at her place and say you were just in the neighborhood and . . .
• Send her an expensive present
• Tell her friends how crazy you are about her
• Tell your friends that you have found Ms. Right
• Send her mom flowers

GET A GRIP! You are out of control. Yikes. She will head for the hills and might even call the cops. Of course, we have exaggerated a bit. However, we have heard of guys who have done all of the above. So what should you do if you feel the urge to hear her sweet voice? *Make certain that the primary reason you are calling is to reinforce your friendship with her.* The call should be as much about her needs as yours. She should welcome your call, not be annoyed by it. Listen to her tone very carefully. If you sense the slightest coolness, cut the call short and give her a few days to stabilize. She needs to know that you have a life outside of the few dates you shared with her.

As far as your wild impulses are concerned — let your madness run in private. Call a close friend or two and ask them to help you get through your anxiety. Count to ten, meaning wait a day or two when you feel the urge to call. The best idea is to go work out. Physical activity will help to reduce the chemical levels that are driving you nuts. Remember — never let 'em see you sweat!

By the way, are you so *sure* that things went as well as you think? Maybe she was just being polite. Here's a thought. *You don't like everyone that you date so why would you expect everyone to like you?*

"Sorry, I'm Busy"

People get busy. An interesting observation is that often the busier a person is, the more interesting they are. Of course, this can work against you. She may not be as available as you would prefer. If you are really interested in her you will have to continue to extend invitations in spite of her difficult schedule. If she is interested, she may suggest an alternative day or time. On the other hand, she may be so jammed up that it may not be possible. Is she starting a new job, registering for classes, moving or taking care of a sick relative? Be patient. Give her a call every week or two and suggest a pleasant evening after chatting for a while. If you suspect that she is "conveniently" busy every time you call or ask her out, that is a different story. This can be difficult to ascertain. You may detect coolness in her tone or she may cut your conversations short. If you come to this conclusion, back off. Try her again in a month or so.

You are in a strong position at this point. With some actual experience you should be able to plan and deliver a successful date. As you continue the dating process, things begin to get more complicated. You may find that your feelings are growing rather quickly. You need a reality check. Take a deep breath and consider what all this really means.

Chapter 22
Dating Psychology 101

"Friendship is seldom lasting but between equals, or where the superiority on one side is reduced by some equivalent advantage on the other."
— *Samuel Johnson, The Rambler, 1750.*

Advance Dating Psychology

Everyone has a hole in his heart. One of the critical aspects constantly before us is to fill this emptiness in exactly the right way. It is a shifting target as we grow. Others are rarely able to perceive the exact nature of these needs and we seldom completely reveal them. The responsibility for the fulfillment of these needs is our own. We must attempt to assess the ability of others to complete our emotional lives. This is, of course, what women are doing constantly. Listen to them. They will tell you.

Now, from your perspective, if you *honestly* believe that you can or do fulfill these needs for her, you are well on your way. Your task, should you accept it, is to deliver what she needs gradually through the dating process *without being overt*. You see, her needs are in her subconscious. You must be clever enough to perceive them and deliver the right words and actions at the right time. This is not easy but the rewards for both of you are great. If you do this gradually and consistently over time she will do the rest. She will fall in love you all by herself because *that is the way that it happens*. If you are the source of her emotional fulfillment, she will forgive your minor flaws, exaggerate your strengths and sell you to herself, her family and her friends. You have certainly witnessed this among the women you have known — sisters, friends, cousins.

Another critical element must be present for love to have a chance and it is tough to accomplish. She must be somewhat *uncertain* about you. People want what they can't have. That's why extremely wealthy people sometimes go over the edge. What is left to achieve or acquire? Our ancient genes tell us to seek — to strive for something better. *You need to be that something.* It is a matter of being less available than she would prefer. How do you do this?

187

Be yourself. Live your life. Let her try to find a place in it. Be aware that women will often behave in this manner.

Your relationship with her has its proper place in your life. You are interested and attentive but she must share your time and resources with others — family, friends, and yes, other women, at least at first. Never give the impression that she is the only one after two dates. She does not deserve an exclusive relationship with the likes of you unless you are convinced that *your* emotional needs will be met. This is an attitude that will keep you from degenerating into a blubbering blob of romantic desperation. Yuck.

Don't Live to Love, Love to Live

This independence is not an arrogant or rude mode of behavior. That would be false and unattractive to women you would like to date. No, you are just a "most happy fella." You were happy before you met her and if things don't work out you will be happy afterwards. Of course, she must believe that you would be much happier in love with her.

So this is the secret. It's not a Porsche, ripped abs or the right pair of sunglasses. *You fill her emotional shopping cart by being an interested, attentive guy who really cares.* You are a pleasure to be with because you are basically happy with yourself and your life. Things are just better when you are around. She misses you when you are away, even if she doesn't reveal it. She is not even sure why. At the same time, you walk this earth as a free and independent spirit with apologies to no one for managing your destiny. This is a very powerful aphrodisiac. You will find a lot of support to achieve this attitude in the other chapters of this book. We are behind you. Go for it.

Let's explore this psychology with a sales analogy. Consider the selling of magazines. They are fairly simple to produce and are available everywhere just like men. However, there are companies and sales people who will go to great lengths to convince you to buy their magazines. This is a tough sell. After all, you have lived this long without their product.
- They will brag about the wonderful benefits of their product, i.e. "I'm the best thing that ever happened to women."
- They will reveal their emotional investment in the sale by appearing overeager and needy, i.e. "Why don't you want to go out with me?"
- They may attempt to make you feel guilty if you don't buy, i.e. "I'm going join the French Foreign Legion if you don't go out with me."

What is your gut-level reaction to these sales tactics? Exactly. *Let me outta here!*

Consider the master fisherman. He carefully studies the natural inclinations and behavior of the trout. He makes certain that his bait is exactly what the trout would find attractive. He may spend hours tying his own flies. He carefully selects the best spot where the most desirable trout are likely to congregate. He chooses a time of day when they are likely to feed. He studies the phases of the moon. Then being as quiet and unobtrusive as possible, he displays his bait, not himself, to the fish. He carefully moves it in ways that the trout finds irresistible. When the trout commits by striking the bait, he commits by setting the hook at exactly the right time. The master fisherman has knowledge, patience and timing. And now some questions for you:

- *How is your bait?* Are you as attractive and desirable as you could be? How much effort have you invested, or are you willing to invest? Can you catch a prize trout with a wad of chewing gum?
- *Do you know where to fish?* Are you still wasting time at bars? What lengths are you willing to go to in order to find the best fishing holes? Are you even trying? Can you catch trout in your bathtub?
- *Do you understand the behavior of the trout?* Do women confuse you? Have you studied their natural inclinations? Do you have lady friends that you can really talk to? Have you read any of the popular books on the subject? Fisherman are well aware that trout will swim upstream at a certain time every year.
- *Do you have a feel for timing?* Do you know when to approach, ask for a date, pull back or come on strong? This is a delicate, learned skill. Experience is the best teacher. Are you trying and learning? Does your fishing line break often?
- *Are you quiet and unobtrusive?* Do you gush about your feelings or are you cool? Do you whine, plead, beg, get angry or generally annoy? How is your self-confidence? Are you living large? Are you living for yourself? Do you display quiet strength? Do you scare the fish?
- *Have you mastered your technique?* Do you know how to treat a lady? Can you plan a date? Can you carry on a great conversation? Do you know how to listen? Can you dance? Do you know how to kiss a girl and when? Are you a good lover? Expert fishermen have complete knowledge of their sport.
- *Are you serious about catching fish?* Are you just passing time by dating? (That's OK, we're just checking.) Are you ready to advance through the stages of commitment when the conditions are right? If the master fisherman does not land the trout, his skills improve and he waits for a better day.

Compatibility Is Overrated

Everyone talks about it. "It's so cool. We like *all* the same things." While this sure makes things easier, it is not as essential as you might believe. The reason is that the common definition of compatibility is *common interests or tastes*. Have your friendships evolved because you both liked Chinese food, the Yankees and reggae? Hardly. Common interests and tastes are very good. They help the relationship along. However, you can have a deep, meaningful relationship with someone in spite of a lack of "compatibility." Conversely, we could put you in an elevator with someone who matches your interests and tastes perfectly and they would scare the daylights out of you.

An interesting twist on this is that people can get along very nicely if their incompatibilities line up. You may have experienced this with roommates. She hates to drive on long trips while you love it. You can't match a pair of socks — her lipstick is keyed to her car interior. You get the idea. It could be a good thing.

The real compatibility you should strive for concerns value systems and life issues. How serious to get and how fast, children, religion, where to live, etc. These are the things that absolutely must line up.

The Whole Package

When you are first dating things are simple. You are spending time with only her. As you advance to steady dating and then to a relationship everything changes. You are now expected to accept her friends, family and that darned cat. This is a good chance to see if you have a future with her. Observe how she treats those close to her. That is the way you will eventually be treated. Observe the way they treat her. Do you think you could fit in? *The closer you become, the more of her life you will have to share.* Of course, the reverse is true. How willing is she to become part of *your* reality? Keep a close eye on this. Many men make the mistake of thinking they can have the relationship without the trappings. Wrong. You have to take the whole package.

Reverse Roles

It may be helpful to imagine what is going on in a woman's mind. Great generals use this technique. What would I do if I were in his shoes — attack, retreat? Of course, the more you know about her, the easier it is. Consider her whole life experience — work, friends, family, finances, etc. Try to walk through her day in your mind. What is it really like to be her? Once you think you have an idea, consider your behavior. If you were her, how would you react to what you are doing? What would you want from a suitor? When you proceed from her needs instead of yours, your odds of success improve. This is not to say that you should ignore your own feelings. We are suggesting that you adjust the *pace* and *intensity* of your attention to match her ability to accept it.

It All Comes Down To Compromise In The End

Show us a perfect match. It's impossible. Eventually, you make *some* compromise. You may have heard of the 80/20 rule — usually stated that 20 percent of the people do 80 percent of the work. Think of it this way. If someone meets 80 percent of your expectations and the most serious stuff is in there, can you live without the 20 percent? It will be hard work with lots of compromise and frustration. Take a look at some veteran couples you know. Ask them how they managed to get through twenty-five years of marriage. Ask them if they are a perfect match. It will open your eyes. To those of you waiting for the perfect woman to come along, please rethink your criteria. Growing old alone is very sad, especially if it isn't necessary.

When men prioritize their lives, they typically put their careers at the top of the heap. They define themselves by their job. I'm an account executive. I'm a fireman. Many men have a very difficult time when they retire because they lose a big piece of their identity. Now they must say, "I used to be in insurance." They will talk endlessly about it. Women often place their relationships and family lives very high on the list. This continues throughout their lives. Maybe that's one reason they live longer than men. Families continue and outlive us. Of course, many women have very productive careers as well. The point is that for most women, her relationship is a big part of her identity. Look at the process after an engagement. She gets a diamond ring. Her friends go nuts and throw parties and showers. Her family plans and pays for the wedding. It's all about her. That's fine, just recognize it. *A relationship is a very important thing to a woman.*

Time

Time can work for you or against you. It's your choice. *If you expect to develop a relationship very quickly, you will find that it ends as quickly.* You can't ramp up too fast.

Consider nature. Some plants grow very quickly. They complete their life cycles in a matter of weeks or months. Common weeds are a good example — here in May, gone in October. Now think about the most successful plants — the redwoods, oaks and some evergreens. All develop very slowly, some over hundreds of years. They become strong and resistant to the destructive effects of the environment. On the other hand, some weeds are crushed underfoot. The species survives by being numerous.

If you *slowly and patiently* address a woman's emotional needs over an extended period of time (at least a year) you greatly increase the chances of long-term success. You have to be in for the long haul — she can depend on you. You will see much weeping and gnashing of teeth if a woman loses the services of someone that she has come to depend on, such as a hairdresser or her favorite aerobics instructor. *You* become a habit. She will turn to you to discuss good news or bad. You always seem to know the right thing to say (more later about how to do this). View the movie, *When Harry Met Sally*. Given enough time you will know each other very well and have an enjoyable time along the way. This, my friend, is the genesis of true love. Why? Because you have become a true friend.

Now, what about "casual dating?" This is a great term. Dating should be casual. It shouldn't be serious or formal. It should be fun. All this philosophy is a bit heavy for your second date — very true. You must still conduct yourself using the above guidelines. You want to be a great date. If you discover that things are not going to work out early on — so what? You had the pleasure of a few enjoyable dates, increased your networking, polished your skills and learned a bit. You also made a nice acquaintance. You will be an even greater catch down the road. And so it goes. You move from date to date getting stronger all the time. On occasion you dwell on one lady for awhile if everything seems right. During these relationships you do your best to make them grow and succeed. With luck (it does have something to do with it) you will go the distance and make the ultimate commitment. When that happens be sure to give this book to a single pal.

Trust

Before his successful career on late night television, Johnny Carson had a show called "Who Do You Trust?" So, who do *you* trust? Why? In all likelihood you trust many family members — probably your parents. Hopefully, you do trust Mom and Dad. The people you trust would not harm you. They have your best interests at heart. They listen to your dreams, hopes and problems. They intend to continue to love you for the rest of their lives. They display genuine affection for you. It has been this way for many years — as long as you can remember. Of course, you reciprocate. You know a day will come when they will depend on you and you will have their complete trust. So, now that you have a working definition of trust, consider the opposite.

We are not speaking of people you don't trust because they have harmed or betrayed you. Think about the first time that you encountered a new group of people — perhaps the first day at a new school, college or a job. At that moment, instinctively, you trust *no one*. Your internal, subconscious mechanisms are urging you to remain free and detached. In this way you remain safe from emotional harm. In this setting, if one person approaches you and is very aggressive about your being his friend and trusting him, what is your natural reaction? You will pull back to preserve your freedom and uncommitted status. The more this person persists — the more you resist.

There is a tale about a competition between the sun and the wind. The wind insisted that it was stronger. As proof, the wind offered to blow the coat off a man walking down a road. Of course, the harder Mr. Wind blew, the tighter the man held his coat close to his body. When it was time for the sun to try, he quietly glowed as warmly as possible. Naturally, the man relaxed and became warm enough to remove his coat. Good lesson.

Now that you have a sense for this natural reaction, you should assume that it is present in every woman you encounter. They have heard it all. Guys have been hitting on them since they got their first training bra. The more attractive and desirable the woman, the more BS she has heard. Therefore, she will have sophisticated internal defenses to overt advances and proclamations of never-ending love. If this is your approach, what makes you think that you are different from all the other guys who have tried? The answer, of course, is that you are not. So what's a guy to do?

Choose your words carefully. What we mean is stay away from any conversation that even hints at fencing her in down the road. Women have built-in radar that looks for meaning in every phrase. They also have perfect recall. (On the sixteenth of last month he said he was considering trading in his sports car for something a bit bigger. Kids?) Men are very loose with their conversation. Be extremely careful about what you say. Keep things light at first.

For example, one mistake amateur gardeners make with seedlings is to kill them by overwatering or overfertilizing. A plant must be strong and mature enough to handle that kind of attention.

A few points to consider:

- Avoid talking about the future, unless it's yours. When you do, don't include her in it.
- Don't hint at future plans for trips or occasions. "Would you rather spend Christmas with my folks or yours?" This is the kiss of death if it's July and your third date.
- Don't send letters or leave cute messages on her answering machine early in the process. If you feel sudden romantic urges, go work out or write them in a private journal she will never see. (We once heard of a guy who recorded every voice message a woman left him while they were dating and then played them for her. She freaked.)
- Don't tell her how attracted you are to her. Keep your feelings to yourself.
- *Let your actions speak for themselves.* Listening to her and sharing in those parts of her life that she is willing to share is more valuable than rattling on about how smitten you are.
- *Get your time frame in perspective.* It takes several months to get to a meaningful emotional level with a woman. You should not be talking about serious commitment for a least a year.

Have you decided that this may be the girl for you? Hold on. Building a strong relationship takes some skill and effort. You may have to change your evil ways. Make her your friend first.

Chapter 23
Friends First

*"Friendship makes prosperity more shining
and lessens adversity by dividing and sharing it."*
— Cicero, On Friendship, c. 44 BC.

Make a New Friend

Although you are very familiar with friendship, stop and think about it for a moment. You acquire friends easily and naturally over time. Most people don't have to work at it. It just happens. Of course, most of your friends are guys. This makes it easy. If you do not already have platonic friends who are women, we urge you to make an effort to do so. *If you can be successful at becoming friends with a woman you have the basis for building a relationship with any woman.* You need to develop the skills and have the experience. Also, you can never have too many friends.

Becoming friends with a woman means meeting her needs as a person.
- You must know her well enough to understand what is going on in her life, good and bad.
- You let her know in simple, gentle ways that you sincerely care for her. You need to be careful at the beginning that this is not too overt. A smile or a little hug will do.
- You think enough of her to be tolerant — no matter what happens or how she reacts. You're not a fair-weather friend.
- You are in touch on a regular basis, perhaps once a week — maybe more, maybe less.
- You are a regular source of positive reinforcement. You notice improvements or successes.
- You naturally become a valuable part of her world over time. She will find herself calling you and depending on you.

Doesn't this sound like a true friend? It's not so hard to do. Actually, what could be more pleasant than to have this sort of relationship with someone you have romantic plans for? Of course, it doesn't stop here. There is much more. However, without this basis any future relationship will have little chance of success. Be certain that your motives are pure. It would be dishonest to pretend to establish a friendship with a woman only to lure her to bed.

How to Listen

Display positive body language. If you were listening to your choice of the most fascinating person in history, how would you behave? Would you be looking around, shaking your foot and fidgeting? No, you would be so fascinated and spellbound that you would not twitch. You would maintain steady eye contact. You would not want to miss a single detail. Behave this way when you listen to her. An occasional nod of the head or other acknowledgment will let her know you are with her.

Don't interrupt. Let her have the floor. Don't bring in your own issues. She needs to know that she can roll on as long as she likes and you will hang with her. She may wander through five different topics. She may need to just vent. Let her run down on her own.

Rephrase when invited. She may pause or look to you for affirmation or reaction. She may ask what you think. *Never give an opinion or judgment.* The only effective response is to reframe what she has said in your own words. This is also an opportunity to provide some empathy. Give the floor back to her as soon as possible.

When you are sure she is completely done, give her hand a squeeze or give her a hug if it seems welcome. Suggest that you do something simple and pleasant for some relief. Go out for ice cream or catch a romantic comedy. Watch for signs that she wants to be alone and respect it. Tell her to call anytime she needs to talk. You'll be there for her.

She needs to believe that she is important and valuable in your eyes. *If you show genuine respect and admiration for her, she will continue to seek reinforcement from you.* She cannot do it for herself. Think of the people in your own life who have provided praise for your better qualities and successes. Don't you hold these people in high esteem? You know that they wish the best for you. They are your fans. If you really care for her provide her with a great cheering section.

This admiration must be sincere and based on your understanding and knowledge of her. This takes time and effort. Learn what is important to her. What is she trying to accomplish in her life? What are the challenges she faces? What qualities and talents does she possess to help her succeed? These are the things you need to praise. Don't forget to link all this to you. These qualities are a big part of the reason she is so important to you. She needs to know that.

Control

An emerging relationship will be driven in one of three ways. In some instances both parties move at the same speed, come to the same conclusion and become equally vested. This is rare, but it happens. *Typically, the process is nudged along by one or the other.* Either situation can be a very good thing. You need to understand the dynamics of each situation in order to monitor and adjust your behavior.

If she is pressing the issue, you have little to do. The laws of nature would suggest that this is an atypical scenario. We mean that as men we prefer to pursue. When hunting is not necessary our perspective may become confused. It is pleasant to have the attention of a woman who is very interested. This presumes that the attention is welcome, meaning that the woman is a potential match based on your needs and criteria. If that is the case, you will control the pace by providing the appropriate amount of emotional intimacy and time. Of course, this must be genuine behavior. *What we are suggesting is that you should control yourself, not her.* The reason you must do this is to make certain that enough time is provided for the relationship to properly develop. (If you allow the pace to be controlled by her emotions, you could find yourself addressing wedding invitations in a few weeks and wondering what happened.) By the way, if you find yourself in this situation often, why are you reading this book? Send us an e-mail and let the rest of us know what you're doing right!

Typically, you will be trying to win the heart of the woman of your dreams. This is a challenging set of circumstances. You must recognize that you are being driven more or less by your emotions. We hope that it is *less.* Your interest is a combination of your chemical balance (or imbalance) and your belief that this woman has great potential as a match. We don't want to drain all the fun out of this. However, the plain truth is that the more you are driven by your emotions, the lower your chance of success. In this situation, you are much more emotionally dependent than she is. *You improve the balance by encouraging her to become more emotionally involved with you.* When you proceed in this way, you will have much more control over the process. Of course, there will be significantly more work and thought required on your part. You must treat the endeavor as a delicate negotiation.

Avoid ultimatums. In general, they are a poor strategy. What you are doing is insisting on a guarantee of behavior in the future to avoid the consequences of your threat. This is no way to conduct a loving relationship. An example from the woman's perspective might be, "If you don't give me an engagement ring by Christmas, we're through." Ultimatums typically start with "if." When you issue one, she will feel threatened. She will not feel closer to you. You will have to monitor her to ensure that she meets your terms. Trust will evaporate. Ultimatums should be a very last resort. They should only be connected to very serious issues. An example would be, "Gina, I am very concerned about your drinking. I care about you and your health. You should get some help, in spite of what you have said. I'm sorry, but if you refuse to work on your problem, I can't continue with our relationship the way it is today."

Going back to the engagement ring example; it may or may not be appropriate. If the two of you have been exclusive for a few years and you are in your late thirties, she may have a valid point. Often ultimatums are based on emotion and a grab for control. These are seldom successful. Avoid ultimatums as much as possible. Also avoid submitting to them.

Building an Emotional Link

This is a basic requirement for love to grow. It may well be the very definition of love. We don't mean to be presumptuous, after all, poets and philosophers have been trying to define love for centuries. We know that women (and men) become dependent on those who meet their emotional needs. If you really have feelings for a woman, how can you build a bridge to her heart? How can you win her love?

You need to be part of her life. You cannot live three thousand miles away. Maybe movie stars can do the bicoastal thing; we'll never know. However, if you are not physically present to listen to her heart and share large parts of her life, you don't stand a chance. E-mail, phone calls, letters and pictures won't do it. You need to be able to look into her baby blues. She will fall in love with the man who is listening to her dreams, pain and day-to-day trivia. Women do this for each other. Bartenders are good at it. You need to be the guy she turns to. You have to be there. You must be in regular contact with her. She needs to be able to contact you easily at her convenience. If you live three hundred miles away, this is almost impossible. Successful long-distance relationships work because the parties were already committed before the separation. *If she is not in your presence on a fairly frequent basis, there is little chance for success.*

Men are not good natural conversationalists. We tend to debate and engage in one-upmanship. We talk over each other and yell. We are competitive and advance all our opinions at one time like a rap artist. This is fine for football games. You need some training for success with her. *The secret is to be a great listener.* Everyone loves good listeners. They are non-judgmental, empathetic and involved. They are a mirror of ourselves. When a woman opens up her heart (remember, that's where you want to be) she will turn to the person who listens and satisfies her need to be understood. When you get an opportunity to be that guy, make the best of it. It is an invitation and the best chance you will have to get close to her.

- *Set the stage* – Provide the right environment and prepare yourself. Provide a quiet, private setting if possible. She will appreciate your thoughtfulness. Tell yourself that you are going to give her your complete attention for as long as necessary. You have all the time in the world. She is important to you. Get a couple of drinks and use the restroom. Visualize how you are going to behave and deliver.

- *Chill out* – Play Buddha. Sit quietly and calmly. Don't distract her with fidgeting and interruptions. When you are not really interested in what is going on, you shake your foot, look at your watch, rip up napkins and chew on straws. Imagine you are going to see a great movie. Relax and give her all the time she needs to get it all out.
- *Keep your mouth shut* – Listening involves the ears, not the mouth. The ratio should be about ten to one in favor of listening. You would do it for your boss. You did it in school. REALLY listen.
- *Send supportive non-verbal signals* – Keep your eyes riveted on hers. Gently nod your head from time to time. If she gets upset, hold her hand or give her a little hug.
- *Give her an occasional word of support* – Listen for pauses and insert a few words that summarize what she has said. Be certain that you are not offering opinions, suggestions or judgments. That is not what she wants. She needs to completely express herself. You can help her by parroting back some of what she has said in your own words, letting her know that you are really tuned in to what she is saying.
- *Be certain you understand your role* – She isn't talking to you because you are such a genius that you will have the answers to all her problems. She doesn't want constructive criticism, analysis or sage advice. She just wants you to *listen, understand and be empathetic.* That is enough.
- *Always be there for her* – Let her know that she can call you day or night if she needs to talk. Do your best to accommodate her. Of course, you need to be on guard for dysfunctional behavior. If she is constantly in crisis and emotional need, she may need a doctor, not a boyfriend. Nevertheless, every time she turns to you it's one more point for your team.

Do you really care for her? Do you have her best interests at heart? Do you want the relationship to move along? While we warn against flowery proclamations of never-ending love, there is nothing wrong and everything right with letting her know that you value her as a person. You admire her. You support her in her struggle to achieve her goals. You want her to do well in her job. You want her to get along with her mother. You are not just another pretty face. You are a guy who cares. You show this care by listening to her, building her up and giving meaningful praise. There is a critical difference between this and expressing your emotional attachment to her. Think about it. She gets to receive rather than being *asked* to give. Don't worry, when the time comes she will figure out that in order to keep all that good stuff coming she is going to have to give up some freedom and independence. You will see the love light in her eyes. It all takes time and patience.

Sympathy or Empathy?

Do you know the difference? It's very important. People generally reject sympathy but welcome empathy. When we are sympathetic we feel sorry for someone. We pity them. When you are empathetic you identify with her emotional status. You understand and share. There is a big difference. You can feel sympathy for people in crisis on the other side of the world. Unless you are actually there to share and interact, you can't really be empathetic. *Learn to express empathy.* It takes more effort on your part but the emotional deposit you make will yield great benefits. Of course, it must be sincere. If you don't really feel it, don't try to fake it. She will know and it will be curtains. By the way, if the relationship moves forward, you will be the beneficiary of empathy from her in hard times.

Keys to Emotional Connection

Listen – Be the one she calls when she really needs to talk. You will not always be especially interested in what she has to say. Learn to listen actively. This is a golden opportunity to make an emotional connection.

Nurture – Provide reassurance and strokes. This can be overdone easily. Look for opportunities to praise her actions and successes. Of course, occasional compliments on her appearance don't hurt.

Empathize – She needs to sense that you really care about her concerns. Share her pain. Use the skills we outline to properly express your support.

Persevere – Be consistent. Don't just call when you feel the need. Contact her on a regular basis, but mix it up. You must balance this in order to prevent the perception that you are needy or desperate. She needs to sense that the level of contact is appropriate. You can judge this by how welcome she makes you feel. Encourage her to call you if she wishes.

Keeping Her Off Balance

At the beginning of the dating dance, you are a blank slate. She knows very little about you. She will be interested in filling in the blanks. In business, she would call references and check you out. Neither of you will have that opportunity. Remember, if she is totally convinced of your intense feelings for her she will lose interest. It's human nature. You have probably had the same experience once or twice. Did you ever have a girl calling you and stopping by at your locker at school, embarrassing you in front of your friends? Well, if you didn't, just imagine it. It's a real turn-off. She needs to be a bit unsure about you. This is not game playing. It is just being prudent. You don't want to reveal large chunks of yourself too soon. A bit of mystique is good. *Here are some tips.*

- *Remember, silence can be golden.* Every once in awhile try a graceful pause in the conversation. Every second does not have to be filled with witty repartee. She will be dying to know what you are thinking. Let her wonder. You are entitled to the privacy of your thoughts. Of course, use good timing. Don't do it at her mother's dinner table — maybe while driving home from a date or waiting for a table.

- *There are other hens in the barnyard.* This is not easy to pull off. It is a good thing if she is convinced that you are seeing other women. You cannot directly inform her of this fact. It doesn't even have to be the case. If the subject of a recent movie comes up, let her know you saw it (be sure this is true.) She will wonder who you went with. Guys rarely go to the movies together. Try these words out: *"I have plans."* They can be used when the general topic of next weekend comes up. Let her overhear you talking about other women she doesn't know in group conversations. "Hey Bill, you should see Karen's new car. She looks great in it." Your date will be wondering who the hell Karen is and why she looks so great. We know this seems a bit dirty, but it is for the best. Besides, are you positive that she is not seeing anyone else? Is that OK with you? Remember, you can't control her social schedule any more than she can control yours. *Never give her the impression that she is the only one you are seeing.* Unfortunately, you can't just tell her. Hence, all the intrigue. Just don't overdo it. All she needs is the impression, not the details. *Gentlemen don't tell.*
- *Dating her is not your number one priority.* Don't forget — you have a life. Every once in awhile try changing your plans. Careful here. We are not suggesting that you be inconsiderate or unreliable. It would be interesting if you had to call and cancel your plans for a good reason with sufficient advance notice. (Be sure it's not her office Christmas party.) If you have a date for dinner and a movie on Friday and you have seen her for five straight weeks, call on Tuesday and beg off. Simply say that something has come up that you need to take care of. Apologize and let her think about it. This works better if you have future plans together. Don't discuss what you were doing. It's none of her business. After all, there is no ring on your left hand.
- *Disappear for a while.* This is the ultimate confidence shaker. It takes a lot of nerve. After a few really good dates, stop calling. Why would you do this? Well, if you are interested in her and she seems aloof and only mildly interested, you have a bit of a problem. You need a paradigm shift. She needs to try the shadows outside the sunshine of your love. It might backfire, but then at least you know. You are calling in all bets early in the game. It doesn't work unless you hold your ground for a couple of weeks. Get busy. She may call or send you a card. If she does, congrats. You're on your way. If it doesn't work, you probably didn't have anything to begin with.
- *Don't forget to come back strong.* The idea is keep her off balance, not knock her off her feet. If you don't extend some hope along with, or after, the doubt the fire will go out. Again, timing is everything. You need to

have some sense of where her head is. If you have let her sit for a while, call and chat. Maybe send a little gift — something friendly and humorous like a coffee mug. You can find these items in gift stores. They can say anything you like. The idea is to create a bit of drama. The art world knows this as *tension and release*. How can you have a happy ending if there is no conflict or doubt in the middle of the play? It is more fun to watch the raging surf than a still pond.

Overcoming Resistance

So, you are executing to the best of your ability by building emotional dependence on you and creating an ebb and flow through doubt and reassurance. Slam dunk? Not likely. This isn't computer programming. There are no expected outcomes. Anything can happen. When objections present themselves you need a strategy.

It is hard to say what might be on her mind. She really likes you and you do all the right things. You sense that something is holding her back. It could be anything. Maybe she has unresolved feelings about another guy. Maybe there are family issues. She may have financial or employment problems. It could be that there is something about you as a person that bothers her such as religion or marital history. These are things she is not likely to want to discuss with you on her own. What you have is the desired emotional link in her heart and cognitive resistance in her head. Be sure that you are not just being paranoid. If you believe this to be the case, you must step in.

- *Intervene at the right time.* When you catch her in a despondent mood, sit her down for a chat. You are not threatened. You are not angry. You are concerned. You care. She probably wants to talk but doesn't know how to approach it. You will offer an opportunity for her to open up.
- *Be sure she is ready to talk and has something to say.* There is a familiar ping-pong game that goes on between men and women. He: "What's wrong." She: "Nothing." We don't know why they do it but they do. Well, maybe there *is* nothing wrong. Just say, "Ok, I thought I sensed something and I care and I want to listen." She wants to be coaxed to open up. Remain available and try some non-verbal supportive looks and touches. Let her know that you are ready and waiting until she is ready.
- *Listen with care and empathy.* You can't fake it. You should be empathetic to her needs. You should want her to be happy. Otherwise you should be questioning the value of the relationship itself. You may be reaching beyond your natural inclinations to provide what she needs but it is worth it.

Just Friends

If you have been friends with a woman and want to switch to dating mode, don't despair. Remember that the best chance for a successful relationship begins with being friends. Unfortunately, not everyone realizes that. Sometimes women tend to categorize men and if you are in the friend category it can be difficult to move up. Indeed, she may have her own reasons why you are just a friend. Changing this requires patience and persistence. If you continue to become a desirable part of her life over an extended period, there's hope. Consider this an advantage.

If things have been going along at a steady pace for several months you will have to shake things up before making a move. The point is to turn her impression of you around and put her off balance. She is used to thinking of you as a friend and has become quite comfortable with you. While this is a good thing, you need a shake-up. Let her sense a coming change in the weather. You will have to get creative. This could be any combination of moves. Change your appearance, habits and behavior. Don't be too shocking. You just need to let her see you in a different light.

When you get to the point where you would like to introduce her to the idea of changing her impression of the relationship, here's some help:
- Rent the movie *When Harry Met Sally* – it's good research for this topic.
- *Keep your emotions under control.* You are at two different levels. You can't expect her to suddenly feel the same way as you.
- *Pick the right time and place.* Find a period where things have gone well for a few weeks and she seems very close to you. Choose an evening when everything has gone perfectly and she is in a great frame of mind. Be prepared to abort your plan if the situation is not optimal and wait for a better time.
- Reveal your wish to become more than friends but give her the option to continue things the way they are.
- *Give her all the time she needs to think about it.* Don't expect an immediate reaction — it will lessen your chances. As a matter of fact, insist that she say nothing right now.
- Give her a big smile, a kiss on the cheek and *get out of there.*
- *Wait.* Don't bring it up again. Give her a few days, then call and suggest getting together for something light and fun with no conditions. Make her broach the subject when you see her next. Don't worry. She's thinking about it because she values your friendship.

Keeping Your Sanity

You need to get in touch with the yearnings that you feel deep inside. Realize that this emptiness (if you feel it) is a *lack of emotional intimacy and sharing.* Men often attempt to satisfy this need with a series of quick physical relationships. Unfortunately, we never experience the satisfaction that we need in this way.

Consider the analogy of hunger. We all get hungry every day. Our bodies require fuel. You have many choices to satisfy this need. You could binge on chocolate, potato chips and ice cream. This will bring immediate but very temporary satisfaction. The junk food is readily available and tastes great while you are consuming it. However, it will not nourish your body and sustain it. A well-balanced meal takes time to prepare and the satisfaction and benefits must be delayed until your body digests and processes the nutrients. Also, you must continue to eat in a healthy way to achieve real, long-lasting satisfaction in the form of good health.

Building a good relationship with a worthy partner is similar to preparing and consuming a steady diet of healthy foods over a period of time. It may help to think of dating as nurturing your emotional health in the same way. While an occasional piece of pie won't hurt you, we all know the end result of meaningless excess.

Reel Life

Television, movies and popular song lyrics have polluted our minds with misinformation about the true nature of relationships. They set standards beyond anyone's realistic expectations. The process is subtle. The words to the song play over and over again in your head. Reruns reinforce situations completely divorced from what we can expect to experience.

Films, songs, romance novels and television require interesting plots that encapsulate romantic notions for their entertainment value. Cultural myths are favorite devices for this purpose. You will notice them frequently once you are aware. The problem is that many people become so conditioned to these ideas that they accept them as fact. Here are a few popular examples you will recognize:

- Love will find a way.
- True love lasts forever.
- There is one true love for every person on earth.
- You will know your true love the moment you meet her. Love at first sight is real.
- Love is all you need.
- Love conquers all.

If you have thought about the material in the previous chapters, you already know the reality of these popular notions.

In the movies and on television incredibly beautiful actresses are thrown into highly dramatic situations with powerful, exciting actors. As they prevail against incredible odds they end up in immediate, passionate scenes of carefully staged lovemaking. Millions of dollars, months of production time and dozens of professionals are dedicated to freeing you from your humdrum life for ninety minutes of fantasy. The wilder and more removed the illusion is, the more attractive it becomes. All this is well and good unless we begin to draw comparisons with our real lives. Why can't I experience romance like that? Harrison Ford always seems to say exactly the right thing to get the girl.

Unfortunately, we sometimes carry over these expectations into our lives. Worse yet, women will do this and be burdened with a life of continual disappointment. Obviously, real life is not just like the movies and television. Did you ever notice how we never get to see what happens after the proverbial happy ending? Do they get married and have kids? Do they rent for a while or buy a house right away? How does he get along with her mother? What is he going to do for a living? Will she continue to work after the kids come along? Who takes out the garbage? Well, of course, the actors move on to the next project (and their next romance or marriage). You, on the other hand, have to deal with all that mundane stuff. Enjoy the entertainment, but put it in the same category as fairy tales and nursery rhymes.

It may take quite awhile to develop your friendship and move toward a relationship. Once you get there, things change quite a bit. If you are serious, you will want to do things right. There is a lot to consider.

Chapter 24
This Is Getting Serious

"Men always want to be a woman's first love – women like to be a man's last romance."
— Oscar Wilde, *A Woman of No Importance*, 1893.

Meeting Her Friends and Family

If she invites you to a party or to meet her family, this is a major sign. Make no mistake about it, Bud. You are about to be put on display. Don't panic. She will prep the audience by telling them all your good points. Her image is on the line just as much as yours. All you have to do is relax, let her do the work and avoid stupid mistakes. This is a situation where less is more. You are on her turf. She's in control. Let her roll.

Get as much intelligence ahead of time as possible, especially if you're meeting the family. Do this on the phone and on the way over in the car. Get the names and relationships right as best you can. Ask questions. "Did you say Jim was married to your cousin?" If you are on the phone, take some notes and review them before the dog and pony show.

When you are introduced, extend your hand, shake firmly and repeat the person's name. "It's great to meet you, Betty. Karen tells me you're quite the skier." The more often you are able to repeat the person's name as you look at him or her, the more likely you that you will remember it. Ask your date for help if you need it. She won't mind and it shows interest on your part.

Listen twice as much as you talk. It is amazing how effective this is. You will learn much more and people will enjoy your company. As strange as it sounds, they will come away thinking you are a very interesting guy because you allowed them to talk about their interests. Don't just listen, ask simple relevant questions. "Wow, that sounds great, Betty. Where exactly is Steamboat Springs?" On the other hand, don't allow some blowhard (they'll be there) occupy all of your time. Circulate, while remembering who you came in with. Under no circumstances, should you spend any amount of time with the great looking blonde in the corner.

205

Drink very little, if at all. Claim you have an early morning, or better yet simply, "I'm driving." No one will argue. Don't gorge yourself. Try a bit of everything. If you know who prepared a dish, hand out the kudos. Walk around the house and make observations and compliments. You can be sure that much effort went into making the place look nice. Careful here — don't be too nosy or enter rooms where you aren't invited.

Sing your date's praise without gushing. "Karen and I have been out a number of times recently. She's a great dancer." People will often ask where you met. There's nothing wrong with letting your date field this one. She may want to put her own spin on it.

Try to keep the evening reasonably short. There are fewer opportunities for mistakes. Be careful not to be insulting, though. Wait until a few people have already left, then check with your date. If she wants to stay longer, cooperate. On the way home, tell her how much you enjoyed yourself and bring up examples of people you found interesting. Again, let her talk. She will be full of trivia.

If possible, you are better off meeting her circle of friends and/or family before introducing her to yours. There is less pressure on her and she will feel more comfortable. If things are still going well a week or two after your debut, go ahead and bring her around to meet Mom and Dad or your golf buddies. If you do, your responsibility is to stick by her side and make her feel at ease. Feed her information about the different personalities so she has a "heads up." "I need to tell you that Aunt Hilda is likely to pinch your cheek. Sorry about that." Follow the same general guidelines outlined above. Keep it short and sweet.

Is She Worthy?

Judge a woman by how she treats her family and friends. Be careful — it is also how you will be treated. You need to be on guard for examples of dysfunctional behavior. Is she constantly whining about the way she's treated by others? Is she manipulative? We can also be guilty of this sort of behavior. You would do well to do some self-analysis. Men often end up treating their wives the same way they treat their moms. She'll notice.

Stay on Your Own Turf

Never move in with a lady. It's a bad idea. You're just playing house. If you feel strongly enough to spend every non-working minute with her, get engaged and then married. Shacking up creates more problems than it solves. It puts a lot of pressure on both of you. Your families will be less than pleased. You are under the false impression that you can have the best of both worlds — the perks of marriage without the commitment. Wrong. It is extremely difficult to break up a live-in arrangement. You don't need lawyers and such but it will be nearly as traumatic. Also, studies show that a very low percentage of live-ins eventually get married. Even worse, the divorce rate is higher for live-ins than the general population.

The 'C' Word

"You better let somebody love you before it's too late."

— The Eagles

It is essentially a waiting game. She must come to you with ideas of commitment. Realize that for her this is a form of surrender. She has to decide for herself that she trusts you enough to give up major portions of her independence and freedom to secure your emotional support and love. You can't help her. She will let you know. If all the pieces fit and she fills the hole in your heart, it is time to close the deal. Life is short. You will not be in this wonderful place many times, my friend. Remember those odds.

Of course, there is the other extreme. If you fail to commit within a reasonable amount of time after she is ready, the offer will go stale. Timing is everything. Women commonly complain about the inability of men to commit. This typically occurs in a relationship that has progressed and has been in place for many months or even years. Remember — a relationship can never be static. It must move forward and grow or die. The lady is ready to get a ring for Christmas, but the guy is not about to go shopping. As you can see this is the complete reversal of what we just described. As the old saying goes, "be careful what you wish for — you just may get it." In this case the man is unwilling to surrender his freedom. The more the woman persists — the more the man resists. Sound familiar?

And so it goes. It can be confusing but this is the nature of our species. What is important is that you understand the natural inclinations of men and women in matters of romance. Then use the information to make good decisions for yourself.

Freedom

People have a natural need to preserve their emotional freedom. You need to recognize this. You cannot press the issue and talk her out of giving it up. She has to come to her own conclusion that a relationship with you is preferable to an independent single existence. The prime reason will be because you satisfy her emotional needs. That is what you must work on. Of course, this works both ways. You will have to make the same sacrifice. That is what makes relationships so difficult. The conditions and circumstances must be right for both parties.

Unfortunately, the Beatles were not quite correct when they sang *All you Need is Love*. You must have boundaries. You probably already do without recognizing them as such. A boundary is an invisible line between you and another person. You have to maintain your identity as a unique person in any relationship. There is an old saying: "good fences make good neighbors." No matter how close and intimate you become with someone, you must preserve your self-respect. Good boundaries make good relationships. They must be in place and clear to both parties early in the dating process. It works both ways. Some men do not respect the boundaries of women. They will be jealous, possessive and controlling. Don't violate a woman's boundaries. Don't let her violate yours.

Chemistry

We hate to reduce the glow of infatuation to chemicals but unfortunately that is the case. You would do well to have some understanding of this. When you see an adorable face and feel that rush you are getting high on a combination of chemicals that will change your behavior and cloud your judgement. Some guys get so addicted to the feeling that they seek it over and over again without ever getting to know a woman well enough to experience a meaningful relationship.

Phenylethylamine (PEA), the love molecule, is an amphetamine-like substance that makes you feel as though you were in a mind-altered state. It is interesting that PEA is also found in chocolate. Oxytocin, Vaspressin and DHEA are some of the other substances that your body pumps out to encourage you to mate. A dose of dopamine is dispatched to your brain to chill you out. Norepinephrine kicks in precipitating the production of adrenaline. You already know what that feels like.

It is not surprising that rational thought can be obscured with all these "love drugs" in your system. Oxytocin, the "cuddle" hormone, triggers orgasm and feelings of fondness. Oxytocin production increases as you become turned-on. Phenylethylamine, norepinephrine and dopamine cause flushed skin, heavy breathing, and sweaty palms, effects similar to those of amphetamines. The body builds up tolerance to these chemicals so it takes more of the substance to get that special feeling of infatuation. People who jump from relationship to relationship crave the intoxication of falling in love and may be "attraction junkies." In the case of enduring romances, the continued presence of a partner stimulates production of endorphins which are soothing substances and natural pain-killers.

The 'L' Word

Next to sex, this is the most powerful benchmark of a relationship. Women put great stock in it. Once you utter the three little words, you can never go back. She will tell everyone that you said, "I love you." It is cause for great celebration among her sisters. You are halfway to the altar. She will immediately respond and say it every chance she gets. She will expect you to say it often and be depressed and worried if you don't. It is like a drug. On the other hand, if she is not in the same emotional state as you, constant repetition of the phrase will only serve to drive her away. Now you can see how powerful these three little words can be.

Of course, you probably don't look at it this way. Maybe you mean it, but you had no idea how heavy the consequences would be. You have now been warned. Our advice? Wait until the last possible moment. This is only fair to her. Wait until you really mean it and you want to ramp up the relationship to Warp Factor 8. That's what the 'L' word does.

Hint: If you want to be sneaky you can write "Love, Jim" on a birthday card and live in that mode for a while. It doesn't have quite the same effect as saying it. If you want to lighten it a bit use the cute spelling, "Luv."

The Real You

Once we are married to someone or in a serious relationship, our true persona begins to emerge. What happens is that people who are interested in each other project an image for survival/biological reasons, to attract the other partner. In most cases, the opposite partner does the same thing. Most of this projection is done unconsciously. But once people become relaxed and comfortable with one another (as in marriage), they stop projecting this image and their true nature reveals itself.

If you think about your own actions, you may find that it is extremely difficult to project your true persona when in the presence of others, even when you are consciously aware of it. Not that your other side is so extremely different, but there are quite a number of traits that do change.

As a simple example, let us say that you dislike rap music. Now, if you are dating a girl who really enjoys this type of music, then you may very likely put up with it because you are highly attracted to her. But once the relationship has progressed past the dating/engagement phase to marriage, you are likely to tell her to turn that horrible music off because you can't stand it. Her reaction might be, "Well... I thought you liked rap? Wow, how you've changed! You're not the same man I thought you were!"

Sooner or later sex will become an issue. We have been cautioning you about this throughout the book. Now it's time to take a realistic look at the subject.

Chapter 25
Sex

"...is there any greater or keener pleasure than physical love?
No, nor any which is more unreasonable."
— Plato, The Republic, c. 6th century BC.

Sex

You nasty boy! Caught you. Now go back and read the rest of the book first! That's OK. Sex is pretty hard to resist. However, you will benefit a great deal if you take the time to plow through the other chapters because they contain important principles that must be understood first. You will be able to frame this material much better if you do. OK, read on.

We want to start this topic with the following thoughts. It is one of the most important issues in the book. Please take it to heart. We want you to be around to enjoy future editions.

Always use a condom unless you are married or in a long-term exclusive relationship. In either case, both parties should have had a recent test for HIV infection. Be aware that there are several other sexually transmitted diseases including syphilis, gonorrhea and genital herpes. There is plenty of information out there on this subject. Be aware. Consult your physician. Always use a condom. Always. No exceptions.

Remember, you are not having sex with each other – you are having sex with everyone both of you have had sex with and everyone each of them has had sex with. The permutations boggle the mind.

People will come up with all sorts of rationales for not using a condom. None of them are valid. AIDS is a one-way street. Socioeconomic position, claims of recent testing or pleas of sensitivity and comfort are irrelevant.

Sex is a loaded topic. There are all sorts of factors here. There is your value system and morality. There are sexually transmitted diseases. There is unexpected pregnancy. We do not propose to address any of that here. You have to go with your own game plan on this one. There is, of course, plenty of help

210

out there for the serious aspects of pre-marital sex. We want to help you with two topics. First, what is the effect of sex on a dating relationship? Second, how does a man seduce or nearly seduce a woman?

You have to make two decisions when you begin to date someone. You have to decide if you will have sex at all. If you decide to have sex, you have to pick the appropriate time. The first decision goes back to the previous paragraph. If you believe that pre-marital sex is OK under the right circumstances, fine. Dr. Laura, forgive us, but we believe a large percentage of the single population feels this way. How many people lose their virginity on their wedding night? Here's the problem. In most cases once the genie is out of the bottle (you have made love) you can't get it back in again. *The first time changes everything.* Here's why. A woman believes that her body and the pleasure it can bring is a very precious and valuable thing. Although she may decide to share it with you in a moment of passion, she will ponder the act intensely for days afterwards.

What It Means to Her

Have you ever heard a woman say, "men only want one thing?" They hate being perceived as a body that just happens to be able to talk. The less attention you pay to her body, the better. Ignore it for now. When she is ready, she will make it clear and give her permission. You must be invited.

The more interested she is in you, the more meaning she will place on "what happened that night." Her imagination will take her all kinds of places. If you don't call fairly soon or don't stay the night, she will feel betrayed. Her nesting instinct will kick in big time. Now, this is not universally true. Not all women will react this way. Some ladies are sophisticated and cavalier about these things. We are going with the percentages. The progression goes something like this. You go out a few times. You do it once. You go out again. You do it again. This continues, although you may not go to bed each time. At some point, she will want to know, with just cause, if you are sleeping with other women. Now what? If you are and you say so, the sex is likely to stop. In most cases if the sex stops, the dating will stop. If you are not sleeping around and you say so, she'll be pleased and consider that the two of you are in an exclusive dating relationship. This is one step away from engagement, guy. Of course, if you lie and say you are not sleeping with others, the result is the same. The difference is that, you're a liar.

Yes or No?

The genesis of all this was your decision to have sex. Realistically, you can delay this decision almost indefinitely. Indeed, persons of high moral position will insist that sex is only appropriate after marriage. But, please remember, we said we wouldn't go there. If you are going to do it, we want you to go in with your eyes open. So what's a guy to do? The simple truth is that guys want to have sex. Guess what? Women want to have sex. The answer is honesty and communication. If you get to the point of the magic moment, *conversations should have already taken place.* You need to discuss the meaning of a physical encounter in your relationship. There will be plenty of opportunity to do this if you are patient and responsible. You will probably do some serious making out on earlier dates. It will probably increase in intensity as time goes on. She will definitely give you signals along the way. If she wants to hold things to a certain level, she'll let you know. She may say something like, "no." She may push you away at a crucial point. There is only one way to handle this. You must smile, reassure her and respect her wishes. Tell her you understand and it's OK. Hold her hand or embrace her. Move on to something else. She needs to know that an expression of her boundary is not a relationship-killer. That wouldn't be fair. Of course, this assumes that you like her and want to continue dating.

Once she has communicated her boundary, you will have to have a discussion at some point. The two of you need to decide how you want to handle your mutual physical desires. This is very personal and can get complicated. We can't do it all for you. The guideline here is that the lady's wishes must be respected. They have to be good enough for you. If you insist on a physical relationship and she is not comfortable with that, you should move on. You are not a match. This is tough medicine but what are your choices? You can't push the issue — that's bordering on date rape. You can't whine and beg. You will appear weak and juvenile. No, my friend, you must recognize things for what they are and adjust accordingly.

Women's Concerns About Intimacy

Before the two of you can become physically close you may have to overcome some fears and objections on her part. Strange as it may seem, many women have an unrealistically negative impression of their bodies. They inspect them regularly, know every flaw and complain about them to their friends. She may even mention a few to you. Be very careful here. Never get into any kind of discussion about the specifics of a woman's body. You will lose. There is no positive position you can possibly take. If you agree and say she is a bit heavy, she will be devastated. If you protest, she will think you're not being honest. You can't win. It is like the old question: "Are you still beating your wife?" Do you answer? Yes or no? If she asks, "Do you think my butt is too big?" or "Do you think my breasts are too small?" — watch out.

Listen sympathetically and let her know that physical aspects are not nearly as important as who a person is. Also, move on to praise other attractive physical assets she has such as her eyes, hair or smile. Never comment on her breasts or her bottom. These are taboo areas. Keep your mouth shut about specifics. She just needs to know in a non-specific way that her body is more than adequate to satisfy you. Consider a statement like, "Well, Karen. Being a gentleman, all I can say is you certainly have my attention in that department." Or "I'll tell you Karen, I believe that sex is more psychological than physical." She wants reassurance and to know that you're not going to run away screaming when you see her in the buff. Remember, just don't get specific. Let her have that dialogue with her friends.

We have already addressed safe sex. You have no choice. You need to let her know beforehand that you intend to use a condom. If you can't have this conversation, you're not ready to sleep with her. The risks of pregnancy (although condoms are not 100 percent) and the laundry list of sexually transmitted diseases is too great to consider anything else. Of course, this is a difficult topic to bring up, but it must be done. You could approach it as a social issue. "You know, Liz, I'm a big believer in safe sex. I think we all have a responsibility to stop the spread of these terrible diseases. How do you feel about it?" Have this conversation after you have a close relationship established and you sense that you are moving closer to intimacy. There is no sense in scaring her off too early.

Another concern is the fear of a one-night stand. She wants to know that she will be seeing you again after you have been intimate. This is a very real concern because it happens all the time. Some men are notorious for this. As soon as the conquest is made, they feel the need to move on. Make it clear that you are interested in a continuing relationship with her. Don't make idle promises or premature commitments. Just share your true feelings and reassure her that the two of you have a future, at least as far as you can see. It might be nice if you had some specific plans for the next weekend to alleviate her concerns.

When?

So when is the appropriate time? This is a tough one. It will vary greatly from couple to couple. *We can tell you that the first date is not the time.* This hurts but work with us here. Do you think for one minute that you are so irresistible that any woman will throw herself at you after three hours of pasta and Merlot? Right. If that were the case, you wouldn't be reading this book and your mail would be addressed: Brad Pitt, Hollywood, CA. No, there's something else going on. Maybe she does this with every guy she goes out with. She might be drunk. She may be extremely desperate for attention from a guy, any guy, and thinks that sex is the quickest way to get it. She may ask you for $100 when it's over! It may be some combination of the above. The question is — is this what you want? Not the sex, dummy, the woman. Do you want to spend more time with her? Are you ready to introduce her to your friends?

What about the second date or the third? OK, this could get silly. Obviously, there is no magic number. All relationships are going to move at different rates and intensities. If you make the decision that you want to move to a physical relationship, what you need is a reality check. *Talk to her!* Do you actually have a relationship going here? Is she part of your life? Do you share a lot? Do you trust her? Are you close enough that you can have an honest discussion about having sex? *If you can't talk to her about it how are you going to get naked with her?* We don't want to remove the passion and make this sound too clinical but it's important that her expectations are properly focused. If you are not ready to commit to an exclusive relationship, the time to reveal that is before you hit the sack. If that's still OK, and the two of you want to proceed, well . . .

What is important is to ensure that neither of you suffers from morning-after remorse. Remember, the focus here is successful dating, not scoring as often as possible. It is important that sex occupy an appropriate position in the relationship. If you want to use dating as a means to have sex, this is the wrong book for you. Successful dating leads to an evolving relationship or relationships. If you are in a physical relationship with several women at the same time, you are not being honest with them. You are not the kind of guy we would like to see dating anyone's sister. You are making it tough for the rest of us. You get the point. We will proceed with the rest of the chapter under the assumption that the two of you have decided to have sex. How can you make it enjoyable and meaningful for both of you?

The Senses

In matters intimate, men are more visual (hence pornography). Women are more tactile ("Just hold me"). When snuggle time arrives, take off your shoes and invite her to do the same — innocent enough. Later, when the time is right offer to rub her feet or shoulders. Take your time. Don't talk. Let her sense of touch set her mood. Go get a professional massage yourself from a woman masseuse (the legitimate kind) and see the effect it has on you. Pick up some techniques. Use *touch* when appropriate. Embrace and caress her. Hold her hands gently in yours. Here is a great tip. Massage her shoulders. Place the fingertips of both hands on her trapezium muscles. They are the large muscles between her neck and shoulders on top. Gently roll your fingertips as if you are playing the piano. After awhile move to her neck and shoulders. Usually this will produce goose bumps. Do it slowly for as long as you can. This will put you miles ahead of your competition.

Satisfy the sense of *sight* by looking as good as possible as previously discussed. Make the environment (the restaurant, your car, your home) as clean and visually pleasant as possible.

Consider the sense of *smell* next — two things here. Be sure not to offend with unpleasant odors (halitosis, B.O. or the aftermath of Mexican food). Entice her with a hint of good cologne and scented candles. You don't have to go overboard — just don't ignore this sense. Taste and smell are very closely related. You already know her favorite foods since you talked to her about this early on. The taste of a good meal should be lingering on her palette.

Hearing is addressed with music and your voice. You should know her preferences because you are interested in her and talked about music on your first few dates. You just happen to have a few CDs she would enjoy. Keep the volume low enough to talk. Remember your voice is low and slow. The closer your lips are to her ear, the better, without being overt. Take your time.

The Secret

Now that the framework is in place for sex in a relationship, it is time to move on to some technique — the art of seduction. This is the best term for it. Unfortunately, it carries a negative connotation. This is historical. Consider Samson and Delilah, Mata Hari, Casanova and Don Juan. The premise in these cases is that one person uses sex with a victim for an ulterior purpose. Please abandon this definition for this discussion. Instead, consider that you are in an advanced relationship with a lady you care about. You are both in agreement that sex is inevitable and you are OK with it. How can you make this a special and wonderful experience? How can you be the lover she has dreamed of all these lonely years? This is a lot of pressure.

We don't mind revealing the secret because it serves women as well as men. Women already understand what it is. Women who are married but unsatisfied with their love lives would be thrilled if their husbands would use some of the skills to follow. This is a case where everyone wins. So, the gloves are off. What is *it*? Let's begin with what it isn't. It isn't looks. It is said that Casanova was actually a homely man. It isn't money, clothes, cars, bulging biceps or the right cologne. All of these are merely accessories that can help the process along. No, my man. The secret is between her ears. It is a woman's naturally active imagination. Voltaire said, "Give me five minutes to speak my face and I will bed the queen of France."

Except under the rarest circumstances, a woman will not be interested in making love unless she is in the proper frame of mind. Men are different. They are horny twenty-three and a half hours a day and would consider making love to a turnip. Women require a great deal more. For a man, it is the act itself. Indeed, the goal of the act is our own climax. All else is secondary. For a woman, it is not necessarily the climax (sometimes they don't have one — worse yet, they fake one). It is everything leading up to the act and everything afterwards. This is exactly what most men find tedious. These things are in our nature. We can't help our natural inclinations, but we can make major improvements in our skills and techniques. How do we put a woman in the proper frame of mind?

First, there is timing. *Timing is everything.* Some time frames are more conducive than others. You can easily observe this if you pay attention. Do any of these adjectives describe her current condition?

Relaxed, dreamy, silly, exuberant, warm, romantic, flirtatious, happy, content.

This is good. Half of your work is done for you if she is already predisposed to making whoopee. Of course, you can contribute to this by doing your best as a date. Flowers, compliments, conversation about her interests and other ideas previously explored can be very helpful.

Sometimes there is nothing you can do. *As a matter of fact, if you try to push the issue at the wrong time you can do terrible damage.* You can come away looking insensitive and inconsiderate. "How can you think about sex when my Mom is so sick?" We don't mean to trivialize, but that's the way it works. Women telegraph their moods. They talk about them all the time to their friends. It is a *huge* topic. All you have to do is pay attention. Look for a different set of adjectives.

Tense, sad, moody, upset, frustrated, tired, cranky, serious, quiet, fidgety.

What you need to do is support her and wait for better times. By the way, are you aware of her menstrual cycle? You had better be. PMS is very real. Obviously, you can forget the week or so after PMS as she will be having her period. The optimal time is during ovulation when she is most fertile. This makes sense. Of course, this presents the most risk as far as unwanted pregnancies are concerned.

Remember how you used to wait for your Dad to be in just the right mood before you asked to borrow the car? You were an expert at it. The same principle applies here. You need to be in touch with her life. Are things going well at work? Is she fighting with her Mom? You should know these things anyway if you are that close to her. Also, you need a setting. You must be alone and have a reasonable amount of time ahead of you. If it's 12:45 AM and she has to get up early for work, your chances are slim. Is she expecting her sister to stop over later? Not likely to happen, pal. *Time and privacy are required.*

If you sense that the two of you are getting closer to intimacy, you can begin to set the stage well in advance by nudging her subconscious in a romantic direction. Do this with images and key words blended in with your general conversation. You might describe a scene from a movie or an article you read. Liberally sprinkle your discussion with words loaded with passionate meaning. If you need examples, check any romance novel. Be sure that you are not leading with a direct suggestion about an interlude between the two of you. You just want to get her imagination moving in that direction. Carefully observe the effect of your words and adjust. If she seems embarrassed or offended take a different tack or back off. If she is reacting positively with body language, keep it up.

If conditions are right, then you are ready to move to the next step. You need to induce a dreamlike state by tapping into her imagination. It is almost a form of hypnosis. Women are excellent subjects. They do it to themselves all the time. Why do you think romance novels are so popular? We would love it if this book sold ten percent of the volume of the number-one best seller in the romance genre. Do men ever buy romance novels? Look at the covers. As a matter of fact, read one if you can stand it. The reason they are so popular is that they are designed to seduce a woman into an escape from reality. It is the woman's version of pornography. Now, not all women are addicted to these books. However, there is a principle here. Women require an emotional framework where they can properly position the sexual act. The physical stuff can't stand on its own. If you don't supply the images, they will often do it themselves. They will close their eyes and picture a romantic island or something exotic.

Tune Up

What you talk about is not nearly as important as how you say it. She knows what you're doing. She wants you to do it. She's cheering for you. After all, if you're successful, she wins too. Learn to adjust the modulation of your voice. This is a fancy word for the tone. It should be as low as possible. Have you ever heard Barry White sing? How about Frank Sinatra or Elvis? These guys were not lyric tenors. *Speak slow and low.* There is a reason why women swoon over the sound of their voices. They were baritones or basses. You want to lower your voice as much as possible without sounding ridiculous. *Speak slowly and softly, include some pauses and keep your mouth as close to her ear as possible.*

Begin talking about something simple and familiar. It should be very pleasant to her. There should be enough detail that you can describe it for quite a while. For example, if she loves the beach (most people do), describe the last time you were there — if you shared a trip there, so much the better. Concentrate on the sensual aspects. How did it feel, sound and smell. Describe the warmth of the sun on your skin, the sound of the surf and the gulls, and the smell of the fresh ocean breeze. Get her to agree with you as much as possible. "Don't you just love falling asleep at the shore?" She may help you along by adding her own images. You will have to develop your own story. It really doesn't matter. Parents will often do this to put children to sleep. Fairy tales are flights of fancy designed to stimulate the imagination of children and put them in a pleasant dreamlike state. We are all children inside. We love a good story. In this case, of course, you are headed someplace more adult and intimate but the principle is the same.

As you continue to talk, it will be possible at some point to segue to more romantic topics. Tell her how wonderful and exciting your relationship is, how close you feel to her. Talk about the things you find most attractive about her. *Avoid any overt physical moves until she is completely ready.* This will break the state. She will let you know. When her stimulation is strong enough, she will be eager for your touch. She will cuddle closer and begin to caress you, play with your hair, etc. You may notice a change in her breathing. It will be deeper and faster. Look in her eyes. Once things are under way, continue to whisper in her ear.

When the moment is right, kiss her. When you move on to more passionate kissing there is a change in your attitude. While you are always a gentleman, you need to exude more warmth and add some passion. Include more caressing but avoid her personal areas for now. Gently stroke her back, neck, face or arms. Move very slowly. Plant gentle kisses on her cheeks, neck and earlobes. (Make certain your breath is very fresh.) As far as open mouth kissing, let her take the lead. Kissing is a more critical precursor to physical intimacy than most men realize. Take your kissing very seriously. She will.

The most important thing is to move more slowly than her. Let her push the process along. Wait for her to move to each new step. This anticipation will only increase her pleasure. The longer this takes, the better. Continue to talk gently, only now focus on her. Tell her how exciting you find her. Talk about the things about her you enjoy the most. *At this point we are going to tiptoe out of the room.* We want you two to be alone. We are going to avoid explicit physical detail here. There are plenty of books on that topic on the market. However, here are a few general guidelines for your consideration:
- Slower is better.
- Delay your satisfaction in favor of hers.
- Slower is better.
- Consider the rest of her body.
- Slower is better.
- Variety is not only the spice of life, it's the spice of love. Use your imagination but be careful. You don't want to exceed her boundaries. How do you know? Ask. An important aspect of this is the ability to communicate during lovemaking. If both of you feel free to express what feels good and what doesn't, your physical relationship will grow.
- Slower is better.

When the main event is over, you need to complete the seduction. *At this point, a lady needs to be held and reassured.* This is sometimes called "afterglow." For many women, this is the best part. Extend it as long as possible. She will let you know when she has had enough cuddling. Enjoy it. It's a beautiful thing. Too many men want to jump up and see if there's a game on TV thirty seconds after the heavy breathing stops. If you break the magic, it takes away some of the meaning. Let her disengage first. Always give her as much cuddling as she wants.

An important note here. *Never ask for an evaluation. This is really stupid. The common question is, "Was it good for you?" You're just asking for trouble.* What if she says, "It was OK." What are you going to do now? Are you ready for an extended discussion about your capabilities? Talk about breaking the mood. Let it be. If there are problems, she will probably let you know some other time. Women are more sensitive to our male egos than we know. Also, avoid discussing other partners in the past — hers or yours. Although she may volunteer, you should be a gentleman and keep your mouth shut. This topic is usually trouble and can be a landmine.

By the way, here are a couple of mundane thoughts that may be helpful:
- Before intimacy, make sure you are as *clean as possible* and you have visited the bathroom.
- Take your socks off before your pants. It looks stupid.
- People should have privacy in the bathroom. Always close the door when you go in. Never barge in when she is in there. Some things are too personal for sharing.
- Clean up afterwards so cuddle time is more pleasant. Sex produces a lot of sweat and stuff.
- Never answer the phone. Take the damn thing off the hook. Turn off your beeper.

Keeping It Going

Once you are in an exclusive physical relationship you face a new challenge. Remember opening presents on Christmas morning when you were a kid and finding that toy you really wanted? You spent hours playing with it. It was great. Then the old saying "familiarity breeds contempt" crept in. You eventually became bored and moved on to other things. After a while you would rediscover it and play with it again. Of course, if your brother tried to touch your new toy, you went ballistic. Now this is a very weak analogy but you have to be on guard not to let your new romance fizzle because of your lack of attention.

Sex does not just keep going by itself. It's very complicated. You know that it's part of a whole relationship, of course. Beyond that you need to keep things fresh and exciting. You also have to be careful to keep outside problems out of the bedroom. Never engage in sexual blackmail. If things are not going well in other areas of the relationship, fix them first, then go to bed. Both partners should be ready. Sometimes one partner will participate to please the other. Always be willing to do this if possible. It goes both ways. The secret is fantasy. Remember the section on seduction. Don't stop trying.

Life is full of problems. Love is part of life. We would like you to consider a few possibilities beforehand so you are better prepared.

Chapter 26
Problems

"...can't live with them, or without them."
— Aristophanes, Lysistrata, c. 411 BC.

He Said – She Said

Forgive us while we generalize. Men and women process information and communicate differently. You cannot ignore this. Recognize it and use the knowledge to improve your circumstances. Men prefer to discuss things and quantities, i.e. computers, cars, baseball statistics, stock quotes. Women will tend to center their conversations around relationships and emotions. Men will speak aggressively and competitively, sometimes to the point of shouting. Women prefer to commune and consider everyone's thoughts, sometimes to the point of weeping. Men look for conclusions and solutions. Women enjoy the process itself and just want to feel better about the issues.

Men	Women
Things and quantities	Relationships and emotions
Speak aggressively and competitively	Commune and consider all sides
Reach conclusions and solutions	Feel better about the issues

With this thought in mind, you can see how men and women can misinterpret what is being said. Sometimes a woman will begin with a question and expect a dialogue to follow. The question may be a precursor to a request. For example:

"Wow. What a beautiful night. I'm glad it cooled down. Are you very tired?"

Possible translation: I'd like to go for a walk.

You can't understand why she wouldn't just come right out and ask. Sometimes she will. The solution is to engage her and play out the thought. Be patient and prepared to follow the conversation through.

"No, actually I caught a little nap this afternoon. What do you think we should do with a night like this?"

This will work much better than just responding with the required information.

"Nope. I feel fine. This cold front will save on the old air-conditioning."

The classic female complaint, of course, is reading the newspaper at the table. Think about it for a minute. Would you do that with your best customer or your boss? We know dealing with this can be annoying but so is driving around for two and half hours because you're too proud to ask for directions!

Women prefer a long phone call to just checking in to say hi. To her it is the process of communication that's important. She will place value on the amount of time and the level of intimacy in the encounter. It's enough for you to just be there and exchange whatever information is required. Bear all this in mind when you are communicating with a woman. We realize that it is gross generalization, but it will serve you well.

We strongly urge you to read *Men Are from Mars, Women Are from Venus* by John Gray, Ph.D. HarperCollins Publishers, New York. This easy to read volume explores the differences in communication styles between men and women.

When the Going Gets Tough . . .

The dating game can really wear you out. If you were to take advantage of all the advice in this book, it would be a full-time job. Also, you will find yourself making significant changes in your life. This is never easy. Indeed, people are very hesitant to make changes unless circumstances force them to. This can work on your last good nerve. You start out with high expectations and make Herculean efforts at the beginning. When results are less than you expect, you find yourself feeling worse than when you used to just lay around and watch TV. That was easy. It's very similar to the mind games you play when you start an exercise program: High expectations+heavy initial effort+minimal return=bad attitude.

Of course, when you think about it carefully you know the process will take a long time to yield the level of result you hope for. But what about right now? First, you must analyze why you are feeling lousy. Do a reality check. Are you like this most of the time? Do you consider yourself an optimist or a pessimist? Do you regularly turn people off with your mood? If that's the case, you have some problems that need to be worked out before you will have much dating success. You see, quality women with good attitudes like to hang around others like themselves. They prefer positive guys who are generally happy with their lives. We highly recommend that you seek some good professional counseling to improve your frame of mind and then return to dating.

What if you are normally a happy-go-lucky guy who is trying to improve his social life and you feel sort of low? Perhaps you've had a few bad breaks lately or maybe you're just tired. You have to figure it out. Get away from everything for a few hours and think it through. What has happened lately to make you feel this way? Can you control any of these issues? Probably you have experienced some rejection or lack of success with several women in a row. Once you understand what the problems are and have done your best to resolve them you can put everything in perspective.

Give Yourself a Break

The idea behind all of this is to increase your personal happiness. If things aren't going smoothly, start by recognizing it. Have a talk with yourself and say, "OK, so the last three girls I asked out said no and the date I had before that fizzled big time. I'm still the same great guy and doing all the right things." *If you have friends you can confide in, give them a call and let loose for a few minutes.* Be certain that you describe your behavior not yourself. If you did something dumb, just admit it. Warn them ahead of time. When you're done, say so and thank them. Move on to something else. You'll feel better.

You may feel a bit down from time-to-time while you are working on the new you. Things could get worse before they get better. You will be abandoning familiar patterns of behavior. This will be painful.

Boxers go back to their corner between rounds to rest. You're allowed to do the same. *Let the whole scene go for a while and let your batteries recharge.* You may be surprised to find that some of your earlier contacts may be calling you! Use this time to increase your energy and your resolve. Treat yourself to something nice — new clothes, a day off, a therapeutic massage.

When you are finished resting, return with a new attitude. Stay away from any negative thoughts such as, "No one will ever go out with me" or "I never seem to meet anyone interesting." Instead, attempt to make some manageable progress. What can you do *today* to increase your success? Workout, go out, call some old friends, talk to the cute brunette at the Laundromat.

We have no evidence but here are some phenomena we have observed. Don't take this stuff to heart. It's just for grins but it's funny how often it happens.

Opportunities come in bunches. You go along for a couple months with next to nothing going on. All of a sudden you have more dates than you can handle. Part of this could be that your self-confidence increases and shows when you have a date or two lined up. Folks in sales will report the same thing if you ask them.

It happens when you least expect it. When you are desperately looking — nothing. Sign up for the French Foreign Legion and your phone rings off the hook. Go figure.

As soon as you start seeing someone opportunities abound. The more serious you are about your relationship — the more flirtatious women become. We suspect that married men look more attractive because their wives are dressing them!

View your journey as a gradual uphill climb. Sometimes the road goes up nicely, then down a bit, then up again — two steps forward and one step back. However, overall you are making progress. It may take a year or more. The important thing is to enjoy the journey. It is making you strong and preparing you to succeed when you get to the main event.

Weekends and Holidays

These can be the worst times if you are not seeing anyone and don't have a date. Planning is the solution. If you have not been successful in lining up a date for the coming weekend by Wednesday or Thursday, it's not going to happen. You have to immediately make some plans for Friday and/or Saturday night. Don't make the mistake of leaving your calendar open "just in case." It is much better to be occupied and have to cancel a movie with your sister if a miracle should occur. This is much better than sitting home alone, or worse, at a bar.

So You Screwed Up On a Date

If you do or say something really dumb, you'll have to admit it and apologize. Maybe you will realize it or maybe she will let you know with her mood and body language. She may even tell you. Don't let the situation simmer. Immediately express your concern that your comment or action has made her unhappy. Tell her it won't happen again and try to lighten things up. If she is so deeply offended that you can't recover, you'll have to ask her if she would prefer to end the date. Tell her that you understand and remain calm. Be a gentleman all the way. It's the only chance you have. She may be willing to go out with you again after she thinks about it and realizes that you made a mistake and acted decently.

If you come to the conclusion that you acted like an idiot after the date is over, you will have to call her and use the above strategy. Be honest and say that you really would like to see her again. Try to frame the situation as a mistake by an otherwise very nice guy. Distance *who* you are from *what* you did. Then evaluate her response. You will know where you stand. If she seems willing to give you a second chance, just ask if you can call her soon for another date. If you sense that she is eager to move on, ask for the date. If she indicates that she isn't interested, say that you understand and thank her for listening. Let her know that if she changes her mind you'd love to hear from her. Don't call again.

By the way, if she screws up — give her a second chance. You may be forgiving the best thing that ever happened to you.

Bad Times

They will come. Surely Mother Theresa argued with someone at sometime in her life. *Disagreements and careless comments occur naturally.* You have to learn to handle these. It will flow both ways. You have to be big enough to let her work through her bad mood and return to her sweet loving self. She should do the same for you. Every good relationship should be able to tolerate a certain number of rough spots.

At some point one of you will commit some transgression. This would be something thoughtless or hurtful. *If it is you, swallow your pride and apologize gently.* Assure her that you will not repeat the behavior and do something nice for her. Move on as quickly as possible and do not over apologize or dwell on it. Actually, it is easier when things are your fault. You can control your own actions — you can't control hers.

If she has done something very wrong, you have to let her know. *First, make absolutely certain that you are right.* You have boundaries. You demand respect. No one is going to treat you that way. Reserve anger for times when she has clearly shown disrespect or lack of consideration. For example, she may have lied or said something rude to you in front of others. Has she been unfairly critical of you? Has she let you down by forgetting an important responsibility? Don't be a Rodney Dangerfield. You deserve respect. Let her know immediately in no uncertain terms that you are not going to tolerate her behavior and make your exit. It's her move. You will now find out what she is made of. Don't call. Give her time to think. If she cares, she will contact you.

People have bad days. People are sometimes oblivious to the feelings of others. People sometimes just look at things differently than you do. It may be your turn next time. Talk about it and let her know that you are disappointed. Forgive and forget.

Here is where you have to show some maturity and character. *If you are satisfied that she has owned up and will not be repeating the behavior, forgive her and move on.* The key is clear communication. She may want to preserve her pride by giving you a shot or two. She may need some more time to think about it. The general idea is you are not up for romance at any cost. You have options.

There are things you should not forgive in a dating relationship. Has she revealed serious character flaws by violating the law or your basic value system? Has she shown a pattern of untruthfulness? (We all tell a white lie from time to time.) You can't change people. It will only get worse. You don't need a project to work on; you need a strong, loving partner. We think you should move on.

Short Timers

There are women who are just fine dating once, twice or maybe three times and then suddenly they bail out. While you can't predict this behavior, you can understand it when it happens. In this way you can deal with it. *Your best strategy is to let it go.* You are only one in a series of men who have played her game. It's not about you. It's about her. *Move on.*

She may be in love with the concept of falling in love. Then she doesn't know what to do with it.

She may have been hurt badly in a previous relationship. She can't bring herself to get serious.

She may thoroughly enjoy dating men — lots of men — often. It was just your turn.

What if you are the one who exhibits these behaviors? That is a serious problem. You will never pass go and collect two hundred dollars if you don't figure out what is wrong. You may need to get some good professional help. However, you can try some of these suggestions to get past the problem.

Do something about it. If you don't see a strategy here that helps, resolve to find a way to turn the situation around. You are, after all, playing mind games with yourself. You know yourself better than anyone, or at least you should.

Try to figure out why. Have you ever had a committed relationship? Did something painful happen? What about during your childhood? Did you have a healthy relationship with your parents and your siblings?

Stay in the moment. Deal with her in the present. Don't try to project what might happen in the future if you continue to see her. Also, your potential with her is completely unknown and not related to your past.

Stretch yourself. Make a good-faith attempt to continue dating her past your usual cut-off point. This will negate ingrained behavior patterns you have developed as a defense.

Give the new situation a chance. This woman is new in your life. She has nothing to do with any painful episodes in your past. Any comparisons or similarities you are drawing are of your own design. Try to put things in their proper time perspective. That was then — this is now.

J P

Not Justice of the Peace. No — *jealousy* and *possessiveness*. This is very bad stuff. These are serious character flaws. Of course, it can work both ways. Either one of you can have the problem. These problems are deeply rooted, require significant effort and, in all likelihood, professional help to resolve.

If you are dating someone who exhibits this type of behavior, it should be obvious to you fairly early. *Our advice is to forget it and move on*. This woman is too unhealthy for a relationship. You will be in for a miserable experience with a bad ending. She will be suspicious of every woman you encounter. She will ask endless questions about phone calls, trips and any time spent out of her direct line of sight.

If you have this problem, you already know it. *Get help*. You will never be able to participate in a happy, healthy relationship. You should not be grilling her about every conversation she has with another man. Some guys really go over the edge with this. They will follow a woman, record her phone calls or go through her possessions. Healthy people do not behave this way. Again, seek some professional counseling so that one day you can enjoy a loving relationship.

Competition

You will face competitors sooner or later. Your response depends on the level of relationship you have with the woman. If you are just dating and there is no commitment your best tactic is to completely ignore her other suitors. Acknowledging them gives them attention and makes you appear weak. Be as bored with her other dates as you would be with your Aunt Hilda's recitation of the family tree.

If you are in a relationship and there are other roosters in the henhouse, you need to have a talk. If your relationship is presumed to be exclusive, start with that.

"You know Jenny, at this point in our relationship, I thought we were exclusive. Am I missing something?"

Give her a chance to explain. If she acknowledges the other dates, you have to reframe the relationship so that everything is fair. Once she admits this, clearly your relationship is not exclusive. You just want the opportunity to play by the same rules. Let her know that.

If you are certain she is seeing other guys and she won't admit it or lies, you have a larger problem. She has a serious character flaw. You need to back off. Don't get angry. You are just disappointed. Tell her.

"Jenny, I'm not so sure we're being straight with each other here. I need some time to think about what is going on. You need to be free to do what makes you happy. Maybe we can talk again in a few days."

Out of Control

"Might as well face it you're addicted to love . . ."

— Robert Palmer

When you let the physical/chemical/emotional aspects of romance dominate your behavior you are surrendering control. You will be directed by these feelings and seek constant "fixes." Unfortunately, the only place you can go for more of the same is the object of your affections. You will reduce yourself to telegraphing your needs to her in the hope of some immediate gratification. When she recognizes this, the opposite will occur. She will perceive a threat to her freedom with little or no basis and head the other way. You will only feel worse.

Slow down. Keep yourself under control. She is the last person who should know that the phenylethylamine in your brain is making you sweat. Don't smother her. Replace your displays of *affection* with regular *attention.*

Violence

There is NEVER any reason to hurt anyone. Society (and law enforcement) takes a very dim view of this. Separate yourself from the woman and get help immediately before you seriously hurt someone and wind up in prison.

Gambling

Gambling should be a form of entertainment, if you participate at all. Moderation, as in many other things, is the key. If it is occasional and the amount of money at risk is no more than you would spend for entertainment anyway, no problem. If you are consistently engaged in various forms of gambling and risking your financial health, stop and get some help. Remember, women are attracted to men who have a sense of security and responsibility. By the way, if she has the problem, think carefully about where the relationship will lead. We suggest that you move on.

Many relationships will end for one reason or another. You need to know how to best deal with this. We also have some closing thoughts for you.

Chapter 27

Pain and Wisdom

"The course of true love never did run smooth."
— *William Shakespeare, A Midsummer Night's Dream, 1595.*

As the Old Song Says, "Breaking Up Is Hard To Do"

However, it happens. If a dating relationship is going to end it is important to preserve the dignity of both parties. We hate the term "dumping." Nobody wants to be dumped and it doesn't have to be that way. There are two obvious possibilities. Either you want to stop dating or she does. Honesty and communication are critical in either situation.

Case 1 – You are ending the relationship.

First, be certain this is what you want. You need to carefully think about her and figure out why you want to end it. Often one person is moving faster than the other. Are you a mismatch because of interests, values or lifestyle? Do you need a break from dating? What are the specific reasons? The reason this is important is that you must tell her. That's right. She deserves it. Wouldn't you?

Don't do it over the phone. Ask her to meet you someplace quiet. It's better than your place or hers. Carry some tissues in your pocket. If you have some of her possessions, leave them in your car and return them if she wishes. Don't beat around the bush. Tell her gently and clearly that you want to stop dating. Don't lie. Tell her exactly why without being critical of her. Don't hold out the lame promise "we can still be friends." That sucks. Perhaps you can but she needs to heal first. Give her some positive thoughts about the relationship. List some of her qualities. Wish her well. Thank her for all the good times. Let her speak her piece. Listen without reacting. She needs to have closure. She may look at things differently. However, do not reverse direction or hold out false hope. *Keep it as short as possible for everyone's sake.* When there is nothing left to say, quietly say goodbye, stand up and leave. Keep your mouth shut. Do not spread the news to everyone you know. Let her do that.

When asked, say that things just didn't work out and it's too bad. Don't call her. Wait a while before dating others. Isn't this the way that you would prefer to be treated?

Case 2- She is ending the relationship.

It shouldn't come as a surprise. There will be signs. You need to keep your eyes open. The ball is in her court. She may call you or ask you to come over. It's hard to say. If you suspect she is trying to end things, try to be communicative and honest. Don't lose control. Never get angry or hysterical. Try not to cry. If there is something you need to know, ask. *When the situation is obvious, there is only one class move. You must stand up, say goodbye, turn around, walk away and do not look back.* Go home or visit a close friend. Do not call her. Don't beg. Don't whine. Be a man. If there is some hope of reconciliation, she will let you know. Then you can decide if it is in your best interests. Avoid dating for a while. You are not ready. You could be subject to the rebound syndrome. Again, keep your mouth shut. Don't discuss the situation with mutual friends. Speak well of her. After all, you shared some good times. Don't wear your heart on your sleeve. If you need to talk, find a confidant — someone you can trust.

Of course, all this assumes that the relationship is ending honorably. If there are serious problems such as deceit, that's a different story. If you're the culprit — shame on you. Clean up your act. Your reputation is at stake, pal. You have some apologizing to do and some crow to eat.

If she's truly guilty of something you need to include that information when you end things. You need to do this for two reasons. First, it will be good for you to speak your mind and let her know how disappointed you are. Second, you are helping her to improve and perhaps saving some other guy from going through this grief. Don't spread ugly stories about her, even if you are angry. When asked, just say, "She wasn't my type of girl" and let it go. It's not worth it. You will come out sounding lame. No one likes sour grapes. Be above it all. Move on.

The Stages Of Grief

Depending on the intensity of your emotional commitment you are going to be hurting. The pain is caused by the loss of someone close and important in your life. You are losing her attention, company, intimacy and affection. There are similarities to the death of a loved one. Psychologists have identified stages of grief that most people seem to pass through as they move toward a healthy acceptance and an ability to love again. You may experience some of these stages such as *denial, anger, bargaining, sadness and integration or acceptance.* Much has been written about this and most counselors can offer support if you are overwhelmed. Don't let the process take an inordinate amount of time but do give yourself permission and time to work through it. The goal is to come out on the other side as a healthy, wiser person who is ready to love again.

Read

There are many valuable books that address relationships. They pick up where we leave off. Continue to learn and develop your relationship skills. The benefits are substantial. Wise people are always in the process of reading something worthwhile. Make it a habit.

Conclusion

We have covered a great deal of ground. It was our intention to address every important aspect of the dating process. We hope that it has been beneficial to you. There is a definite logic to the order in this book. You must begin by making essential improvements to your body. You can then turn to your life circumstances and behavior. Finally, you will be ready to address the techniques and psychology of dating. We urge you to proceed in this manner. The ancient Greeks espoused the concept of striving for a balance of body, mind and spirit. We believe they were right.

We wish that it was possible for us to accompany you on your journey but we have our own. Seek the friendship of others, especially women. Share your experiences, failures and successes. That is the way that we learned. Try to help others with their journey. Keep your focus on the long-term goal. Think in terms of months and years, not hours and days. Never give up. We are behind you. We wish you the best of luck. Take very good care of yourself and your loved ones. God bless you.

The End

Appendix

Annual Check List   Year -

Complete Physical Checkup by Your Physician	
Review Dream Girl List	
Review Self Inventory	
Assess Wardrobe	
Check Body Fat Percent Measurements	

Monthly Check List   Month -

Review Finances/Budget, Pay Bills	
Haircut/Style	
Review Social Calendar/Add Events	
Review Flirting/Dating Progress – Set New Goals	
Start a New Activity	

Weekly Check List   Week of -

Trim Nails	
Do Laundry/Cleaners	
Clean Car	
Clean Home	
Explore New Activities (Check Paper, Radio)	
Plan Weekend (On Monday-Wednesday)	

A Man's Field Guide To Dating

Daily Check List

Shower/Shave	
Brush and Floss	
Work Out/Physical Activity	
Drink 64 Ounces of Water	
Take Multivitamin/Aspirin	
Approach 3-5 women	
Eat Three Healthy Meals	
Read	
Self Affirmation Exercise	

Pre-Date Check List

Clean Car (3-4 Hours Before)	
Make Reservations/Plans/Pick Up Tickets	
Leave 15 minutes Earlier Than Needed	
Visualize Success/Set Expectations	
Control Emotions	

Before You Go Out

Check the Mirror	
Hair?	
Shaved?	
Breath?	
Shirt/Sweater – Clean/Pressed	
Pants – Clean/Pressed	
Shoes – Clean/Shined	
Business Cards/Pen	

Some Sexy Ideas to Keep the Fires Burning

Tell her that you love her body.
Watch the sunset together.
Take showers together.
Give her a back rub or massage.
Listen to classical music and cuddle in the dark.
Hold her with your hands inside the back of her shirt.
Whisper to each other.
Cook for each other.
Make out in the rain.
Kiss every part of her body slowly.
Hold hands.
Wear her favorite cologne every time you're together.
Shampoo her hair.
Kiss every chance you get.
Bubble baths.
Kiss and smell her hair.
Hugs.
Look into each other's eyes.
Very lightly push up her chin, look into her eyes,
  tell her you love her, and kiss her lightly.
When in public, only flirt with each other.
Walk behind her and put your hands in her front pockets.
Read to each other.
Let her sit on your lap.
Kiss her stomach.
Hold her around her hips or sides.
Comment on her hair.
Dance together.
Call when on a trip to tell her you were thinking about her.
Remember your dreams and tell her about them.
Brush her hair out of her face for her.
Hang out with her friends.
Learn to say sweet things in a foreign language.
  (Italian and French are good.)
Dedicate songs to her on the radio.
Stand up for her when someone talks trash.
Never forget the kiss goodnight.
  And always remember to say, "sweet dreams."

Assorted Positive Thoughts

The saddest words in the English language are, "If only I had . . ." Don't come to the end of the road regretting your lack of action.

Keep your expectations low. It will minimize disappointment and heighten success.

Be the first to show interest.

Make flirting part of your personality.

Resist the logic that says, "I will be happy next month" (or year, or when I have a new job, or whatever). It will never happen. You will only shift the goal to something else. Be happy today.

Treat yourself to something really nice at least once a week. You deserve it.

Smile and say hello to almost everyone.

Always look your best. Work on it.

Be the person you seek to date.

If you're going to be rejected, get thrown out the front door in front of God and everyone with your head held high. Don't slither out the back door.

Be a work in progress — always improving, never complete.

Be proactive. It is the natural role of the male of our species.

Assume that you are going to meet the love of your life in about six weeks. You don't know exactly what day. Spend the next six weeks getting ready for that meeting, and the next six weeks after that, etc. Success is the residue of preparation.

Remember — flirting is a heartfelt, sincere, complimentary gift. It is the nicest thing you can do for a woman. Even if nothing happens, it will brighten her day. Be liberal with this gift.

Don't be in the habit of constantly saying "I'm sorry." Reserve those words for times when you have hurt, offended or done something wrong. Say "excuse me" or "pardon me" instead. When it is not merited, "I'm sorry" makes you sound weak.

Some Eternal Wisdom

Three of the Ten Commandments

IX – Thou Shalt Not Covet Thy Neighbor's Spouse – Keep your eyes and attention on the lady you are with.

XIII – Thou Shalt Not Bear False Witness – No one likes a liar. Trust is essential for love.

VI – Thou Shalt Not Commit Adultery – The destructive power of infidelity is legendary.

The Seven Deadly Sins

Pride – False pride and arrogance are repulsive to women. Braggarts are merely displaying their insecurity.

Envy – Be content with what you have. There is nothing wrong with striving for more but don't compare yourself with others. Jealously is very discomforting and unappealing.

Gluttony – If you eat too much, you get fat. You also get unhealthy.

Lust – When lust is your primary motivation you reap dead-end encounters and can never achieve a healthy relationship. Controlled passion follows emotional intimacy and some level of commitment.

Anger – Except for rare circumstances, anger is not appropriate behavior. Anger hurts and drives people apart.

Covetousness – Jealousy will eventually destroy a loving relationship. You cannot control another's behavior. They must be in the relationship because they want to and it benefits them.

Sloth – Men who are lazy and lack energy are very unattractive. Don't be a couch potato. Have some ambition. Be proactive.

The Seven Heavenly Virtues

Faith – You must have faith that your efforts will improve your circumstances. Faith may be all you have on some Saturday nights when you are home alone.

Hope – Hope will keep your enthusiasm high and your spirits buoyed through your quest. You should enjoy the journey.

Charity – Be as generous as you are able. Have sympathy for those less fortunate. These are irresistible qualities.

Fortitude – Change takes courage. You will need plenty.

Justice – Be fair to everyone. Those you date and those you don't — and also, your competitors.

Temperance – Moderation in alcohol consumption as well as other addictive behaviors will keep you healthy and desirable.

Prudence – Proceed with wisdom, common sense and discretion. Good judgement will keep you from harmful relationships.